Minnesota
CURIOSITIES

Help Us Keep This Guide Up to Date

Every effort has been made by the author and editors to make this guide as accurate and useful as possible. However, many things can change after a guide is published—establishments close, phone numbers change, facilities come under new management, and so on.

We would appreciate hearing from you concerning your experiences with this guide and how you feel it could be improved and kept up to date. While we may not be able to respond to all comments and suggestions, we'll take them to heart, and we'll also make certain to share them with the author. Please send your comments and suggestions to the following address:

GPP
Reader Response/Editorial Department
PO Box 480
Guilford, CT 06437

Or you may e-mail us at:
editorial@globepequot.com

Curiosities Series

Minnesota

CURIOSITIES

Quirky characters,
roadside oddities &
other offbeat stuff

Third Edition

Russ Ringsak with Denise Remick

Guilford, Connecticut

The prices, rates, and hours listed in this guidebook were confirmed at press time. We recommend, however, that you call establishments to obtain current information before traveling.

Maps by Daniel Lloyd © Rowman & Littlefield

All photos by the authors except as otherwise noted.

Text design: Bret Kerr

Layout artist: Casey Shain

Editor: Tracee Williams

Project editor: Lauren Brancato

ISSN 1541-3438

ISBN: 978-0-7627-6979-7

Printed in the United States of America

Distributed by NATIONAL BOOK NETWORK

To our mothers:
Ruth Baker Ringsak and Ruby Rydeen Remick

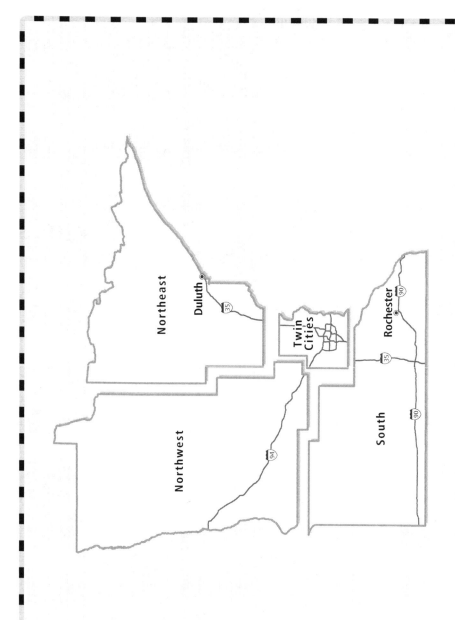

Northeast

Duluth

Northwest

Twin
Cities

Rochester

South

Overview

contents

acknowledgments

*I*t requires a certain measure of confidence to offer oneself up as a subject for a book titled Curiosities. Some of us would be flattered to be considered Interesting or Unique or even Different, but a Curiosity is not that far from an Oddity in many minds, and Odd is just a step from Weird—and Weird's not a goal we generally set before our children. One doesn't look at one's new baby and happily think that someday this kid might create the world's largest ball of twine, a ball so big it will take a crane to lift it.

But of course that's the whole point. Few of the contributors here set out to follow established protocol; this is a collection of people who dared to not follow the arrows painted on the pavement. These folks saw what needed doing and they did it, and where the hotel lacked cats they furnished them, and where the town lacked the spectacle of wood tick racing they invented it.

And it is to these folks whom we are most grateful. The bold, the innovators, the persistent, the bearers of the ridicule who carried forth and in the end achieved the huzzahs. And we thank those who helped us find them: the dedicated people at the historical societies and libraries around the state, the various chambers of commerce who assisted, and the Minnesota History Center in St. Paul.

Thanks also to the Rick Christenson family in Winona who opened the door for a couple of strangers to a number of exotic finds; to the writer Neil Haugerud, the former sheriff of Fillmore County and author of *Jailhouse Stories,* who directed us to the Hanson Museum; and to Charlie Warner of the *River Valley Reader.* Thanks also to Jan Elftmann for her help in the metro area.

And a particular measure of gratitude goes to Nick and Candy Tollefson, not only for the driving and photo assistance but also for enduring the constant boring references to Das Buch. And to Wendy, Jolene, and Linda, for constructive advice and impartial critique. And to our pal Jim Cox, just on general principles.

preface to the third edition

Most books don't get a second chance at the market, much less a third. Most books are sweated over for months or years, assembled and reassembled, comma by comma, adjective by adjective; every nuance and understatement inspected, studied, rejected, and reinstated. There is a labored flurry at the end, and then they are packed up and mailed late at night to meet one last deadline, sent off full of doubts and regrets. They fly to the publisher, leaving behind a distant gnashing of teeth, and they stand or fall just as they were when they left the house for the last time.

This book is one of the favored few that get a second resurrection. We dug out thirty-three additional curiosities, which, or who, in some way, small or large, help define Minnesota as it now sits. (We're not claiming the state is now drained of unexamined oddities, though; the big book of all the curious things, here or anywhere, would be too heavy to haul in a dump truck.)

But like the latest pickup trucks, it's a little bigger and the styling is a bit smoother, and it has more interior area without a big price hike, so it's an even better value than the 2008 model. Entries have been updated, along with various phone numbers, and there are a slew of new website addresses. And it has, as we mentioned, the thirty-three new features. We had to lose thirteen when Lillian's Grocery in Amherst closed its doors, the Tank Ride moved to Florida, the Anderson Hotel in Wabasha closed, and some of our stars passed on. So, all in all, we think you made a heck of a good purchase here. Thanks.

Minnesota is bound by waters, with the Minnesota and Red Rivers on the west and Lake Superior and the St. Croix and Mississippi Rivers on the east. On the north it's complicated, with the big Lake of the Woods, the Rainy River, Rainy Lake, Namakan Lake, the Loon River, and a string of Boundary Waters lakes, which are: La Croix, Iron, Crooked, Basswood, Ensign, Knife, Ottertrack, Saganaga, Gunflint, North, South, Rose, Watab, Mountain, Moose, North Fowl, and South Fowl.

The state is called the Land of 10,000 Lakes, but it actually has 11,842 lakes larger than ten acres and more than 63,000 miles of rivers and streams. That's 7,762 square miles of water in all—an area of water as large as the entire state of New Jersey. (No mention of acreage is complete without some reference to New Jersey.) There are 90,000 miles of shoreline here, more than California, Florida, and Hawaii combined.

It is the only state to contain the sources of three major river systems: the Red River, draining north to Hudson Bay in Canada; the St. Lawrence, draining east through the Great Lakes to the Atlantic; and the Mississippi, running south to the Gulf of Mexico. The most popular name for a Minnesota lake is Mud, but there are also lakes named Hole in the Day, Ball Club, Bad Medicine, Big Spunk, Hanging Horn, Height of Land, Ice Cracking, Pomme de Terre, Spider, Split Hand, Stalker, and Whaletail. There are Lake Lida and Lake Lizzie, and Woman Lake, Man Lake, Girl Lake, and Boy Lake. Only two counties, Rock and Olmstead, have no natural lakes at all.

It's a land of contradiction. It's the only state to vote for the Democratic presidential ticket for the last thirty years straight and it has a long history of liberal politics, but here "liberal" usually means "restrictive": Liquor stores close at 8 p.m. and all day Sunday. You can't buy wine or spirits in grocery stores. You can't buy a car here on Sunday and you can't buy fireworks at any time. There's plenty of public gambling—busloads of elderly hauled to casinos daily—but you can't scalp tickets to a baseball game or any other game. It's the only state to put a famous professional wrestler in its highest office and where you see faded bumper stickers that proudly read: OUR GOVERNOR CAN BEAT UP

YOUR GOVERNOR. And it has an official state muffin: blueberry.

It contains the nation's oldest rock, the oldest indoor mall, and the largest shopping mall, which is also the nation's most visited attraction, a larger draw than Disney World, Yellowstone, and the Grand Canyon combined. However its most famous small town, Lake Wobegon, cannot be found by anyone because of a surveying error. Another surveying anomaly called the Northwest Angle added a little piece of Canada to the state, now the northernmost point in the lower forty-eight.

International Falls, called the Icebox of the Nation, is only the fifth coldest town in Minnesota. In February 1996 the official thermometer at Embarrass broke from the cold; unofficial thermometers read sixty-four degrees below zero. The town bought a new thermometer that reads to seventy-five below.

Minnesota taste in sculpture runs less to nubile maidens, nude athletes, and full-breasted robed goddesses and more to prairie chickens and walleyes. There is very little in the way of classical European sculpture here and not much of the soldier up on a fiery steed, like they favor down south. Even serious art here tends to run toward the whimsical, and on the less serious side there is a frightening amount of large roadside sculpture in the state, generally done in bright glossy colors: 74 animals and birds, 24 fish, 32 mythological creatures, 18 Indians, 8 voyageurs, 62 miscellaneous objects, and 54 advertising statues; 272 in all, plus whatever has been built last week. There are twenty-six statues here having to do with Paul Bunyan, everything about Paul from the cradle to the grave, including both the cradle and the grave. And a lot more, including his ax, his ox, his girlfriend, and his CB radio. They say his statue in Bemidji is the single most photographed attraction in the United States.

The University of Minnesota's mascot is Goldy, the Golden Gopher, called Golden to cover the fact that it's a rodent and a pest to farmers. It's very likely the only state wherein counties currently post a bounty on their own mascot.

Minnesota has been compared to Wisconsin by Michael Feldman in his funny book, *Wisconsin Curiosities,* and most of the points he made were directly on the mark. They are certainly more casual over there, and a couple of degrees warmer and a couple of degrees goofier than we are. Most of us here bear neither rancor nor envy to the state of Wisconsin, despite their thirteen world pro football championships compared to our none, our *big fat zero,* which Michael was too much of a gentleman to mention. Most of our feelings toward his state are feelings of gratitude, because they give us humor, Sunday liquor, fireworks, and concert tickets when we need them; best of all, they provide a nice heavy cushion between us and Illinois. They are an overstuffed pillow between ourselves and the overstressed and overcrowded masses of the East. And if their freeways are lined with billboards reading CHEESE that's no problem for us. Whatever it takes.

P.S. In the summer of 2002 the state legislators gave us permission to light sparklers and snakes; some took this as an insult and others saw it as a relaxation of tyranny. Either way, it has led to an increase in the number of illegal fireworks shot off on the 4th of July, especially from the forbidden launch pads on the docks of lake cabins.

1

South

The concept of *a Southern Minnesota is not in itself a curiosity because it's different from the northern two thirds. Minnesota is somewhat like Europe itself, with blondes in the north suffering the biting cold and brunettes down in the comfy part, enjoying thirty-five fewer inches of snowfall and ten more degrees of sultry heat.*

The north of the South lies along the Minnesota River Valley and the east falls off the Mississippi bluffs; the west and south borders are straight-line survey lines with generally friendly neighbors.

Highlights of the South include a glockenspiel, a brewery, a waterfall, Indian petroglyphs, a professional football training camp, pipestone quarries, pioneer museums, many lakes, and the Jolly Green Giant. Plus a fabulous Owatonna bank designed by Louis Sullivan and a restored 1901 Opera House in Fairmont, and in Northfield, the very bank the James Gang tried and failed to rob.

And in the eastern high bluff region, one finds Amish shops, the National Eagle Center at Wabasha, and Niagara Cave and Mystery Cave. Winona offers the Great River Shakespeare Festival, a Beethoven Festival, and the Maritime Art Museum. And Redwing is a very cool old river town.

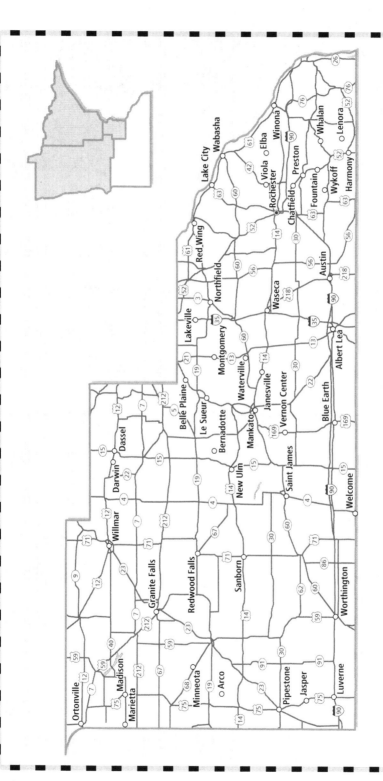

South

Christensen Rock Garden
Albert Lea

Near the city of Albert Lea in southern Minnesota is a hidden rock garden, which, unlike most things, is far more than its name implies. Its actual name is the Christensen Rock Garden and it is known as the Itasca Rock Garden, after the township in which it sits, but properly titled it would be called something like Your Wildest Dreams Built in a Stone Fantasy.

In 1925 a retired farmer and beekeeper named John Christensen set out to build a root cellar to store vegetables. Apparently realizing he

Itasca Rocks.

had talent, he went on to construct a marvelous vision of castles and pools, waterfalls and walkways; this at a time when there was a lot of spontaneous artwork being done across the land, much of it in stone. The rocks themselves are beautiful; a stunning collection that includes stone from forty-eight states, most of which would take an expert to identify.

He hid bits of humor throughout this yard of pathways. Two sets of cat ears stick up from behind a wall, and on the top of a turret on the small castle there sits the head of the Ancient Mariner—skull cap, mustache, and sunken eyes looking off in the distance; a Buddha sits on top of the main roof of that castle. When the light hits a certain way, rocks with faces appear in other places along the tour.

What is referred to as the small castle is six stories tall and looks like a luxury hotel in Switzerland. It is built at the far end to a slightly smaller scale, giving an illusion of distance. The large castle is big enough to walk inside and has massive towers and a bridge flying over the walkway. Other arched bridges crisscross a creek and ponds.

It's hard to imagine that this much rock could be hauled from around the nation back in the days of horse-drawn wagons and the skinny-tired Model A Ford. Even now, local people who travel will sometimes find unusual stones and bring them back and leave them on the doorstep. In the pile there are stones from Tennessee or Kentucky called Indian paint rock, with pock marks that will yield a gold or red powder when broken open.

Mr. Christensen worked on his garden until 1938, and he died in 1939. He built this large complex in a third of the time it took to construct the world's largest ball of twine. It is no longer open as a tourist attraction, but the current owner is not unfriendly. He is a working man with a real job, and if you are lucky enough to find him at the right time you may be treated to a real wonderland.

For more information call the Albert Lea Convention and Visitors Bureau at (800) 345-8414. Tour buses can be arranged. Donations are welcome.

Stone Gas Station

Arco

It's a tiny town on the prairie, population one hundred (give or take a few), and it once held a Texaco station so sensational that busloads of tourists would stop to see it. In 1949, four thousand visitors dropped in from all over the nation.

The building and some sculptures remain. It's not what it used to be, but, as with a lot of us, there is enough left so you get the idea. It was built by H. P. and Ricka Pederson and their boys, M. M. and Vernon, a natural progression from the rock sculptures they were already

H. P. Pederson thought the rocks in his fields were a bonus. In the 1930s he and his family created a stone fantasia of the town's Texaco station.

★ ★

making. Farming in the early 1930s would yield rocks in every plowing, and H. P. broke them with a sledgehammer, mortaring pieces around wire frames to make ashtrays, lamps, flowerpots, and bookends. There was a market for them in town.

In 1936 they bought the Texaco station in Arco and set out to give it the stone treatment. By then they had a lot of stone, some collected on annual trips out west, some donated by neighbors. They covered the entire exterior and built a flowing parapet on the front wall, with

Hugo the Ram.

five open circles rising to the center, a metal Texaco star in each circle; they set a colorful stone Texaco star in a circular recess above the front door. Before they were done a fantastic stone garden flanked the station, containing an elegant stone-domed pergola, archways, a Liberty Bell shrine, a life-size mountain goat, and a dramatic Statue of Liberty, plus a Dutch windmill, a snake wrapped around a petrified log, a lighthouse, and a large Viking ship. Even its sail was stone. A stone pelican perched on one of the arches. There were also a number of miniature rock sculptures, including a house and church, an entire farm, and a railroad scene complete with depot, elevator, and stone locomotive. There was stone in there from every state in the Union, of every kind and color, from quartz to jade, coral to petrified wood, and even a bit of pipestone: the stem of a stone apple, still there beneath a windowsill.

The building today is vaguely reminiscent of the Alamo, although it's occupied as a house; the metal stars are gone from inside the five circles on the parapet, and most of the garden sculptures have disappeared as well. But the goat, the Liberty Bell, the Statue of Liberty, and part of the garden wall are less than a mile away, in a park on Lake Stay.

Take County Road 19 west of Marshall for nineteen miles to Route 7, then head four miles south to Arco.

The Spam Museum
Austin

A visitor enters the new Spam Museum beneath a wall of Spam cans, 3,390 of them, all empty but impressive nonetheless. The original Hormel Foods museum was set in a local mall in 1991, on the company's one hundredth anniversary, and contained just three items related to Spam. Even then it was such a success they had to expand it. It now covers 16,500 square feet in a refurbished Kmart building.

They had been in business for forty-five years when Jay C. Hormel proposed the idea of canning ham to his father, George A. They say

George didn't think much of the idea at first but went along with it, calling the new product Hormel Spiced Ham. They wanted a catchier name and held a contest, and at the 1936 New Year's Eve party at Jay's home, Kenneth Daigneau, a guest, won a hundred dollars when he took out the five middle letters of *spiced ham* and came up with *Spam.* At the current rate of 435 cans per minute, two shifts make 417,600 cans a day, so it could be argued that Mr. Daigneau will be, and in fact already is, the planet's most read writer—a man who wrote only one word, a word he himself invented and a four-letter word at that, conceived at a New Year's Eve party and now copyrighted in 111 countries: 6.3 billion copies in print. End to end, the twelve-ounce tins would reach around the equator sixteen times.

Minnesota isn't the state where the most Spam is consumed—that honor belongs to Hawaii—but Spam is to Minnesota what barbecue is to Texas; it's our Austin gift to the world, our flagship delicacy. Our contribution to American culture, folks, and remember: It wasn't barbecue that helped our boys win World War II. And it wasn't barbecue that carried Russian and British troops through the darkest days, either. Nossir. Old Nikita Khrushchev himself said so, and Maggie Thatcher said the same thing. In fact, that wasn't barbecue in the famous Monty Python skit, and it wasn't Wisconsin cheese curds; it was good old spiced ham from Austin.

These and many other facts can be found at the new museum: One learns, for instance, that it was in 1954 that Haile Selassie I, Ethiopian emperor and father of the Rastafarian movement, visited this very plant. They say that in South Korea, Spam is considered a delicacy even to this day. And they display a letter from President Dwight D. Eisenhower, written during World War II, about the role Spam played in feeding the Allied Forces.

A four-hundred-foot-long conveyor belt runs through portions of the museum, carrying more than eight hundred cans and simulating the production line: It gives visitors the chance to put on hard hats, rubber gloves, hair nets, and earplugs just like the folks who work in the real

There are those who say the Vikings discovered Spam.

plant (Oh, boy!). A five-foot replica of a Spamburger hamburger is suspended in the exit corridor, adjacent to a seventeen-foot burger-flipping spatula. There is a Spam Exam, an interactive quiz show that allows participants to show off their Spam knowledge. And of course there is a gift shop, selling more than four hundred different Spam items.

Follow the signs off Interstate 90 to the corner of North Main Street and 1937 Spam Boulevard. The museum hours are Monday through Saturday 10 a.m. to 5 p.m. and Sunday noon to 5 p.m. No admission fee. Call (800) LUV-SPAM or (507) 437-5641 or visit www.spam.com for more information.

Two-Story Outhouse

Belle Plaine

A souvenir shop called the Booger Hollow Trading Post near Dover, Arkansas, claims to have the "World's Only Double-Decker Outhouse," but it's just another claim out of Arkansas that can't stand up to scrutiny. Theirs is not only not the only one—it's not even one at all: The upstairs is a fake, with a sign that says UPSTAIRS CLOSED TIL WE FIGUR OUT PLUMMIN'. One suspects there's no Boogers there either; but hey, it's a souvenir shop.

"America's Only 2-story Outhouse" in Gays, Illinois, was an outhouse and was connected to apartments above a store, but the store has been torn down and the outhouse, although restored, stands alone and is kept locked. There is a tidy two-story in Phelps, New York, attached to the Dr. John Q. Howe residence, built in 1869, of brick. A two-story outhouse called "Big John" has been spotted behind an old hotel in Nevada City, Montana; they say there is also one in Cedar Lake, Michigan, that was once part of a railroad station.

But in Belle Plaine, Minnesota, there stands a historic and handsome white house with an outhouse on the side connected by a skyway to the second floor that, if it were given to boast, could truthfully call itself *The Only Two-story Outhouse in the Nation That Is Connected to a Real House and Isn't Made of Brick.*

You'd build a two-story outhouse too,
if you had eleven kids. Samuel Bowler built this
three-seats-up, three-seats-down loo in 1886.

It's now a serious museum and belongs to the Belle Plaine Historical Society, so if you go there for the novelty and stay for the historical
interest, that's fine with them. It's called the Hooper-Bowler-Hillstrom
House and was built in 1871 by a businessman from New York named
Sanford Hooper. He owned a hotel, a machine shop, a foundry, and
a riverboat, and had a hand in getting the first bridge across the Minnesota River built.

It was bought in 1886 by Samuel Bowler, founder of a local bank and owner of a lumberyard. He added a kitchen, an office, a bathroom with a copper-lined tub, and the now famous outhouse, three seats up and three down, with glass windows and curtains and a ventilator shaft. It's finished inside and built on a stone foundation. Theirs was a large family—eleven children, mostly girls. There is a double wall behind the ground-floor seats, as you might imagine, and the outhouse is connected to the house at the second floor only; the ground level opens to the outside.

Alfred Hillstrom bought the place about 1900; a member of this family lived here until it was sold to the historical society in 1975. It's been restored and furnished in three periods: 1850s, late Victorian, and early 1900s.

Asked if there were any funny stories about the place, a museum volunteer said, "Not that I know of, but it's never been tipped over."

The Hooper-Bowler-Hillstrom House, located at 410 North Cedar Street, is open to visitors from Memorial Day through Labor Day on Sunday from 1 to 4 p.m. and other times by appointment. Call (952) 873-4433, (952) 873-6109, or (952) 873-2963 for more information.

The World's Largest Indoor Cow Collection
Bernadotte

Rather than trying to sidestep the bad puns, it might be best to just cleanse the page quickly—run through them all and be done with it—and have no more references to mooseums, moosic, amoosing, mooving, mooment, cowllector, cowllectable, cowabunga, cowabilia, cowzy, udderly, udderly cowzy, like no udder, and dairy-air. Done.

She grew up on a dairy farm near New Ulm, did Ruth Klossner, and was given her first pet calf at the age of four. She showed cows through her childhood, winning the 1966 Champion Holstein ribbon at the Minnesota State Fair 4-H show with a cow named Princess. She was named National Holstein Girl at a convention in Milwaukee in 1968 and picked up a B.S. degree in home economics from the

University of Minnesota in 1970. In 1979 she earned a master of agriculture in animal technology and agricultural journalism at the U of M. In 1983 she began working at the *Lafayette-Nicollet Ledger* as a photographer and part-time staff writer, building a private photography business on the side. She is now the full-time editor of the *Ledger*.

And somewhere around 1980 she began to collect cows. Ruth has a record of doing well at whatever she puts her mind to, and right now she is really good at editing a newspaper and accumulating cows; at this writing she has more than 13,822 cows. She has her

More cows in here than in a Spaghetti Western.
PHOTO BY RUTH KLOSSNER

own version of the fabled King Ranch in Texas, which once covered nine counties, only without the heat and the dust and the flies.

When you come in and sign the guest book and you reach for a cow candy in the cow dish, it moos at you; from there on, it just gets better. Cows on and of everything: cow toys, napkin holders, pictures,

The Doris Group

Twenty-three kids began first grade in Storden in 1959, according to the official history of the Doris Group: "7 boys and 15 girls." It makes you wonder if the parents of the other child were just not saying, or if nobody bothered to ask. Still, the more remarkable fact about that class was that the teacher and four of their mothers were named Doris, as well as another teacher hired a few years later. With six of them in the school and a few others nearby, Doris Jean Halvorsen, the new teacher, got the idea that they should get together for coffee.

It never quite happened, and Doris Jean passed on in 1991. But her idea still hung in the air, and finally on February 22, 1995, ten local Doris' assembled in her honor at the Cafe in Storden. (They have concluded, over the years, that Doris' with an apostrophe is a preferable plural to Dorises.) The ten were Ewy, Vaupel, and Olson from Westbrook; Torkelson of Redwood Falls; Bierman and Barker of Jeffers; Bottem of Lamberton; and Lerohl, Nelson, and Olson of Storden. It reads like a poem.

Ten became twelve that fall in Lamberton; the next year in Sanborn there were sixteen, and then twenty-one in Tracy, twenty-three in Redwood Falls, twenty-four in Milroy, and thirty-one in Wabasso. They met for the eleventh time in Bird Island on April 26, 2000; by then they had eighty-two members. The youngest Doris, Konold, was statuary (small, medium, and large), a cow rocking chair, wooden wall hangings, alarm clocks, Chicago cows, New York cows, watches, books, caps, shirts, hand towels, greeting cards, belt buckles, pencils, ties, banks, jewelry—even COW beauty soap from Japan. There are cow booby traps, including one that moos at you when you open the refrigerator door,

four years old, brought in from a nursery school (she is now sixteen); the oldest, Kolander, was driven in from a nursing home. A banner was hung in the dining room with the name of the event: Doris Day. The meeting's main order of business was to decide where to have the next one, and Dallman of Wabasso turned to Bickman of St. Louis Park (a Minneapolis suburb) and said: "Don't volunteer; I don't want to come to the Cities." It got a big laugh.

That fall when they met at the Redwood Falls Pizza Ranch they had become 109; the Doris Group was experiencing exponential growth. Otterson of Alexandria says, "We're an organization for people who have difficulty remembering names." And as of February 2012, there were 278 members. Doris Olson, one of the founders, says, "It's just a social event. We don't have officers or presidents or anything. I just have the list of names. We get together and everybody talks. . . .

Some of these ladies, I don't know who they are. I know their name is Doris, but that's about it. Mostly we just gab a little bit and get acquainted."

And if you're wondering, Doris Day is an honorary member, even though she still hasn't been to any meetings. She did send them an autographed photo.

For more information about the Doris Group, call Doris Hennen at (320) 235-7764 or e-mail her at dhennen@charter.net.

and cow cookie jars that do the same. Cow refrigerator magnets, key chains, calendars, salt and pepper shakers, and butter dishes. International cows from Russia, Poland, Switzerland, Denmark, Belgium, and Norway, and a sixteen-pound cast-iron cow from Japan; cows rare and elegant and cows common and ordinary. There's a room called the shirt shack, with the walls covered with cow T-shirts, where Klossner can grab a shirt to wear right off the display. Mechanized cows, cow mailboxes, cow nativity figures, and even a cow carved from a dried cowpie. A resurrection of sorts.

Visitors are welcome to the world's largest cow museum, where Ruth is up to her eyeballs in cows and, apparently, wouldn't have it udderwise.

The museum is located in Bernadotte on County Road 10 and County Road 1 northeast of New Ulm. For a tour of the Ruth's Cow Collector's Mooseum, call Ruth Klossner at (507) 240-0048 or send your message to cowlady@centurylink.net.

Jolly Green Giant
Blue Earth

Not surprisingly, the biggest piece of roadside art in the state is a smiley guy in a skimpy green outfit, with pointy green shoes and his hands on his hips and looking satisfied at what he sees. Which, of course, is mostly green fields in summer and miles of snow in winter, and somewhat of a mess in between.

He's fifty-five feet tall and was built just in time to oversee the completion of Interstate 90 on September 24, 1978, the last piece of it between the coasts; sort of like the driving of the golden spike when the railroads joined, but at a lower level of excitement. They used concrete mixed with gold powder from Germany so that roadbed sections near the rest areas are now paved in gold for depth of color; the governor, Miss Minnesota, and Miss America were on hand for it, and the giant has been grinning ever since. Ho ho ho.

He's big and green and jolly all over.
COURTESY OF BLUE EARTH AREA CHAMBER OF COMMERCE
AND CONVENTION AND VISITORS BUREAU

Blue Earth is also the birthplace of the ice cream sandwich, but that's been overshadowed by the big fellow. Had it happened in some other town, a town that didn't already have a Jolly Green Giant, they might have put up a big ice cream sandwich statue.

If you turn south onto US Highway 169 from Interstate 90 (exit 119) at Blue Earth . . . as they say, you can't miss it. For more information call (507) 526-2916.

Bandtown USA, Certified by the USPS
Chatfield

Chatfield lies southeast of Rochester on US Highway 52, in Olmstead and Fillmore Counties; the line cuts the town in half, east to west, so cleanly that it goes right through a house. They've learned to live straddling that line—even though the garbage pickup is on different days in the two counties—and in fact it may explain their civic unity; Chatfield is one of the few towns in the state that has a tax levy for a city band. It's been that way since 1885, a band for anyone who wants to join—no audition required—and its size varies, usually from twenty-five to thirty players.

There was a band here as early as 1882 but things took off in 1969 when Jim Perkins revived the community band concept; he called as many of the old timers as were around for a rehearsal and sixteen people showed, six of them tuba players. They went on to establish a reputation: In 1978 Governor Anderson proclaimed Chatfield "Bandtown USA," and in 1982 they played for President Carter at the John Philip Sousa Memorial Concert in Washington. In 1983 the US Postal Service sent them forty thousand thirteen-cent commemorative stamps and permission to use a cancellation stamp: "Bandtown, USA, 125th Anniversary, 1858–1983."

The band is good enough that it has played alongside the US Marine Band, but what really put the town name on the musical map is the Chatfield Brass Band Music Lending Library, the only one of its kind in the world. Perkins started that, too, by asking people from all over the country to donate sheet music; when he took the band over there wasn't much of anything. He also donated land and got a grant to build their three-thousand-square-foot library building.

It now holds more than seventy-five thousand items, all cataloged and filed by volunteers. The categories include marches, overtures, waltzes, operettas, serenades, Dixieland, religious, patriotic, special holidays, and so forth. And one called "trombone smears." It has become a national resource for old band sheet music; they get calls from directors from all parts of the world.

Chatfield is on US Highway 52, between Rochester and Preston. The Music Lending Library is open Monday through Wednesday, 8 a.m. to noon and 1 to 4 p.m. The phone number is (507) 867-3275. If you can't stop in you should at least check their terrific website online at http://chatfieldband.lib.mn.us. They can also be found on Facebook.

World's Largest Ball of Twine
Darwin

One thinks of a ball of twine as a comfort, fitting nicely into the hand and a good thing to have around if one is recycling cardboard boxes. To farmers, especially those who deal with cattle and hay, it's much more; but no matter one's pursuits, it seems at home in the barn, in the garage, or in a kitchen drawer. One buys it at a certain size and over time it loses mass, like stars do, and eventually it becomes a black hole and one goes to buy another.

In Darwin a fellow named Francis A. Johnson had a ball of twine that just kept getting bigger, in direct contradiction to prevailing Ball of Twine theories, until it found itself in the *Guinness Book of World Records* and the subject of a song by Weird Al Yankovic. It began in 1950, when Francis wrapped two fingers with twine and then just kept wrapping, four hours a day, until the ball got so big he had to move it with railroad jacks to keep the growth circular; ultimately he had it raised off the ground with a crane so he could work all sides.

It grew in his yard for thirty-nine years, until Francis died in 1989 and left it to the city of Darwin. They moved it a block south to the base of the water tower, where it sits inside its own Plexiglas gazebo in the Twine Ball Compound, which naturally includes a souvenir shop. It's forty feet around, more than twelve feet in diameter, and weighs 17,400 pounds. It's the size of an asteroid; we're glad it grew here and didn't fall out of the sky. It abuses the notion of what a ball is, especially a ball of twine. Which, of course, is the whole point.

Now, there are other twine balls around that claim to be larger, but some of those have plastic twine in them—an abomination to the purist—and aren't nearly as heavy; and the main thing they aren't is that they aren't wrapped by one person. None of them. They are all team efforts, which really isn't the same thing at all.

And if any one man was destined to create the World's Largest Ball of Twine Rolled by One Man, it was probably Francis. He had the initial pressure of being the son of someone famous—US senator Magnus Johnson—and on top of that was a compulsive collector; he claimed to have five thousand pencils, two hundred feed caps, and an unknown large number of wooden ice cream containers. The twine caught the public's imagination, however, and catapulted him into the fame he enjoyed, which is today greater even than that of his father the senator.

Darwin celebrates "Twine Ball Days" on the second Saturday in August, just in time to catch motorcycle traffic returning from the big Sturgis Rally in South Dakota. You don't want to miss it.

The Ball of Twine Museum is on County Road 14, which runs south out of Darwin off US Highway 12. Hours are April 1 through October 1, Monday through Sunday 9:30 a.m. to 4:30 p.m. For more information call (320) 693-7544 or visit www.dasselenterprisedispatch.com/twine-ball-darwin.html.

Ergot: From Blight to Blessing

Dassel

The Universal Laboratories building in Dassel is on the National Register of Historic Places, not for architectural reasons but because for thirty years it was by far the largest producer of ergot in the United States. It began as Rice Laboratories, a maker of yeast for livestock feed. In 1937 they built an addition and named it Universal Laboratories, and the manager, Lester Peel, began the collection of this strange fungus. He knew it was a blood coagulant and that it was in demand at hospitals and by the military.

She's still at work, perhaps looking a bit stiff.

The most famous fort in the ergot war.

During World War II local women sat at tables here and sorted ergotic rye from the healthy grains, the social experience enhancing the good they were doing for wounded troops overseas. Those with small children were given bags of the grain to sort at home, and for many rural women it was their first actual paycheck.

But for centuries ergotism was a terrible and mysterious killer, going back to the beginnings of mankind's using grasses for edible seeds. Its properties were known to Plato and Socrates in the third millennium BC, and a potion made from ergot called *kykeon* was drunk for a thousand years in ritual Grecian ceremonies of the Euleusinian Mysteries. Initiates said they were "forever changed." It killed the same way it saved, by constricting arteries and by blocking the blood flow.

Spartans recorded symptoms "like fire" in 430 BC; thousands died from it in the Rhineland in 857, in Paris in 943 and Rheims in 1041. By the middle of the fourteenth century there were over fifty epidemics reported in central Europe and many more in Russia, where it stopped Napoleon's army in its tracks. It came in two varieties, gangrenous and convulsive, both types too painful and hideous to describe in a fun book like this; it killed six or seven of every ten infected. Domestic animals were not immune.

The connection of the fungus to rye and grains wasn't understood until 1673. The symptoms from ergot poisoning became known variously as Angel Fire, Holy Fire, St. Anthony's Fire, and the St. Vitus Dance, it found its way into the Salem Witch trials and burnings in America in 1692.

Researchers have since developed a synthetic version of ergot for medical uses and Universal Laboratories is now the Ergot Museum, where vintage fashion mannequins stand beside the old factory equipment and dramatic paintings of the plague and the witchcraft trials hang on the walls.

Marnach House

Elba

In the last thousand years not many countries on the planet have been run roughshod upon by neighbors like Luxembourg has. They've seen the boots of Italians, Huns, Spaniards, French, Dutch, Franks, Prussians, Austrians, and Nazis. Some made multiple visits.

It's not that big, 999 square miles, and less than half a million people live there. Not surprisingly, a good percentage of them speak three languages. French is the official language, but the Germans also plopped down enough times to pass on their melodious tongue. And they have developed their own specific language, Letzenbuergesch, probably out of sheer defiance. A little over a century ago they adopted a national motto: *"Mir wolle bleiwe wat mir sin,"* meaning "We want to remain what we are."

Luxembourg leaves its mark on a quiet valley.

All of which helps explain why it was a big deal to restore the old Marnach house in the Whitewater River Valley. It is the last remaining authentic stone home of the settlers who came over to Winona County from Luxembourg in the 1850s. They were enthusiastic farmers but they overcut the trees, and in thirty years' time cornfields began eroding right down the river. Whitewater State Park was created in 1919, and as failing farmland slowly became available the entire valley evolved back into a game refuge.

John Marnach was a stonemason and built his house in the traditional "Quereinhaus" style, which means there are six rooms, three up and three down, with no corridors and each with one window, facing south. A curved stairway goes from the kitchen in the center, where the doorway is, to the room upstairs. It has limestone walls more than two feet thick, with hand-sawn oak timbers and wood-pegged joinery. The square window openings are truncated, larger on the inside, and a straight ladder goes up to the attic. It was finished in 1860 and was occupied by John's descendants and later rented, until the property was bought by the Minnesota Department of Natural Resources (DNR) in 1949.

The DNR has no funding to maintain historical houses, so it fell into serious disrepair. The west wall cracked and moved and the roof was about to fall in when in 1991—just in time—stonemasons and carpenters were sent from Luxembourg as a donation. In a slow-moving drama over three summers they poured a new concrete beam around the base, rebuilt the west wall, and replaced the roof; they also put in new flooring and new doors, windows, and shutters. On August 12, 1993, they had a grand celebration, with international dignitaries, in the nearby town of Rollingstone. (Which is a good name for a town full of Luxembourgers, who are known for their ability to remain in one place.)

The Marnach House is on a 1.6-mile hiking trail that begins 3 miles north of Elba on Highway 74. For more information call the Minnesota DNR Information Center at (651) 296-6157 or (888) 646-6367 or write to Whitewater State Park, Route 1, Box 256, Altura, MN 55910. Also check out "Reflections of Luxembourg" by Suzanne L. Bunkers at www.intech.mnsu.edu/bunkers/marnach_house.htm.

Sinkhole Capital of the USA

Fountain

Looking at a black-and-white aerial photograph of Fountain, population 315, one immediately assumes the paper has been used for target practice with a 12-gauge shotgun. It's hard to count exactly how many, but within a mile and a half of the town there look to be about four hundred hits.

These are not potholes, which form in rock at the base of waterfalls or where sand and gravel are swirled in a stream, but are karst sinks, formed when underground limestone collapses from the action of rainwater; the underlying stone drops, and the topsoil drops with it. (To most Minnesotans, potholes happen when ice and salt freeze in the road surface and kick up huge shards of pavement, leaving axle-cracking craters big enough to homestead.)

Pietenpol Air Camper

In 1924, three years before Lindbergh crossed the Atlantic, a man named Bernard Pietenpol in Cherry Grove built an airplane powered by an engine from a Model T Ford; he knew how to build one before he knew how to fly. He managed the takeoff but not the landing and ended up nose-diving into a field, flopping the plane forward onto its back—the forward-roll maneuver that aviation instructors now encourage pilots to avoid. In 1928 he did successfully build and fly an aircraft that came to be known, through a journalist's remark, as the Air Camper, a design still being built today. You can order plans for it, and with a minimum of tools and a little welding you can be airborne for a few thousand dollars. They've been built now for more than seventy years, and it'd be hard to argue with the claim that this is the most successful airplane design in history.

The Air Camper has an open cockpit and weighs forty-three pounds less than a Harley Davidson Fat Boy (another open cockpit design); although it's not quite as fast as the Harley, it doesn't have to deal with road construction and carries the same number of passengers. Bernard's first one was a single-seater that had a frame built of wood from the local lumberyard, covered with bedsheet material painted with clear varnish. The landing gear was built from gas pipe and motorcycle wheels, the fittings were made at a blacksmith shop, and the engine was a water-cooled Ace four-cylinder, turning a propeller hand-carved from black walnut. It was flown fifty hours in its first two months.

There are about 5,750 karst sinks in Fillmore County, varying in size from 30 to 150 feet across; the deepest go down 30 feet, and in winter kids slide down the sides. They can't do this in all sinks, though, because most have a tree growing right smack in the center. Others have steep

Bernard made some changes in the landing gear and began using Ford Model A engines for power. The final two-seater design and drawings were finished in 1934 and haven't changed since. A factory was set up in Cherry Grove and another in Wykoff, and airplane kits were shipped from both places until World War II broke out in 1941, when Bernard officially became an aviation instructor. Over the years other engines have been used: Ford V8, Velie, Kinner, Lycoming, Franklin, Continental; when the Chevy Corvair was introduced in 1960, Bernard built an Air Camper to use its air-cooled engine. It was lighter and smoother and put out more power with less fuel. Modified plans are available for mounting various engines. The baggage compartment is still where it's always been: The passenger climbs in and you put the luggage in their lap.

Bernard's son and his grandson are both still in the home-built aircraft business. The garage where it all started was also hand-built, originally as a place to repair Ford Model Ts; the building is now on the National Register of Historic Places. Different times now; hard to picture some guy designing a moon rocket that you could build yourself out of stuff from your hardware store. Hard even to imagine going out in your yard and building a garage that would someday end up as a National Historic Place.

The Pietenpol Scout 1932 plane can be seen at the Fillmore County Historical Center at 202 County Road 8 in Fountain. Call (507) 268-4449 or visit http://fillmorecountyhistory.wordpress.com/ pietenpol for more information.

walls. This is also the reason you can drive all the way through Fillmore County and not see a single sinkhole; you look out in a wheat field and think you're seeing twenty-foot trees sitting out there, but they are actually crowns of forty-foot trees in twenty-foot holes.

People used to throw their garbage in the steep ones, until it became obvious the garbage was soaking down there at the same level as a lot of wells and was feeding springs to boot. So they don't use 'em for landfills anymore. Instead the town of Fountain did what most places do when they have some less-than-useful aberration: turned them into a tourist attraction. It worked on us.

There is a sinkhole at the entrance to the city, near the welcome sign, and a viewing platform not far away. The town brochure mentions other attractions: "The warm and friendly people of Fountain welcome you! The small town atmosphere is perfect for a pleasant and relaxing visit. . . ." And so forth. The Proud Sponsors of the brochure like to use mottoes: A cafe is "Open 7 Days"; a car wash says, "A Clean Car is a Happy Car"; and Willie's Grocery and Locker says, "Where You Meat Your Friends."

Fountain is located south of Rochester on US Highway 52. You can see sinkholes from almost any road in the county, especially on County Road 80 between Wykoff and Fountain.

World's Oldest Rock
Granite Falls

It's not something you'd expect to find in soybean country, but in the parking lot of the Yellow Medicine County Historical Museum just south of downtown Granite Falls, there is a sign that says WORLD'S OLD-EST ROCK. There's a lichen-covered outcropping there of Morton gneiss (pronounce it *nice*) that's 3.6 billion years old. It's hard as rock; they'll let you sit right on it, even though it's that old.

The planet itself is 4.5 billion years old; most rock that reached the crust in the early eons has long crumbled into dust, or been drawn

A rock older than dirt.

back down into the mantle. But the stone in this outcropping has been through an incredible series of geologic events, the most recent being when Lake Agassiz—a huge glacial lake that is now the Red River Valley—burst through a natural earth berm on its lower end and cut a trench through southern Minnesota. It was 180 feet deep in some places and took off an enormous amount of soil, revealing the shiny edge of solid rock that can be seen, here and there, for sixty miles along the Minnesota River; veteran rock from the Archean eon, when the earth's crust and oceans were formed. Geologists from around the world come here to visit it.

Now, 3.6 billion years is what they call "deep time"; time unimaginable. If a grown male spreads his arms and stretches his fingers out as far as they can reach, and if that distance, fingernail tip to fingernail tip, represents the age of this rock, then one firm stroke of an ordinary nail file would scratch off all of human experience, all the way back to before the beginnings of the Neanderthals. Two hundred thousand years, gone in one quick scratch.

It's impossible to grasp even the time in that scratch; getting a grip on the age of this rock is right up there with trying to understand the distance across the Milky Way. For those of us who can't even remember the last Super Bowl, a more useful mental exercise might be just to sit on the rock and try to imagine the next birthday coming up that we'll get in trouble for if we forget.

The Yellow Medicine County Historical Museum is at the convergence of Highways 23 and 67 and US Highway 212. Call (320) 564-4479.

Niagara Cave

Harmony

Niagara Cave has all the ingredients of a good road stop: history, mystery, fossils, a granddaddy stalactite, a wishing well, sunflower coral, a wedding chapel, and a sixty-foot-high underground waterfall.

In 1941 a touring Al Capone and his wife stopped in; this of course was after his Alcatraz tour. But it was popular with the local population before the celebrities discovered it. There have been hundreds of weddings down there, too—enough that older people coming to the place are often couples who were married there in the 1950s. A catered prom dinner was once held in the cave.

It's a fissure cave, as opposed to the tunnel type, meaning that it consists of interconnected underground cracks in a stone plate, if you can call a room 130 feet tall with a creek and a waterfall running through it a "crack." The granddaddy stalactite is 8 feet long and is in a big room 225 feet below the surface, with a bunch of his relatives. The sunflower coral is actually 350-million-year-old algae from the time of the first insects—the late Devonian epoch, when the Appalachians were formed and everything was all one continent. The various fossils are older yet, dating back 450 million years, to a time before life grew on the land. The limestone plate itself is five hundred thousand years old and was at one time situated on the equator.

The cave was discovered in 1924 by farm boys looking for three missing pigs, according to the story. They found a narrow sinkhole, peered in, and heard squealing way down below; professionals went down and found the pigs and a whole lot more. Must have been quite an experience for those boys; they were probably telling the story the rest of their lives, to anyone who would listen. When word got out the three cavers formed a partnership and leased the place. By 1934 pathways had been built and lighted for the tourist trade. The present owner, Mark Bishop, is a caver himself—a term now favored over *spelunker*—and has explored most of the network not open to the public; it extends well past the one-mile underground tour.

It is an amazing place. In the last room you look way down and see the creek disappear into a sheer wall. It travels in primeval darkness south through a few miles of rock to the river bluffs, where it reappears

Tilt-A-Whirl

You could ride a Tilt-A-Whirl a hundred thousand times in a row, if the carnival were in town long enough, and every single ride would be different. This was not the exact goal that woodworker Herbert W. Sellner set out to achieve when he invented and built the machine in 1926, but mathematicians using computers and the latest Chaos Theory formulae have taken it upon themselves to analyze what it takes to make fun fun, and they've proven that unpredictability is a big part of it.

Herbert had already pioneered breathtaking fun in 1923 when he invented the Water Toboggan Slide, a fabulous large wooden structure built out over the water where you would climb the ladder with your sled and then slide down at a high rate of speed and go zinging along the water for a hundred feet or so; they were "installed at beaches around the world."

The first Tilt-A-Whirl was operated at an amusement park in White Bear Lake, Minnesota. It was built mainly of wood and had nine swinging cars, each pivoting on its own platform about its own center; the cars rotate together over a roller-coaster track, causing each one to swing in different ways. As the mathematicians put it: "When the motion is chaotic . . . the resulting plot, known as a Pinker section, shows points scattered across the plane . . . the system is constantly shifting from one unstable periodic motion to another, giving the appearance of great irregularity . . . the movements of an individual car resemble those of a friction-impaired pendulum hanging from a support that is both rotating and being rocked back and forth while the pendulum swings."

as two natural clear-water springs, the Hawkeye and Odessa Springs, along the Upper Iowa River, which runs east into the muddy reality of the Mississippi. The temperature down there is a constant forty-eight degrees, all year long.

Easy for them to say.

At any rate, the Tilt-A-Whirl was an instant hit, with hundreds sold to parks and carnival operators across the United States. The Sellner Manufacturing Company is still in Faribault, where it began, and is still in the hands of the family; the president is Erin Sellner Ward, fun-loving Herbert W.'s great-granddaughter. Her husband is vice president and general manager. They sell other rides the company has designed, but the Tilt-A-Whirl is still the biggest seller. It has changed somewhat, now having seven cars instead of nine and being built of steel, aluminum, and fiberglass, but it is still rugged, reliable, easy to assemble, and very popular. Lately the company has been getting requests from people who want one in their own backyard; a new status symbol, apparently, in some level of our amazing society.

It is a fun ride for the operator, who has control of the overall rotating speed. He or she can pick out one car and, by just a slight acceleration at precisely the right second, can fling that car into a high-speed spin. Once they master that, some operators move up to the Advanced Hysteria Level in which they can accelerate two cars at once. And since each car carries different weight in different positions, no two ever behave quite the same way. The added benefit to the operator of maximizing the spin velocity—above the extra squealing—is that it means more change spills out of riders' pockets.

Physicist Richard L. Klutz of the National Institute of Standards and Technology says: "Ride designers have been fairly adept at finding chaos without appreciating the mathematics underpinning what they're doing."

Niagara Cave is located two miles south of Harmony on Highway 139, then two miles west on Niagara Cave Road; it's one mile north of the Minnesota-Iowa border on Highway 139. The cave is open daily from May through September, 9:30 a.m. to 5:30 p.m.; April and October it is open weekends only. For more information call (800) 837-6606 or write Niagara Cave, PO Box 444, Harmony, MN 55939.

The Windmill Collector
Jasper

On a collecting difficulty scale of one to ten one might find matchbooks or free catalogs down there in grade one, cigarette lighters and calendars probably two; from there on up you'd get into larger items like silverware, tools, fishing tackle, and snowmobiles. After that, vintage cars, farm machinery, and bulldozers. But at the top of the scale, collecting windmills has to be right up there with cabooses (are they cabeese?) and railroad bridges.

Terry Rodman started this collection about ten years ago when he fixed up an old windmill and then was offered another by a neighbor. People took notice and would say, "You lookin' for windmills? I got one you can have." After moving and renovating a few of the domestics, most of which were made in Illinois and Ohio, he developed an interest in overseas machines and found one over the phone in Australia; it took two and a half years of perseverance to get it here.

Then came another, from Mexico, and then Canada, Argentina, and even China; he found one in Brazil that took nine months in transit. It seems US Customs doesn't deal real well with windmills.

He now has a couple dozen of them up and operating and there is a large boneyard of parts and sections waiting across the road. His collection has been on national television.

Windmills are referred to by size—an eight-footer is one with an eight-foot-diameter fan; the height of the tower doesn't count and can be anything from eight to sixty feet tall.

The greater the fan diameter, the deeper the well can go. He has an old twenty-footer from Texas that goes down 1,520 feet and he's

All we need is a little breeze.

not sure how they could drill that deep back then. And a particular gem in the collection is one of only two three-legged Airmotor fans still standing.

He also has a twin fan twelve-foot irrigation windmill from Kansas, the blades rotating in opposite directions, which can pump a remarkable six hundred gallons a minute. Most are down in the one-hundred- to two-hundred-gallon range. The gears and bearings of the mills are generally very quiet, especially considering the terrific power they develop.

He's been to Holland a number of times and has built a half size version of the classic flood-control Dutch windmill with an outside walk-around deck; the inside is about the size of an average kitchen. On winter nights the four blades rotate slowly with their lights on.

You can view them from State Highway 23 just one mile north of Jasper on the east side of the road. You can't miss them. Terry Rodman can be contacted at PO Box 366, Jasper, MN 56144.

Hot Sam's
Lakeville

The HOT SAM'S ANTIQUES entry sign straddles the tall wheel of a deconstructed hay rake, as if it had been pulled in from the field and crashed there. You get the camera out, as do thousands of others when they see the place; it is a magnet for fashion shooters, set designers, and photo classes.

Here you'll find a hood and front fenders of a red, white, and blue Buick with the Statue of Liberty apparently standing in the front seat; a bare-metal short-track racing car parks on a two-wheel trailer nearby. A fifties-era Hudson pursuit car with spotlight and a roof-mounted siren sits across from a faded old Tijuana taxi.

A small biplane, red and yellow and shiny metal, sits near a rusted wrecker, lifting an even more rusted early-thirties sedan, utterly dilapidated, roofless, doors hanging by single hinges, wood spoke wheels, flat tires.

The problem was that he'd chase 'em down one at a time.

A shiny stainless two-story-tall guitar lies horizontal on a trailer, with real frets and strings. A small submarine rests nearby.

Nosedived into the weeds on the other side of a pond stands a yellow-winged open-cockpit plane with MOSQUITO CONTROL painted on the tops of the wings—and you are still getting acquainted with the place.

It all began ninety years ago when an Armenian emigrant stowed away on a freighter to get clear of the endless fighting with the Turks; he came to America, started a junk business, and raised a family. His daughter Gladys grew up to race stock cars with her husband in Michigan—in 1954 she won a national NASCAR women's meet—and they ultimately came to Lakeville and took up the antiques trade.

Gladys's son Robert joined the navy and spent nine years in Vietnam, returning to a country he barely knew. He said he had spent his youth in warfare and had nearly forgotten the language here. He joined the business and, with the passing of Gladys in 2011, is now the proprietor of this remarkable ten acres.

A well-furnished red Railway Express Agency caboose sits coupled to a green boxcar on rails across from the antiques store at the west end of the yard. A flock of black chickens patrols behind the store.

There's a lot more—literally a story with every artifact. They've been drawing crowds here for twenty-seven years. It's a terrific find. Hot Sam's is located at 22820 Pillsbury Avenue in Lakeville. Take Interstate 35 West south of Minneapolis to County Road 70 (exit 81), turn left to Kendrick Avenue, then turn right on Kendrick and it will become Pillsbury Avenue. Watch for the sign on the right. The phone number is (952) 469-5922.

The Hanson Wildlife Museum
Lenora

It's like reviewing a hidden Metropolitan Museum of Art, this place; more than a person can comprehend in one dose. Bruce Hanson began collecting as a kid, when he was walking behind his father's plow and saw an Indian spearhead disappear beneath the soil. He couldn't find it and says he's had his eyes on the ground ever since.

The museum, at the end of a driveway lined with bowling balls, is a campus of eighteen buildings in hilly country, most of them small farm structures built for raising poultry and the like. They remind you of oysters, funky and rough on the outside and quite something else inside. Like medieval churches in Mexico. They contain amazing collections from around the world; wildlife has been Bruce's main interest, but there is a building full of antique cast-iron kitchen utensils and Avon products; a building featuring small metal sculptures, and one of natural wood oddities, burls and Florida knees, ginseng roots, mushrooms, and so forth; and yet another of beautiful wood carvings from artists far and wide. He gathers these pieces at auctions, estate sales, and junkyards, through word of mouth, and by pure chance.

A building contains a jaw-dropping collection of horns and antlers, from Cape buffalo to roe deer from the Black Forest and including the not-as-rare-as-you-might-think jackalope, a half-jackrabbit half-antelope critter commonly seen in saloons in the American West. Another shed holds a fantastic collection of knives like you never quite imagined knives could be. Yet another is full of axes and hand tools, including an ax that looks like it was designed for beheadings but was actually used to trim logs for house construction. A separate building contains 1,400 wrenches, plus gripping tools of all types.

There's a collection of wild animal pelts, including one of the now extinct civet cat and also featuring marmot, mink, weasel, marten, Alaskan wolverine, Canadian bobcat, and fox of many breeds—an inventory of the wild fauna of North America. Another little building contains the fantastic seashells of the world, thousands of them, causing visitors to *ooh* and *aah* uncontrollably. Bruce has the fossil of a giant squid, found on his own land.

He has the ordinary as well as the exotic: figurines, license plates, horseshoe collections. A thousand bottles and cans take you through the history of American patent medicine and beer, and although Mr. Hanson has never been a beer drinker, he has five hundred brands of it on display, including the famous J. R. Ewing and Gilly's brands from Texas and Billy Beer from the ex-president's brother. (Ne'er-do-well relatives seem to be a common affliction of Democrat presidents.)

He's farmed this land since taking over from his dad, sheared sheep—five thousand in one year—and worked for a while for a well-known fur buyer, once skinning a hundred raccoons in a single night; he's also hunted ginseng, especially back when it was plentiful and when the searchers would only take a portion and leave the rest to grow. He says it was not uncommon for him to have a hundred pounds of it dried for sale at the end of the season; asked if he used it himself, he replies: "No. . . . It ain't good for nothin'." He's worked as a logger, selling timber from the property, and as a taxidermist.

Nothing says "welcome" like
a collection of animal skulls.

The security system consists mainly of nine dogs, penned in the day and loose at night, and an alert owner; you aren't sure what other measures are in place, but the single robbery attempt against him was foiled quickly and he hasn't been bothered since.

School kids are brought here on field trips, although, he says, the next-door neighbors have never been through the place. They just don't know what they're missing.

The Hanson Wildlife Museum is on County Road 24, one and a half miles west of Lenora. Lenora itself is not easy to find, but it's about seven miles east and two miles north of Harmony, down there close to the Iowa line. The museum has no phone.

Blue Mound Mystery

Luverne

In southwestern Minnesota near the South Dakota border there is a large outcropping of Sioux quartzite rock—rock formed at the bottom of a sea a billion and a half years ago—called the Blue Mound and now part of the Blue Mound State Park. One side of the formation drops off into cliffs that may or may not have been the site of Plains Indian buffalo jumps—a discussion one would think would be easy to settle just on the evidence.

A more interesting mystery sits not far away: a line of rocks a quarter mile long lying on an east–west azimuth. Twice a year—at the spring and fall equinoxes—the sun rises directly at the east end of this line and sets on the west end of it, meaning that twice a year at least a dozen people climb the mound and sit and wait for dawn. The land is fairly quiet most of the rest of the time; it contains a goodly stand of big bluestem grasses, which can grow an inch a day and get to seven feet tall, and a herd of bison numbering forty-five animals. The Minnesota Department of Natural Resources has reintroduced a hundred different native wildflowers to the park, and there are patches of prickly pear cactus on some of the shallow soils on the rock; in late June and early July, they bloom yellow.

There has been no agreement as to who built the line of rocks, though it's accepted that they have been in place for many centuries. Some like to think they were set by white men from a time even earlier than the Norsemen's arrival; others say they were set in place by ancient peoples who predated the known Indian tribes, and may be related to other celestial references in stone scattered around the American West and in Canada. Nothing fires the imagination like big rocks with unknown histories.

Blue Mound State Park is two miles north of Luverne on US Highway 75, the King of Trails.

The Birth of Waterskiing

In 1922 the tomb of Tutankhamun was discovered in Egypt, the USSR was formed, the BBC began broadcasting in England, and Mussolini came to power in Italy; here in the United States, Prohibition had been in effect for two years and we were about ready to party, and at that critical juncture in history a reckless eighteen-year-old kid from Lake City, Minnesota, invented waterskiing. It didn't exactly hurl us into the Roaring Twenties, but it did nothing to hold us back, either.

His name was Ralph Samuelson. His youth was spent as a Huck Finn river rat; he dived for clams in the thirty-mile-long and three-mile-wide spot in the Mississippi known as Lake Pepin, two blocks from his home. The clams were sold to a now long-gone factory in town that made them into shell buttons.

Samuelson used snow skis for his first attempt at waterskiing. After he was dragged like a boulder behind his brother's twenty-four-horsepower boat for a couple of hours, he decided they weren't wide enough. Barrel staves didn't have enough curl, and he was dragged for another few hours. He went to a lumberyard and bought two eight-foot pine boards, nine inches wide. He boiled the front ends in water and clamped them around a curved surface to curl the tips. After two more days of being dragged around the lake in front of the whole town, he got the idea of keeping the tips up when his brother hit the power, and on July 2, the last day before his nineteenth birthday, he rose upright out of the water, driving his friends on the shore wild. He had to zigzag to stay up because the boat could only reach twenty miles an hour.

He made better skis and found more powerful boats, up to one with a propeller and an airplane engine that could hit fifty miles per hour. He built a greased ski jump and would amaze vacationers by jumping sixty feet and landing upright. He went from the boat to a World War I Curtis-Wright flying boat, and sometimes at eighty miles an hour it'd get airborne in spite of itself and carry him twenty feet above the water. The first time he lost a ski he invented slalom skiing right there. He invented barefoot skiing when he lost both of them. The young man never got hurt doing this.

And he never made any money at it, either. Bought a yellow roadster and toured the country and did sensational shows from Florida to Detroit, but he'd only take enough to pay his expenses. His son Jon later said, "That was Americana in those days. The whole country was filled with people who were unique and didn't invent something to become famous and rich, but just to try something new."

Samuelson injured his back and wrist in an accident unrelated to waterskiing and eventually moved back to Minnesota, to Mazeppa, and the nation forgot about him. He became a success at raising turkeys and was married in the late 1940s to a woman named Hazel, who said, "When I married Ralph, I didn't know anything about his death-defying waterskiing. But I knew we were defying something to raise turkeys."

He was rediscovered in the mid-1960s and recognized for what he'd done, and for the last ten years of his life rode in parades and made speeches on behalf of the state. In 1977 Ralph was invited to Winter Haven, Florida, for groundbreaking ceremonies at the Water Ski Hall of Fame, where he was a charter member. Hazel said later: "He shouldn't have gone—we wanted him to go back to the Mayo Clinic—but it was important to him to make that trip. As soon as he got home, he passed away."

Another Lake City resident, Dennis Francis, traveled the entire navigable length of the Mississippi on water skis in the summer of 1973. It was 1,842 miles; his expenses were $17,000. He started on July 3, Ralph's birthday, and reached the Gulf of Mexico thirteen days later, where, according to a newspaper account, "Some twenty dolphins formed a welcoming party." At $9.32 a mile, they should have brought champagne.

Lutefisk and Outhouse Races
Madison

The World's Largest Codfish sits in J. F. Jacobson Park on a base that reads:

MADISON MN

LUTEFISK CAPITAL

USA

It was commissioned in 1982 when two members of the city council proposed they give themselves that title because they had been holding lutefisk celebrations in town for a long time. They probably didn't need to add that the title was vacant, that it had always been vacant, and that it was unlikely anyone else would ever want it, *lutefisk* being the Norwegian word for gelatinous remains of codfish slabs packed in lye in wooden barrels to withstand the rigors of long trips in sailing ships. It's often slimy and doesn't smell all that great, but boiled and buttered it's really not that bad. To a Scandinavian, anything boiled and buttered can be pretty decent.

The statue was finished in 1983 and turned out real nice; twenty-five feet long, fiberglass, finished in bright acrylics. It has ten fins and a fat belly, and a wide-awake fish-eye openmouthed look of surprise and wonderment. It was named Lou T. Fisk and in 1984 was hauled to other places named Madison, as in Wisconsin, Ohio, New Jersey, and Connecticut, with a stop at Madison Avenue in New York on the way. This put the town on the map, however briefly, when the story was picked up by CBS-TV, NBC-TV, the *Wall Street Journal,* the *New York Times,* the *Chicago Tribune,* and the *Christian Science Monitor.*

More than thirty years later, Norsefest (also known as Stinker Day) is still going strong. The annual celebration features ethnic costumes, dumplings and ham, krumkake, rommegrot, lefse, and lutefisk. And outhouse races, possibly less dramatic than NASCAR racing; there's just one outhouse, which is open, with a roof and a toilet seat. It's pushed around a pylon-marked timed course, three to a team, and it

You can tune a piano, but you can't tune a cod.

features the so-called Norwegian steering—turn right, go left. And it's very touchy, so people get flustered and run into curbs and pylons. It makes for amusing racing.

And for all the other excitement, the highlight of the Norsefest Evening of Entertainment is the Lutefisk Eating Contest. It's not an event for the faint of heart; the winner generally needs to put down about eight pounds of lutefisk. Many of us get queasy just looking at a single serving.

For Madison information call the chamber of commerce at (320) 598-7373 or visit www.madisonmn.info.

The Mystery Boy

In the small town of Janesville there is a roadside park with a small memorial containing a time capsule. It's a sweet little place, worth stopping for, but the icon for which the town is famous is nothing as grand as that; it's just a life-sized figure in a high gabled attic window of a two-story frame house by US Highway 14.

A young boy, maybe five, stands behind the glass. He has a round face, his head tilted to the right and down, looking to the street as if expecting someone. He has chubby cheeks and far-spread eyes; a short nose. There is an expression of interest about the mouth. He's wearing a jacket or shirt with a collar, and has what appears to be a bird on his head. But it could be a hat.

If you ask a teenage girl in Winona if she knows of any unusual places around there, she might say, "Well, there's that boy in the window in Janesville," and her mother will say, "Don't tell 'em about that. That's nothing they'd be interested in." But of course we would, and so are a lot of people. He is a compelling figure up there; not unlike the statue of the woman in the Savannah harbor, looking out to sea, waiting for a certain sailor whom we all know isn't coming back.

Motorists stop and take pictures. At least once a week a stranger will ask about it, and years ago someone called the county nurse and reported a boy held captive. The house has been in the family for a hundred years, but no one is quite sure when the boy first appeared in the window. The owner, Ward Wendt, is friendly and will show you an interesting parlor full of antiques, but he has little to say about the mystery boy.

So without a ready-made legend from the household itself, people have made up their own. Some say the clothes are never changed; others say they're changed daily. Some say there was a terrible

For Sale: three-bedroom, two-bath house; small child in attic.

tragedy, and others claim he's actually not a boy at all but some creature in disguise, one capable of putting curses on people. Some say there is a camera hidden up there. There are dozens of versions, which become more intense around Halloween.

A great favor this boy has done for his neighbors, to loosen so many imaginations. And to show us what can be done with a simple figure and a long and sustained silence.

Janesville sits on US Highway 14 about nine miles east of Mankato. You can see the Mystery Boy at 114 West First Street, a block before the main street in town, or visit www.youtube.com/watch?v=lPxHLY1XAJo.

Salt Lake

Marietta

There's a 250-acre lake on a country road in Lac Qui Parle County near the South Dakota border, surrounded by grasslands and open country. The only structure visible is a platform, accessible from a gravel parking lot, and a sign remembering Mrs. C. E. Peterson. It is the most alkaline body of water between the Atlantic Ocean and Great Salt Lake.

Goodman Larson lived next door to Mrs. Peterson, as a boy in neighboring Madison in the 1930s; she was a pharmacist and one of the few birders in that part of the country in those days. She'd take him along to help band birds, and she'd often spot unusual species at the lake, ocean birds and birds like Marbled Godwits, Snowy Egrets, Cattle Egrets, and Eared Grebes, as well as Horned and Western Grebes. She'd report these to Dr. Roberts, then the curator of the Museum of Natural History at the University of Minnesota, and, as these are not Minnesota birds, he'd occasionally question her accuracy. "So . . . she would catch one in a trap and then, while she's a lovely lady, to prove that she was right, she'd squeeze it until it died and she'd send it to him," says Larson.

It was through her early interest that this lake was preserved; she personally banded thousands of birds, more than anyone ever had at the time, and she brought the place to the attention of naturalists who would later rescue it from becoming a dumping ground for farm machinery and general junk—a status it was well on the way to acquiring. It is now a major station for the MOU, the Minnesota Ornithological Union, drawing birders worldwide to see migrating Avocets and Sandhill Cranes, Tundra Swans, Snow Geese, and Red-necked and Wilson's Phalaropes. Whoever heard of a Phalarope in Minnesota?

And it's developed into a social event for the town as well: In spring the Sons of Norway put on an evening banquet and the town of Marietta serves a breakfast and a noon lunch for birders. Other towns in the area are jumping into the competition; with hundreds of strangers coming in from all over the world, it's getting to be a big deal out there.

Marietta sits five miles north of US Highway 212 on County Road 7, two miles from South Dakota; Salt Lake is one mile west and three miles south of town. Visit online at www.wildlifeviewingareas.com/wv-app/parkdetail.aspx?parkid=461.

Box Elder Bug Days
Minneota

They are a polite bug, clean and handsomely marked in red and black, formal and neatly shaped, especially when compared to box elders themselves. They don't eat crops, spread disease, smear the roads, foul the waters, buzz, bite, sting, or stink. But in September you couldn't get enough zeros on this page to number them, and they all want to get in your house and spend the winter with you.

And small towns in this state like nothing better than to identify a local nuisance and celebrate it with a weekend named after it. Farming's becoming more solitary all the time; some of those folks need to have a reason to come to town and have some fun.

It began in Minneota in 1985 as Town and Country Day, the first Saturday after Labor Day; after a few years they decided to juice it up a little with some humor, and in 1990, after local writer and poet Bill Holm assigned the insect as a poetry subject for his college students and published a book of the resulting verse, it became Box Elder Bug Day. In 1991 they added another day, and in '95 made it three days. They hide a wooden box elder bug named Olaf and the finder gets a fifty-dollar bill; they have a street dance, a beer garden, a queen and her court (". . . yes, child, your grandma Britney was once the Box Elder Bug Queen of Minneota, Minnesota . . ."), arts and crafts stands, a kiddie parade, antique tractor plowing, a magic show, a chili cook-off, quilt shows, puppet shows, pony rides, a whopper feed, bull riding, a softball tournament, a sheep-to-shawl weaving demonstration, along with rock bands, a horn band, a Dixieland band, a Grand Parade, a sporting clay shoot, and a lot more—including of course box elder bug races.

(Continued on page 51)

Big Honza's Museum of Unnatural History

It's not a large museum but it holds a lot of funny flummery, mostly centered around Big Honza Giganticzech, a supersized Czech in the spirit of the Nordic Paul Bunyan and the vegetarian Jolly Green Giant: oversized and approachable.

The museum offers group day tours that include a musical variety show, an ethnic specialty lunch, and a tour of the museum containing a

"I can't get him to leave."

good bit of droll memorabilia, such as a model of the truck Honza hand-lettered during a bout of dyslexia: REVE-PIRD GNIFOOR CO. (Ever-Drip Roofing Co., now defunct). You can also view the World's Largest Nit, Big Honza's Airplane/Corn Shredder, the 2-Person Alarm Clock, a Honzertina—The World's Only Chain-Driven Concertina, and Big Honza's Navel-Lint Dreamcoat Sweater.

One may purchase Big Honza's Little Misfortune Cookies, inspired by a Chinese railroad foreman who worked south of Montgomery. Inside they have such useful aphorisms as, "Sometimes when you leap, planning to hit the ground running, you just hit the ground," and "You will be gratified to learn that several of your friends have recommended you for a personality transplant."

If you are not amused by the Big Honza you may want to have your humor trigger Czech'd out. For information on the museum visit www .bighonza.com.

(Continued from page 49)

You race your box elder bug on the same track you race your wood tick; athletes start in the center of the circle and the first to reach the outer ring wins. If they panic and fly it's a match disqualification. No exceptions: gotta have at least one of the six feet on the track at all times. You can buy racing bugs at the Bug Market there, and you can also buy a book of authentic box elder bug poems.

Box Elder Bug Days are held the first weekend after Labor Day in Minneota. For more information call the Minneota Bug Days Committee at (507) 872-5252 or visit www.boxelderbugdays.com.

Glockenspiel
New Ulm

There are two tons of brass bells hanging in a forty-five-foot tower smack in the middle of this city. The biggest bell, a low C, weighs 595 pounds, and together with its associates it plays a series of tunes every day at noon, 3 p.m., and 5 p.m.; when the bells play, figurines in the tower dance, seemingly in spite of themselves.

This is an analog timepiece, with four clock faces with huge hands and a lot of gears and very few microchips, harking back to an age when there were only one or two clocks in a whole town and the knowledge of the correct time was held by very few. The tolling of the time sent a message of power beyond the imagination of the average miserable peasant—later to become our ancestor—and was a source of pride and wonder. Time wasn't something you carried around back then; you got it from the authorities, when they wanted to give it to you. Now children carry time on their wrists more precise than observatories in those old days. Digital timepieces sell for the price of an hour's pay at an analog hamburger joint, or free for opening a bank account.

With analog time this large you also get large analog music, real bells with real strikers inside, and you don't have the options you get with your digital devices, such as the type of ringer and the tune—for instance, you can't choose a Hungarian Dance or the Hokey-Pokey or

A town where no one asks you for the time of day.

Hermann the German keeps watch
over New Ulm's 14,000 residents.

the Waltz Militaire, or even the Regular Ring. The options belong to
the person at the keyboard, and you get what they give. But it's free.
It's not only free, but you get it whether you want it or not. There's a
lesson in there, children; who can tell me what it is?

New Ulm, a city of fourteen thousand, is a natural place for the first
freestanding carillon clock tower in the United States. It was built here in
1980 with donations from people in thirty-one states and fifty-one Minnesota towns, and it fits right in with the town's ongoing celebration of
all things Germanic. It was settled that way on purpose, by a contingent
of Chicago immigrants from the province of Württemberg, where Ulm
is the main city, and has kept many of the original names, costumes and
holidays. Oktoberfest and Fasching are big here: lots of lederhosen and
polka bands, a time of tubas, bratwurst, accordions, and beer.

Bandwagon

An obituary notice captioned
CHUCK PASEK—TV HOST, 76,
read as follows:

Mankato, Minn.—Chuck Pasek, the longtime host of a weekly television program featuring polka and old-time music, died Tuesday after a long illness. He was 76.

Mr. Pasek was the host of "Bandwagon" on KEYC-TV in this southern Minnesota city for more than 30 years until he retired in 1995. Mr. Pasek also was program director for many years while working on air as sports director, then as a news anchor.

Before going into television, Mr. Pasek did sports and news reporting for KYSM-AM in Mankato.

A nice little notice but not that unusual—except that it was printed in the *San Diego Union-Tribune.* His wife wrote: "I received notes, letters & cards from people all over the US—old Mankato residents that had grown up listening to him. His death was carried in many cities in the US."

The show is still carrying on, the longest-running live polka show in the country. Almost thirty years ago the *Mankato Free Press* ran a story on the show's amazing longevity. "The Bandwagon Show has been so successful it's almost embarrassing," wrote Tim DeMarce. "In the last 10 years the show has always been in the top 10 of all Nielsen-rated programming on the station, including the best that CBS has to offer."

Bandwagon went on the air November 21, 1961, when the station itself was only a year and a half old. It's always been local bands and local dancers, people whose friends are watching them on television. Chuck Pasek once said: "Why, they come in here on Monday nights, and they're celebrating their fiftieth wedding anniversary, and Mom's in a long gown, and Dad's in his best suit, and they've got boutonnieres on, and they slip me a note to say they're in the audience. Their relatives are all at home watching, and after they leave here they'll go out and buy Ma dinner. I can't hardly ignore it. That's golden. . . . We try to make 'em part of the show."

It's been forty-five years of fun, and a hitch or two; a streaker furnished a memorable *Bandwagon* moment back in the 1960s. And a man fell down with a heart attack on the dance floor one week and was back the next.

They do receive the occasional complaint. Pasek was quoted: "They're mostly from people who weren't raised around here, some professor from the college or somewhere. I call 'em the 'intelligencia.' They say it's corny, but I don't argue with 'em. I've never claimed it was great art." Pasek became the "sex symbol of the over-60 set," getting him squeals from the ladies and sometimes packages of dressed chickens, or pork chops, or homemade bread. He said, "They're really nice people, and if this is what they enjoy instead of Beethoven, then that's their right."

Bandwagon is recorded Monday nights at 8 p.m. at the KEYC-TV studios, 1570 Lookout Drive in North Mankato. Dancers are welcome. It is broadcast the following Saturday from 6 to 6:30 p.m. central time. For more information call (507) 625-7905 or visit http://keyc .dayport.com/bandwagon. Tell 'em we sent you.

On a high hill overlooking the city stands the heroic figure of Hermann the German, his sword upraised. Hermann the German was the man who freed them from the rule of the Romans—this was back in Europe of course but it's kept the Romans from bothering them over here as well.

The Glockenspiel is in Schonlau Plaza, 4th North and Minnesota Street, in New Ulm. For more information visit www.newulmweb.com.

Charles Hanson Duck Collection
Ortonville

Charles Hanson has been interested in water birds since he was a farm boy in the 1940s, admiring the fabulous plumage of ducks and geese brought home by his dad and uncles in hunting season. They lived near Artichoke Lake in western Minnesota, right in the middle of the migratory flyway, and he was witness to a rich variety of Teal, Pintails, Mallards, Wood Ducks, Bluebills, Redheads, Canvasbacks, and Goldeneyes.

A fascination with preserving the birds put him into taxidermy and he got good at it, and when he had the chance to hunt farther afield he went, ultimately making seven trips to Alaska, for the Emperor Goose and other exotic coastal species. The Kodiak and St. Lawrence Islands yielded sea ducks: Eiders, Scoters, and the beautiful Harlequin Duck. The collection contains birds from everywhere, including the Baikal Teal from Siberia, the Chiloe Wigeon from South America, and the Capercaillie Grouse of northern Europe, the world's largest Grouse at twelve pounds. Charles hunts birds on a one-of-each basis, as an entomologist hunts bugs; it's not about the meat. He might carry the same two shotgun shells in his pocket for weeks in the field.

The result of this life's work in the marshes of the world is a collection of more than five hundred species of waterfowl, including even the extinct Labrador Duck. He didn't help this bird to extinction—it was already gone—but he put together a dead-accurate re-creation of it using markings and features from a Common Scoter, a Red-breasted Merganser, and a White Call Duck.

Clearly, Hanson was a man with his ducks in rows.

In addition to the waterfowl, he has gathered and displayed a large number of American Indian artifacts, vintage cars, and old John Deeres. He and his wife have traveled to Latin America, India, and Asia as volunteers, helping to build schools and hospitals, and he has reconstructed, moved, and donated the old Artichoke Lake Trading Post, built by his uncles of ax-hewn logs, to the Big Stone County Historical Society. It is in this original log building that his bird collection is on display, and it is most amazing; especially that one man, with help from no college, trust, or government, could have assembled and constructed what is very likely the most complete collection of waterfowl in the world.

You can see the Charles Hanson Collection at the Big Stone County Historical Society (320-839-3359) located at the junction of US Highway 75 and US Highway 12.

Shootout

Some like to say that Northfield's famous bank holdup was the last battle of the Civil War, fought eleven years after the fact on the main street of a prospering northern small town. Jesse James of Missouri, who had fought with Quantrill's Raiders, was said to harbor a deep dislike for two of the First National Bank's stockholders, one a Union general and the other a notorious carpetbagger.

It happened in the nation's one hundredth year, the year Alexander Graham Bell invented the telephone; on September 7, 1876, ten weeks after George Custer and his troops were killed at the Little Bighorn and just a week after Wild Bill Hickock was shot in the head in Deadwood—and fifty-four days after the first major-league no-hitter was pitched, by George Bradley of the St. Louis Brown Stockings against the Hartford Dark Blues.

The James brothers, Frank and Jesse; Cole, Bob, and Jim Younger; along with Charley Pitts, Clell Miller, and Bill Chadwell, rode north to Northfield with more than vengeance on their minds; the bank was rumored to hold $200,000 on any given day, and a sleepy little Minnesota river town didn't seem likely to be a problem. After ten years of successful armed robbery in Missouri and Kentucky, they were well dressed, well armed, and well ponied. And they were cool.

Northfield was a town of hardworking farmers, millers, and storekeepers, mostly of Swedish descent, and eight strangers riding in on fine horses and wearing suits and fancy long coats and shiny black boots, Colts on the hip and new Winchesters in the scabbards—well, they kind of stood out. They'd never had a bank robbery in Northfield, but they had an idea of what one might look like, and this sort of had that look. Especially when Jesse, Bob Younger, and Charley Pitts went into the bank, with Cole Younger and Miller standing outside, while Frank, Jim Younger, and Chadwell sat on their horses at the end of the street and didn't say much. A barber told a customer to wipe the shaving cream off his face and get ready to fight.

A hardware store owner from across the street, J. A. Allen, came over to the bank, walked up to Clell, and asked: "What's going on here, young man?" Miller is said to have replied, "Shut your damned mouth and git," and shoved him off the boardwalk. And just that quick the street was full of men with shotguns, revolvers, cleavers, knives; whatever was handy. Rifles magically appeared in upstairs windows.

And inside the bank a teller named Joseph Heywood refused to open the vault. Cole stuck his head in the door and said they had trouble outside, and Pitts gratuitously shot Heywood in the head on his way out. On the street they were met with a hail of gunfire; Miller and Chadwell were killed, Pitts was mortally wounded, and all three Younger brothers were hit, later to be captured at Madelia, Minnesota, and sent to prison.

The James boys got away; Jesse put a new Missouri gang together and robbed trains—his last four in 1881, the same year Louis Pasteur developed an immunization for anthrax. Jesse was killed the next year by Bob Ford, another outlaw, for the ransom, and Frank turned himself in and was never convicted of anything.

They hold a reenactment, "The Defeat of Jesse James Days," the weekend after Labor Day. It's a lot of fun.

For more information call the Northfield Chamber of Commerce at (800) 658-2548 or visit www.northfieldchamber.com.

Pipestone Quarry
Pipestone

> *At an ancient time the Great Spirit, in the form of a large bird, stood upon the wall of rock and called all the tribes around him, and breaking out a piece of the red stone formed it into a pipe and smoked it, the smoke rolling over the whole multitude. He then told his red children that this red stone was their flesh, that they were made from it, that they must all smoke to him through it, that they must use it for nothing but pipes: and as it belonged alike to all the tribes, the ground was sacred, and no weapons must be used or brought upon it.*

An artist named George Catlin wrote this in 1836; it is a Lakota account of the beginnings of pipestone. Other versions come from other of the Plains Indians: the Crow, the Pawnee, and the Blackfeet. Stone pipes from two thousand years ago have been found in Ohio, but indications suggest that pipes from this quarry were first carved sometime in the 1600s, when Indians first acquired steel tools through trade.

Catlin had set out to document North American Indians in oil on canvas; although he wasn't the first white man there, his was the first published account of the quarries and of the petroglyphs around the base of three nearby granite boulders, called the Three Sisters. The Indians considered them the guardians of the sacred red stone. The formal name of the stone is Catlinite; a rare honor for a painter, to have an entire class of rock named after him.

The general public didn't become aware of it until a poet began his most famous narrative with: "On the mountains of the prairie / On the great Red Pipestone Quarry. . . ." This was in 1855, Longfellow's *Song of Hiawatha,* an epic that is reenacted yearly at the nearby amphitheater built specifically for the purpose.

Our first national monument wasn't signed into existence until 1937, when the Pipestone National Monument was opened to the public, with quarrying limited to Indians. The first park ranger was a great man, an Ojibwa named Standing Eagle, also known as George Bryan. His skill and artistry at carving pipes was such that Presidents Truman and Eisenhower were presented with them; a beautiful example hangs in the Smithsonian Institution in Washington. He carved the largest peace pipe in existence, the Buffalo Pipe, which hangs here at the visitor center.

His son Richard recently retired after twenty years with the National Park Service; he and his family carry on the legacy, carving pipes as they have been carved for hundreds of years. Patiently, and with great artistry.

You can visit the monument every day of the week throughout the year. The hours are 8 a.m. to 5 p.m., with extended summer hours. It is located north of the city of Pipestone on US Highway 75, then west on County Road 67. Contact the Pipestone National Monument, 36 Reservation Avenue, Pipestone, MN 56164; (507) 825-5464, ext. 214.

Das Boot

Red Wing

On a high knoll overlooking US Highway 30 in Hallam, Pennsylvania, there stands a structure billed by some as the World's Largest Shoe. Built in 1949 as a promotional tool by a man in the shoe business, it would more properly be called the World's Largest House in the Shape of a Shoe—because it's a house.

Don't fall for it. The official World's Largest Shoe is in Red Wing, Minnesota, made on a giant wooden shoemaker's last from actual boot-making materials: eighty leather hides held together with twelve hundred feet of nylon rope and three hundred pounds of adhesives; sixty gallons of urethane in the sole, which is flexible, plus eighty gallons for the covering of the sole. It was lock-stitched together with the same thread and sewing machines used in the making of the company's regular work boots. Eighty pounds of brass was used for the eyelets and the shoelace is 104 feet long, and a person had to be lowered into the boot with pulleys to do the final stitching. The gusset label was sewn on a tapestry loom in Italy.

The *Guinness Book of World Records* certified it in February of 2005, replacing the previous title-holder, a Filipino pair 18 feet long and 6 feet tall. This one is a single Red Wing signature work boot for the left foot, a classic Model 877 with the crepe sole and the white stitching, a size 638 1/2 D (European size 850)—twenty feet long, sixteen feet tall, and seven feet wide. It would fit a one-legged workman standing twelve stories tall; if a two-legged one showed up they'd have to spend another few months to build the right one. A guy that size would probably put 'em on and then walk up to Bemidji

W. W. Mayo House

William Worrall Mayo was born in 1819 in the village of Eccles, near Manchester, England. He studied medicine in Glasgow and London and sailed for America in 1845, working first in New York City's Bellevue Hospital and then moving on to the Indiana Medical College; he married Louise Abigail Wright in 1851. He didn't take a straight-line path to becoming a doctor: He was at various times a tailor, a census taker, a farmer, a justice of the peace, and a ferry boat operator. In 1854, while suffering one of a number of bouts of malaria he caught in Indiana (perhaps it's more like India than we think), he hitched a horse and wagon and told his wife he was going north: "I'm going to keep on driving until I get well or die." He found the weather to his liking and moved his family to St. Paul.

In 1859 he built with his own hands a beautiful little Gothic house at 118 North Main Street in Le Sueur. He set up his first medical practice in an upstairs room, nine feet by ten feet, and became known as the Little Doctor; he was five feet, four inches tall. In 1861 his first son, William James, was born in the house.

in sixty-foot strides and knock Paul Bunyan on his keister, just for sport.

It took sixty volunteers and retirees thirteen months to design and build the masterwork, working mostly at night. It's now the center-piece of their handsome new museum, along with 17,000 square feet of the company's 105-year heritage, all done in photos, interactive displays, and original paintings by Norman Rockwell. For all the statistics,

In 1863 he was appointed examining surgeon for the Civil War draft board of southern Minnesota, headquartered in Rochester, and the following year he moved his practice there, where his second son, Charles Horace, was born; ultimately the doctor and his sons founded the Mayo Clinic.

The house in Le Sueur was bought by Carson Nesbit Cosgrove; three generations of the family lived in the house from 1874 to 1920. C. N., known as the Little Giant, was five feet, three inches tall and the driving force and the first president of the Minnesota Valley Canning Company; his son Edward and his grandson Robert were each born in the house that Dr. Mayo built, and they both served long and well at the company C. N. built. In 1950, under Robert's leadership, it became the Jolly Green Giant.

Two of Minnesota's proudest organizations, both hatched in a modest but elegant white house made by the careful hands of a surgeon, in this quiet river town.

The Mayo House is located at 118 North Main Street in Le Sueur. It is open May, September, and October, Saturday only from 1 to 4:30 p.m., and June through August, Tuesday through Saturday from 10 a.m. to 4:30 p.m. Call (507) 665-3250 or (507) 665-6965 for more information.

the four-pound eyelets and the 104-foot lace and the fact that it would be a couple sizes too big to fit the Statue of Liberty if she happened to be wearing work boots; it is beyond all that. It has a feel and a spirit to it that goes beyond the marketing and into a celebration of the working people who wear them.

The Red Wing Shoe Company and Museum are located at 314 Main Street in Red Wing. Call (800) RED-WING, e-mail customer service@redwingshoe.com, or visit www.redwingshoe.com for more information.

Minnesota Inventors Hall of Fame
Redwood Falls

The building that houses the Inventors Hall of Fame, just west of Redwood Falls, was for decades the Redwood County Poor Farm, a large and handsome brick building with arched window openings and stately evergreens in the yard, a scene that would fit nicely on a college campus. The kind of building that would make some poor people uncomfortable. But poor farms went out of style some time back, and it is now the Redwood County Museum, where one room is given over to the Inventors Hall of Fame. It's kind of a hidden Hall of Fame, not considered a big enough deal to mention on the town's website, or even on the museum's website.

There aren't a lot of displays right now in the Hall of Fame, and it's open only in summer. The walls are hung with pictures of inducted inventors, but if you are looking for splashy displays of astounding inventions you have to wait until the second week in June, when the Minnesota Inventors Congress meets in the big Redwood Falls Community Center and conducts "the world's oldest Invention Convention."

There's wistful talk of someday building their own building and having a real Hall of Fame, but for now they are just One of the World's Least Famous Halls of Fame.

For information on the convention, which is famous and open to the public and draws huge crowds, call the Minnesota Inventors

Congress at (800) INVENT-1 (that's 800-468-3681), e-mail halloffame@ minnesotainventors.org, or visit www.inventhelper.org.

Transparent Man
Rochester

He might be less interesting if he were younger, but this anatomically correct guy has been standing utterly naked with his head back and his arms upraised for eighty years. He is actually less than naked. You can see right through his skin. His physique is an inspiration to men in their late seventies and a model of encouragement to youngsters.

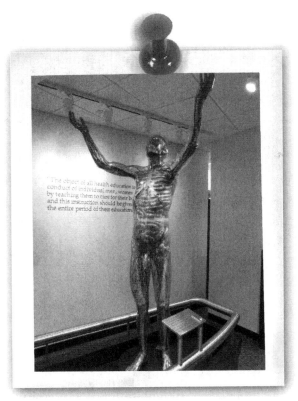

"I'm tellin' ya, that fish . . ."

Obviously too transparent to go into politics and too stiff for general labor, he might have been employed to hold up one end of a scaffold. Or he could have been fitted with a discreet camera in the base and been given security work—in 1931 the Leica 35mm camera was already six years old—but it was a time before the public would have put up with hidden scrutiny.

So he stayed in public relations. Born at the Dresden Hygiene Museum in Germany, his first real job was to pose proud and famous at the Mayo Clinic exhibit in the Chicago World's Fair in 1933, showing off his liver, his heart, lungs, muscles, brain, teeth, blood vessels, and all those bones.

From 1935 to 1988 he was the superstar of the Mayo Clinic Museum in Rochester, until the displays apparently fell out of fashion and were closed. He now stands in the clinic's Patient Education Center on the subway floor of the Siebens Building.

It's not exactly the World's Fair, but hey, eighty years old, still on the job and standing tall—nothing the matter with that.

World's Largest Ear of Corn
Rochester

In the game of the world's largest there is no uniformity of scale, no standard minimums or maximums; it's a lot like the old western frontier. No law at all and anything goes. For instance, everyone knows a prairie chicken is larger than an ear of corn, but the world's largest ear of corn is a whole lot bigger than the world's largest prairie chicken. Even the world's second largest ear of corn, also in Minnesota, is bigger than the world's largest prairie chicken.

And if any petty little fussbudget comes along and whines that this is just a water tower painted to look like an ear of corn so it's not really qualified, you say, if it's your tower: "What does it matter what's inside? Sure there's water in there. Do you know what's inside the world's largest prairie chicken? Or the world's largest otter? We admit there's water in there. Others aren't so forthcoming. Who knows

Not only the largest but also the
highest moisture content.

★ ★

what's inside some of these world's largest creatures? They could be full of Swiss cheese or Swiss francs, for all you know. The world's largest otter could be a piggy bank, but he'd still be the world's largest otter."

Sullivan's Jewel Box

The mechanical butter churn was invented in Owatonna in 1889, and by the time Louis Sullivan came to town in 1906 the place was known as the Butter Capital of the World, producing more butter in sixteen square miles than any other sixteen square miles anywhere in the known universe. After the opening of the Farmers' National Bank building in July 1908, they were still first in butter but they were also home to "Sullivan's Jewel Box"—the last masterpiece in the career of the man who invented the skyscraper and who is arguably our greatest and most influential architect.

If you were to visit but one architectural landmark in the state, this would be the one; in 1958 the Postal Service featured it on the eighteen-cent stamp, one of only four buildings in the United States so honored. The reason for all the hullabaloo is that it's gorgeous.

Sullivan couldn't have done it without a willing client. Carl Bennett was vice president of the Farmers' National Bank and was given the job of seeing to the completion of a new building. He had earned a degree in fine arts from Harvard in 1890 but gave up his plans for a career as a concert pianist to return to the family business. And although he was a dedicated family man and a strong Baptist, he selected a nocturnal hard-drinking agnostic architect. They built a mutual respect and a lasting friendship.

Bennett's collaboration with Sullivan and draftsman George Grant Elmslie, Chicago artist Louis Millet, and sculptor Kristian Schneider

The world's largest ear of corn was completed in 1932 by the Chicago Bridge and Iron Company, for what was then the Reid-Murdoch Company and is now Libby Foods; it's 151 feet to the top of the light

One last masterpiece from the man who invented the skyscraper.

produced a building that created a sensation among critics and architects, as well as in the banking trade. The remodeling in 1958 drew the attention of the *New York Times*: ". . . In 1908 the design was perfect, and it was functional. A noted Dutch architect, Dr. Hendrick Berlage, considered it superior to anything of its kind in Europe. In recent years architects have recognized it as one of the great buildings in the United States."

Sullivan himself fondly called it a "color symphony," probably as good a description as any of the fabulous interior. Go there.

The bank is located at the intersection of Broadway and Cedar Avenue in downtown Owatonna. Bankers' hours there are 8 a.m. to 5:30 p.m. Monday through Friday and Saturday 8 a.m. to noon. For a tour of the bank call Julie Troft at (507) 455-7500.

and 90 feet to the top of the standpipe, so the ear itself is 60 feet tall and has a capacity of 50,000 gallons. And it's designed to the proper proportions; counting the rows and kernels gives a standard ear of corn. The root is a bit deeper than standard; it's drilled down to what they call the Jordan level, which is about 310 feet below ground, and to the scale of the ear that's about a 16-foot root. In real life 16-foot roots would take a lot of the humor out of raising corn.

The *New Yorker* magazine ran a picture of it once. Mr. Al Whipple, who retired as the plant engineer after forty years, said it serves the canning factory on a seasonal basis. They start in spring with peas, moving on to lima beans, sweet corn, carrots, and mixed vegetables; the season is over in November, and they spend the winter doing heavy maintenance work. The tower looks the same whether it's work-ing or not; its main job is to be an ear of corn anyway, and it does that year-round.

It's easily seen from the intersection of US Highways 14 and 63 in south Rochester.

Arts and Cats
St. James

It's pretty much cats all the time in this neat but unassuming St. James house, but they aren't always the stars here, no matter how sleek and well groomed. To the neutral visitor it's more about the house, as Camp Snoopy to some folks is more about the roller coasters than it is about the riders. Having said that, it's still a task to describe the place.

Kind of a shock, really, to walk in and find oneself in the most interesting space puzzle in the state, or what is likely its most intrigu-ing three-dimensional network. And it will surely be some of the best domestic carpentry you've seen. The rail detailing and the fit and finish of the place are all first class, and to call it elegant wouldn't be over-stating it.

A cat can traverse the entire three floors, go outside, and come back in, without ever setting foot on any floor. They simply own the

Cat moving through Minnesota.

joint and you can't go where they go. Catwalks, ledges, stairs both curved and straight, all lead in and out of thirty-eight wall passage-ways hand cut into a variety of shapes, from the geometric to the whimsical. Stop sign, heart shape, Minnesota, Charlie Brown's head, rabbit, jay, circle, square. A continuous pathway of catwalks a foot-ball field's length—three hundred feet—is curled and folded into this house.

Feline access doesn't depend on the regular doors; with all doors in the house closed they can still move vertically and horizontally throughout the entire house, the attached garage, and their outdoor hut in the fenced catnip forest.

It's an impressive remodeling, all done by the owner, Greg Krueger, who calls the cats the Fur Kids. One considers all the wiring, plumbing, and heating changes he had to make and asks about his carpentry skills; he laughs and says he got a D-minus in wood shop class.

The walkways are generally overhead, where the cats seem to like it best. There are five Maine Coons and one other breed, all big curious types. Multiple show winners, they are graceful and quiet, giving an air of English aristocracy to the place. You can't quite picture anything but cats living here; small dogs just wouldn't look right and probably wouldn't take to living in the trees, as it were.

So it's all cats and naturally so. Krueger may have even started an architectural style here. Something like Cat Deco, or Arts and Cats.

Sod House on the Prairie
Sanborn

It's an unlikely teenage dream come true, this simple one-room house made of dirt. Stan McCone's great-grandparents homesteaded in South Dakota in the 1880s; he himself moved from Iowa to this western part of Minnesota in the 1970s and finally in 1987 began work building the house that had been bugging him since he was teenager, the replication of his tallgrass ancestral home.

It sits just a few miles up US Highway 14—officially the Laura Ingalls Wilder Historic Highway—from Walnut Grove and the banks of Plum Creek. It's twenty-one by thirty-six feet, the walls are two feet thick, and it features a fir plank floor and a grass roof. It's heated by firewood, lit by oil, watered from a bucket hauled in; there's an outhouse back behind somewhere and that's made of sod, too. And if this all sounds like fun to you, you're not alone. Stan and his wife, Virginia, have turned it into a B&B and if you have a mind to stay there you need to sign up ahead of time.

Stan cut the sod from a neighbor's field, a hard-to-find patch of virgin prairie. He rode a horse-drawn sled with side blades and center cutter to slice it into strips, which he cut with a knife into two-foot

We sure don't build 'em like we used to.

lengths. They were hauled four miles on a hay wagon and then stacked in double rows for the walls; he said the wall would settle as much as eighteen inches during drying, for which the builders would have to make allowance when they put in the wooden window and door frames.

With its decent floor and plastered walls, Stan calls this his rich man's soddy. Back in the 1880s it would have cost about fifty dollars. He has also built a more typical house of the era, the poor man's soddy, smaller, with a dirt floor and leaky roof and a price tag closer to five bucks, to show visitors a more accurate version of the hard realities of the time. There were no courthouses or railroad depots, no concert halls or corporate headquarters, ever made of sod; Stan's rich man's soddy is about as good as sod construction ever got.

Virginia has furnished it with two beds, a fainting couch with a buffalo robe, gingham curtains, books on sod house living, and a set of Wilder's works, and she brings guests breakfast in the morning: turnovers, bacon, eggs, and coffee, on dishes from the time. The surrounding acreage has been restored to bluestem prairie grass and wildflowers.

Visitors come from as far away as Japan: birders, history fans, Wilder readers, ordinary curiosity seekers. Virginia says, "Everyone who stays here, no matter where they're from, goes home feeling refreshed. They get a chance to get away from television and cell phones and to realize what's important again: spending some real time with people you care about."

The Sod House is located one mile east and a quarter mile south of the junction of US Highways 71 and 14 near Sanborn. It's open daily April through October. For more information, call (507) 723-5138, visit www.sodhouse.org, or write to 12598 Magnolia Avenue, Sanborn, MN 56083.

The Cairn of Peace
Vernon Center

At a rest area half a mile north of Vernon Center on US Highway 169 stands a dignified rectangular monument built of Kasota stone. In the face are set twenty stones, each from a different country; two are newer than the rest, from Northern Ireland and Yugoslavia, both of which finally arrived thanks to a determined citizen from each of the two countries. Why they were missing in the first place is a mystery— perhaps somehow lost or misplaced during construction—but they are in place now and they complete the chronicle of a remarkable event.

Just across the road from here, on the farm of Mr. Bert Hanson, people from around the world gathered in 1972 for the first-ever Farmfest, held in conjunction with the nineteenth Annual World Ploughing Contest. "Ploughing" is similar to what we call "plowing" except it has a more international feel to it and it's done on a smaller scale; nothing like our monster ten-bottom plows and eight-wheel-drive articulated tractors.

The contestants from the twenty nations used tractors we don't see around here: Steyr, David Brown, Leyland, and Deutz, along with the more familiar Massey-Ferguson and Ford. Ploughs carried names like Fiskar, Gassner, and Kverneland. Accounts from the time don't go into the arcane details of judging the ploughing, but one gets the impression that it's a quiet and precise activity—as opposed to, say, the tractor pull, which is all noise and horsepower.

Speaking of which, there were quite a few politicians on hand for that first Farmfest, held in an election year; George McGovern made a campaign speech and Nixon's secretary of agriculture, Earl Butz, made a counterspeech, and a number of others put in appearances. Roy Rogers and Dale Evans did a show here, and country singer Charlie Pride sang for 50,000 who broke into applause at the beginning of every tune. Bob Hope drew 80,000 people; a couple was sent here on a date by *The Dating Game,* along with a chaperone. The Air Force Thunderbirds put on a low-altitude high-speed spectacular that raised the adrenaline level in the county to unheard-of levels.

It was quite the deal. And when it was all over, stones from the twenty competing nations were quietly set in place in a monument by a patient stonemason named Bud Reed—who placed temporary ones for the two that showed later—and everyone went home. A woman who operated an overworked grocery store in nearby Garden City said of the foreign visitors: "I'll tell the world—those people were the most wonderful people I have ever met."

A bartender in Vernon Center said: "They were much better behaved than some of our people."

An elderly woman expected "sit-ins and maybe demonstrations" when McGovern spoke, but she said, "It's surprising, but there weren't any hippies in town."

The Cairn of Peace can be seen on US 169, north of Vernon Center on the way to Mankato.

Giant Canadians

In the 1920s the Mayo family in Rochester had a small flock of captive geese at their cabin southwest of town on Mayowood Lake, on the Zumbro River. Migrant geese from Canada dropped in out of curiosity and found out they were related. And according to Minnesota custom, once they found a place at the relatives' where they could stay for free they came back the next year, and they brought the kids with 'em, too. They began to drop in, so to speak, on their way down to Mardi Gras. And drop in again on the way back.

And in 1947 a grateful patient of the Mayo Clinic who had heard about the family geese donated twelve bigger geese from Nebraska, to be released on Silver Lake right there in the middle of town. Well, bigness seems to draw more bigness, and that dozen caught the attention of a few quite larger geese; the newcomers liked the warm water from the power plant so much they stayed all winter, and next year there were more. Biologists had believed the giant Canada goose to be extinct, but on a fine morning in January 1962 they came to town and were able to confirm that this alien bunch were indeed the last known *Branta canadensis maxima.* They are the largest of the eleven nations of Canada geese, weighing eleven to fourteen pounds apiece and sporting wingspans of nearly six feet. Their next-largest relatives weigh from eight to ten pounds, and even that seems like a lot of weight to fly with.

Now, at the peak of migration in a typical year, downtown Rochester is home to 30,000 to 35,000 giant geese, one big goose for every household. At 10 pounds per bird, that would be 300,000 pounds: 150 tons of goose, three times the weight of both houses of the Minnesota legislature, and you could throw in a good-sized governor to boot. In a small park setting, 150 tons of just about any creature deposits a considerable daily slipperiness to the landscape, and a crabby minority of the citizens of Rochester would be just fine with it if everyone just grabbed their goose and they all had a big old barbecue.

But the majority is proud of the city's giant geese. The *Rochester Visitor* says, "The waterfowl using Silver Lake are an integral part of the Rochester community . . . and even though Minnesota's seasons change, the beauty and magic of Silver Lake's giant Canada geese stays the same." The ordinary person is moved once more to ask: So is this a great country or what?

Counting Gophers
Viola

Addressing the mystery of how a farming state could adopt a rural nuisance rodent as a mascot, you find it originated from a satirical political cartoon in 1857—one depicting nine railroad "tycoons" on striped gopher bodies pulling a "Gopher Train." This in protest to the state providing a loan to the railroads to build trackage farther west.

Minnesota mascots or not, they're still rodents.
PHOTO LICENSED BY SHUTTERSTOCK.COM

The cartoon was widely circulated and Minnesota became the Gopher State, a derisive moniker. It was accepted as much out of simple indifference to sarcasm, it seems, as out of anybody ever actually naming it. The university ultimately took it for their mascot.

A farmer would have found that strange and perhaps amusing, like a hunter might feel if the deer tick should be so honored. But there it is. It's as if the Mets had accidently been named the New York Rats.

The town of Viola sits in gopher country, as does most of the state, and when the problems of broken cattle ankles and sinkhole-jammed machinery became serious enough they put a bounty on the critters and had a celebration on counting day, when they would tally the tails and settle up.

The first formal event was held in 1874, one year before the first Kentucky Derby, and it's been a tradition every year since. It's the second-longest-running celebration in the country and the only such event in the known world. The town has a population of about seventy, but three thousand or so show up for Gopher Count.

And the gophers have become but a small part of the fun; Wednesday is Family Day with a 5K run and a 1K walk, followed by a talent show and big fireworks. Thursday is the Grand Parade leading into the soap box derby, the crowning of the royalty, a doll buggy parade, a pie eating contest, ladies nail-driving contest, tug of war, races, and a polka dance in the town hall. There is a street dance at night under a big tent. And that's it. Two days.

A number of the usual animal rights protesters show up to express their moral indignation, followed by eager reporters—in this case, all the way from LA. The locals put up with it without much more than a rolling of the eyes. It's the old protocol: Start having fun, and you'll surely attract a fringe of the righteously indignant. All you can do is smile and outnumber them.

For information visit www.gophercount.com.

Horse Thief Detectives

In June 1862 Orrin Pease of St. Mary had two fine horses stolen; he was new to the area, and his neighbors were outraged at this terrible welcome. Three men were ultimately caught and convicted of larceny, but they broke out of jail pending appeal. It was one of many such incidents, leading people to conclude that the southeastern part of the state was infested with a gang of horse thieves.

They organized the Waseca County Horse Thief Detectives on February 16, 1864; between then and 1900 only one member lost a horse to a thief. And once the story got out that the WCHTD were after them, two suspect families left town and that was the end of it.

But the association lives on, with 1,200 members around the world, some from as far away as Oman. The current president, Wayne Breck, says: "We only meet for a picnic once a year—it's a carryover from years ago—they really had an association that met monthly and went after horse thieves and all that stuff—but there's no horse thieves around now, at least I haven't heard of any. . . . Maybe 150 people come every year, and a lot of them are descendants of early settlers in the county, way back to the 1870s—so we just have a potluck dinner and we play games with the kids and then go home. It's only an annual thing, we don't do anything in between. We sell memberships for three dollars and you get a bumper sticker and a card and a little brochure. . . . We give prizes to the members who come from farthest away, and the newly marrieds and the new babies, and the oldest married, and stuff like that.

"We always meet on the Fourth of July, at noon, west of town here at the orchard . . . everybody knows they're supposed to be there at noon with a dish to pass, and we have a nice picnic."

Asked about the hard history, he says, "We have on record, about three or four times where they caught horse thieves, back in the late 1800s . . . but they never actually hanged anybody in Waseca County for bein' a horse thief. Mainly the organization was to alert all the farmers to look out for each other."

The membership card specifies three obligations:

- "I am obligated to keep a sharp lookout for stolen horses; to return them to their rightful owners and to aid in discouraging horse thieves.
- "At the call of the Captain of the Riders, I shall mount my best horse in pursuit of thieves and carry a rope for use by the Vigilante Committee if so ordered.
- "I will not leave my saddle during posse duties except for fatigue and/or other reasons."

Contact the Waseca County Horse Thief Detectives, Mr. Wayne T. Breck, 432 10th Street Southeast, Waseca, MN 56093 or visit www .snorky.com/hthieves/index.html.

Bullhead Days
Waterville

You don't hear much talk about bullheads in the sporting world; you never see them on the covers of *Sports Afield* or *Outdoor Life* or *Fishing World.* They don't have scales and they don't get big like their catfish relatives; they have floppy whiskers and are shaped in the classic Don Rickles physique: wider across the mouth than the chest. Not to put too fine a point on it, but they're an ugly nuisance. When the bullhead herd gets large, they muddy up the water and make it unusable for both game fish and waterfowl, they have sharp spines that sting when swimmers step on them, and they pretty much seem bent on destroying every lake in the state. All of which means that bullheads, like a lot of other bottom feeders, have a real public relations problem.

Problems have a way of finding each other, and when Waterville needed something to build a spring festival around they turned to the nasty bullhead population in Lake Sakatah. Early in June, members of the sportsman's club go into the lake with nets and haul out anywhere from eight thousand to sixteen thousand bullheads, skin 'em with pliers, clean 'em, cut off the heads, and lower them into boiling oil; one of those things that sounds bad in print but in fact is a lot of fun.

Besides the big fish feed, Bullhead Days have featured events like tractor pulls, demolition derbies, water parades, pickup pulls, horse rides, and fireworks on Sakatah Bay. Refreshing beverages are made available and they crown a queen, tactfully titled Miss Waterville. We talked to a contestant from twenty-plus years ago, Julie Gross. She said she was sixteen at the time and didn't have any talent other than her cheerleader pom-pom routine. The lady who ran it said, "Well if you don't have no talent, why don't you clean a pail of bullheads?" Julie said she knew how to fish but had to learn how to skin bullheads.

They had the usual formal part, and they modeled sportswear instead of the usual bathing suits, and then came the talent contest. She wore bib overalls, a straw hat, and her dad's old boots. She had a pail of about twenty bullheads and asked the woman how many she should do; the woman said she better do 'em all.

She told a couple of stories as she cleaned, sitting there behind three pails: a regular pail, where "they were floppin' around alive," a second pail for the good part of the bullhead, "and then the guts and the skins went in the other pail."

"It's something that you'll never forget . . . and you know how the older ladies like to get the front seats? It was in the school cafeteria where we had it, and I was up on a platform. The guts were flyin' in the pail and all around, and all I could see were these little old ladies covering their faces. . . . I ended up gettin' first runner-up. The girl who sewed her own clothes was second attendant and the girl who sang was crowned Miss Waterville."

Word has it that if you go to the festival you should get there early and get your basket of deep-fried fillets and your bread, because it's usually sold out before Saturday night.

Bullhead Days are held the first full weekend of June, Thursday through Sunday. Call the chamber of commerce at (507) 362-4609 or visit www.watervillemn.com for more information.

Curbside Fountain

Welcome

You see movies of crowded cities a hundred years ago and get a feel for what it must have been like—all those big animals, the motion, the air filled with noise, the heavy barn smell, the creak of leather harness and wooden wheel, barkers calling out.

But in the movies you seldom see a downtown horse getting a drink of water. It of course happened, and in the latter half of the 1800s both the Society for the Prevention of Cruelty to Animals and the Women's Christian Temperance Union had taken an interest in street fountains for horses and humans, and they built them by the hundreds across the country.

"Keep to your own side, Buster."

City water wasn't always germ free and beer was considered by many to be a health beverage. The WCTU didn't buy that argument and set horse and drover fountains in front of saloons to offer the option. The SPCA just wanted animals to be comfortable and so built similar ones, some with a second lower basin for dogs, but with the idea that a person might not stop if they couldn't get a drink themselves.

Fountains embellished with horse statues seem to be all over European history, but the earliest one we found at which a live horse could actually drink was the exquisite Petrovskiy Fountain on Theater Square, carved in Moscow, Russia, in 1835. It is Moscow's oldest fountain, and numerous water carriers used the fountain along with the horses.

The one in Welcome is not so grand as that one. It is of simple sheet metal design, shaped like a small rocket or a robot with a vertical main tube and a long conical hat; the two attached dish shapes look vaguely like hatches that might be on backward. The horse side gets a nice big basin and the people get a smaller one on the sidewalk side, where neat stone steps rise for shorter patrons.

What it really has going for it is that it's still here, whereas most of the thousands that were built never survived the arrival of the combustion engine.

You can find the fountain in Welcome Park on the corner of First Street and South Dugan Street across from the City Hall.

Standstill Parade

Whalan

A thin line it is between wackiness and brilliance: Ptolemy's notion that the world was round is a case in point, and so is Dave Harrenstein's idea that if a town is so small that a parade can't move in it, then the parade should stand still and the crowd should move. It gets back to physics: In the case of the parade, you have an organized rectangular solid (sort of) confined to a rectangular space and you have a disorganized fluid, the spectators, able to flow around it, and what could be more sensible?

Marriage Mill

The republic was founded with a few specific duties given to the federal government, like raising an army, but most of the lawmaking given to the various states. The founders knew about regional differences and decided to leave the hammering-out process to the locals. Combining this wonderful tolerance with a sensible economic system meant a lot of state borders offered business opportunities; this is why Minnesota is today bracketed east and west by fireworks and Sunday liquor.

Back in the early 1960s the southern border of the state drew young people from Iowa, and especially from the Waterloo area, who wanted to get married and didn't feel like waiting. Word had it that up around Preston you could get a waiver of the three-day waiting period, and for a few years some people in town were doing a modest business in out-of-state late-night quickie marriages.

They don't like to talk about this in the current climate of obsessive responsibility, but it may not have been as bad as it sounds. Much as politicians like to stand up and shovel out ever more restrictive laws, especially as regards the behavior of reckless youth, some of us consider the idea of kids getting liquored up and running off and getting married to be preferable to them getting liquored up, running off, and not getting married.

There's no monument there to these few years of history of course but it would be interesting to know how many of those who sneaked across and were married without the wait—and it wasn't illegal—are still married, and how many children are walking around as grown-ups who would not exist at all if not for that judge signing that stack of waivers for the clerk of court and the two justices of the peace. Who all, by the way, got in hot water over it; the lid came off when a couple had a car accident on their way home and were questioned by troopers.

But one has to wonder: Did any of those couples, or any of their children, ever come back and thank those guys?

Whalan is a town of ninety-four, eight-four, sixty-eight, or sixty-four people, depending on your source, sitting along the abandoned Milwaukee Road tracks; the rail line is now the beautiful Root River Bicycle Trail and site of the wildly popular Sykkle Tur (Norse of course for "bicycle tour"). Towns along the trail hold festivities to open the season in the middle of May; in 1996 Fountain put on a sausage and pancake breakfast, Rushford had historic tours, Peterson opened a museum, and Lanesboro had an all-city garage sale. Preston held a trout-fishing contest for kids and grown-ups. And Whalan had a Standstill Parade that ended up on the CBS Television news.

In the parades since, and all the festivities on the side, they've had bluegrass bands, square dancing, kids' tractor pulls, bed races, antique cars, a display of American flags, rummage sales, book sales, and boxing demonstrations. There are floats of all kinds and constant *lefse*, made right there and best when it's warm. And live snakes and lizards, live exotic birds, a Norwegian display, face painting, plate painting, soap making, lace making, quilting, and crocheting. Pony rides, petting zoos, a calliope, nonmarching bands, and free blood-pressure checks.

One year an organic farmer dumped a wheelbarrow of dirt on the street and planted green things, and a masseuse gave free massages. A man from Rushford sat in his mint 1932 Packard Super 8 and a fellow from Fountain City, Wisconsin, rode his 1884 high-wheel bicycle—a bike he once rode coast to coast. A couple showed their pet goose, dressed in a colorful outfit, and every ten minutes they'd change the outfit. In 2000 they held a real wedding in the parade.

The parade's first Grand Marshal, Adeline Larson, born in Whalan in 1908, sat in a convertible and waved to people. She said, "Seems to me eighty-eight years is a long time to wait for something like that parade. I'm really too old for something like that, but, well, it wasn't so bad."

The Standstill Parade takes place in downtown Whalan on the weekend closest to Sykkle Tur, which is May 17. Whalan is east of Lanesboro on Highway 16. Call (507) 467-2696 or (800) 944-2670 or visit www.standstillparade.org for more information.

Stephen Taylor's Grave

Stephen Taylor was born in New York State on March 23, 1757; he was with Ethan Allen's Green Mountain Boys on May 10, 1775, when on a narrow strip of land between Lake George and Lake Champlain, in New York, they forced the British surrender of Fort Ticonderoga. It was a surprise attack and our critical first victory in the War of Independence from the British.

History records Ethan Allen as having demanded the surrender of Fort Ticonderoga "in the name of the Great Jehovah and the Continental Congress." But there was no Continental Congress at the time, and Virtual Vermont says, "according to historian and folklorist B. A. Botkin, one Israel Harris was present at the time, and later told his grandson (the late Professor James D. Butler of Madison, Wisconsin) that Allen's actual words were 'Come out of there, you goddam old rat!'" However delicately Ethan phrased the demand, they did come out, surrendering without firing a shot.

Stephen Taylor was listed as a resident of Sheffield in Berkshire County, Massachusetts, when six years later he went from "the 83" and enlisted in the First Massachusetts Regiment, "for three years or the duration." He served as an enlisted man in three different regiments of General Washington's Continental army, taking a British rifle ball in the battle of Yorktown that left him partially blind. He was honorably discharged as a private on December 27, 1783.

He returned to Sheffield and then to Seneca, New York, where he raised four children and a stepson with his wife, Abigail, who became bedridden and died at the age of thirty-six. He applied for a veteran's pension in 1821, stating his occupation as a farmer and listing his assets as "5 old chairs + 1 old table, an old desk, an old looking glass, 2 pr. old curtains, pots and pans, 4 old pails, 4 old barrels, dishes, a churn, an ax, an old chest, 4 old books, a cow, 2 pigs, 3 fowl and a teakettle"; altogether it was worth exactly $51.89. They granted a monthly pension of eight dollars.

He moved to Minnesota Territory with eleven other Taylors in 1854, at the age of ninety-seven. The locals remembered him as a large and robust man, temperate, never known to be sick. He qualified for 160 acres of land; the grant was approved March 10, 1856. He died in June of the following year and was buried at Money Creek Cemetery, a landed private at the age of one hundred.

The family moved away and his grave remained unmarked until Memorial Day in 1880, when the caretaker of the cemetery, Captain Matthew Marvin, with his own money erected a stone with a brief biography. In 1933, with the assistance of the Wenonah Chapter of the Daughters of the American Revolution, the remains were moved to a memorial in Woodlawn Cemetery in Winona. The memorial

Fort Ticonderoga—from where the British fired not a shot.

is a ten- by twenty-five-foot stone replica of Fort Ticonderoga, four high walls with towers at the four corners. A marker with a metal plate is set over the grave, inscribed:

A COURAGEOUS SOLDIER, MEMBER OF ETHAN ALLEN'S IMMORTAL BAND OF 83, WHO TOOK PART IN THE SURPRISE ATTACK ON THE BRITISH GARRISON AT TICONDEROGA AND THE ONLY REVOLUTIONARY WAR SOLDIER KNOWN TO BE BURIED IN THE STATE OF MINNESOTA.

Woodlawn Cemetery is located on the southwest side of Winona. To get there take US Highway 61 south to Huff Street, turn right, and take another immediate right onto Lake Boulevard. The cemetery is a quarter mile down on your left.

Great Gobbler Gallop
Worthington

Worthington's annual King Turkey Day goes back to 1939, when a flock of turkeys led, or were driven by, a parade down the main street of town; the publicity releases on the event don't mention that they went on to the processing plant while the rest of the parade took a right turn. The media were there and so were the politicians and it was a big success. Next year it was bigger yet, featured in *Life* magazine and in movie newsreels across the country.

In Cuero, Texas, a similar event had been held since 1912, sometimes with as many as twenty thousand birds; it was inevitable that a challenge would be issued—turkeys being what they are—and in 1973 a group of handlers brought a turkey up from Cuero to race against Paycheck, so named because he went so fast. The Texas bird was named Ruby Begonia because she could handle a paycheck, and she did, that year. The names are always the same, regardless of the birds. That's because we know turkeys, and we know they don't know the difference. Turkeys know the difference about almost nothing, truth be told. Change your clothes and you're a stranger to your own birds.

The race is staged in two heats, the first up here in September and the second down there in October, at the Cuero Turkeyfest, formerly called the Turkey Trot. (Is *Turkeyfest* more politically correct than *Turkey Trot*?) The athletes are chosen from wild flocks in the two counties, but the visiting team has the disadvantage of bringing just one bird, a bird who gets very cold in the cargo bay of an aircraft. The home bird is drafted that morning from a flock and is presumably well rested and aggressive. In the race there is a thirty-second penalty if the turkey flies off into the crowd or refuses to run, and a two-minute penalty if the handler picks the bird up and runs with it. The winner is the one with the lowest combined time from both heats.

The winner's trophy is three feet tall, of walnut and gold, and is called the Traveling Turkey Trophy of Tumultuous Triumph. The winner also claims the title World's Fastest Turkey; loser gets the Circulating Cup of Consummate Commiseration.

Before the gobbler race on Worthington's King Turkey Day there is a free pancake breakfast and a parade, a 5K walk for humans, and a 10K race for humans. The Texas celebration features food as well, but of course instead of grim running they have live music and street dances.

King Turkey Day is the second Saturday after Labor Day. Check with the Worthington Chamber of Commerce at (507) 372-2919 or (800) 279-2919 or visit www.kingturkeyday.com/index.html for more information.

Ed's Museum
Wykoff

A tin of salmon from the 1950s recently exploded in Ed's Museum and coated the place with a remarkable odor; they've cleaned it up, but there are others sitting there swollen that could go any minute. They are considering drilling small holes in the bottoms to relieve the pressure, but it would take away a lot of the dramatic tension in the place. Right now it's not unlike visiting a museum of unexploded hand grenades. You find yourself in a heightened state of awareness there, ready to hit the deck at any sudden noise.

The building was built in 1876, the same year the town was founded; it was a brewery and a saloon, with a harness shop in the basement. In 1915 it became a grocery store, and Ed Krueger bought it in 1933, selling the Jack Sprat line of goods. There were five grocery stores in town at the time and he did the best of any of them, but his wife passed away in 1940 and keeping things in order became difficult. In the late 1960s and '70s, Ed kept the place open but also took work as a painter, specializing in church steeples; he'd go to work early and then come back and open the store and sell pop and candy bars for the kids. The counter remains the way he left it, the slumbering candy bars still there along with the unstable canned goods.

Esther Evers with Ed's last cat, Sammy.

Mainly what Ed left behind was a huge and complicated mess, but he deeded it all to the city in his will, stipulating that it be made into a museum. After his passing in 1989 local women took on the project and turned it into a detailed odyssey of a man's life through most of the twentieth century, as recorded in a small-town grocery store. It's an amazing place, containing everything Ed ever owned, right down to his gallstones. In another little jar are his gold teeth. They also have his last cat, Sammy, in a plastic shroud in a cardboard box sitting on a shelf in the basement.

They have three sets of Jack Sprat figurines in the original boxes, very valuable, and the Shirley Temple dishes that used to come in cereal boxes. Ed had a son named Fred and all his toys—even though they were well used and shared—went back into the original boxes.

To get to Ed's from Interstate 90, take Highway 16 at Dexter, go twenty-two miles to Highway 80, and take a left into Wykoff. Ask at the Bank Gift Haus for a tour or call (507) 352-4205.

Angle Inlet ○

NORTHWEST ANGLE
STATE FOREST

75

59

11

11

32

89

72

Argyle

Warren

1

1

75

59

1

Crookston

92

75

2

89

71

Funkley

29

Fosston

2

Bemidji

200

92

2

Bena

200

75

32

113

71

8

Walker

200

59

Akeley

34

Longville

Moorhead

10

Dorset

Hackensack

94

Rollag

34

Menahga

64

Sabin

New
York Mills

371

Cuyuna

9

Rothsay

10

Crosby

210

Motley

Brainerd

Fergus
Falls

210

78

Vining

10

25

27

55

59

71

29

9

Alexandria

27

Little
Falls

Royalton

Herman

94

27

28

10

23

169

27

Kensington

28

94

Sauk Rapids

28

75

Chokio

9

Starbuck

Collegeville

59

29

55

23

Villard

Cold Spring

Northwest

2

Northwest

They get the cold waves and blizzards first, taking some of the edge off to make them easier on the folks farther south. They are also the part of the state that raises sugar beets, potatoes, and hard grains and, in the southern part, corn.

Snowmobiles are locally raised here, by Polaris in Roseau and Arctic Cat in Thief River Falls, and insulated windows and hockey sticks come from Warroad. These industries seem natural at the junction of the northern conifers, the eastern hardwoods, and the great Red River flatlands.

The right side of the region is peppered with thousands of fishing and boating lakes surrounded by woods for hiking and hunting. There are large unpublicized peat bogs here and the big Upper and Lower Red Lakes plus long-time favorites like Winibigoshish, Cass, Leach; the Mississippi River begins southwest of Brainerd, in Lake Itasca. There are also quite a few Indian reservations, which is a subject all to itself.

And somehow this region also distills down into powerhouse high school hockey. This year the northern prairie schools of the Mariucci League—Warroad, Roseau, East Grand Forks, Thief River Falls, Bemidji, and Crookston—once again had the best combined record of any league in the state. Their whole town is often smaller than the student body of one big metro school they compete against.

Perhaps it's the big sunrise and poetic sunsets that do it, or that the kids inherit strong hands from forbears who milked cows. Whatever it is, it's been that way out there for more than fifty years.

The $110 Bridge
Argyle

The best thing about this bridge is not that it cost about one ten-thousandth the price of an average bridge; the best thing about it is what a sweet little bridge it is, and how good it looks sitting there.

The Red River Valley of the North is about as flat and as fertile a place as exists anywhere on the planet; topsoil there runs pure black and five feet deep in places. But it's known more for what it doesn't have, like surf, mountains, forests, waterfalls, tropical fish, volcanoes, painted canyons, fabulous big-city nightlife, or any of the other standard tourist attractions. Two highways and a river run through it, but there isn't a vast category of fiction written about it; it's not exactly the antebellum South.

So it's never been a hotbed of tourism, but they've made some game attempts; one of the highways through it is US Highway 75, long called the King of Trails and now, in the southern part of the state, designated the Laura Ingalls Wilder Historic Highway. Back in 1920 they marked it with a sixteen-inch bright yellow band around the telephone poles with black block letters, a K above a T, and it was "the best-marked road in the United States." They planned for it to run from Winnipeg to Mexico City. It made it to Winnipeg and south through Sioux City, Omaha, Topeka, and Tulsa, and then seemed to lose its identity in Texas, somewhere around Dallas; a familiar story.

But for now it's enough that it takes you through these flat and subtle fields, and past the little park at Argyle. The Lorangers' 1878 log cabin sits there, and a three-acre piece of land across the Middle River was added in 1974. They priced pedestrian bridges and then found this old well-traveled wood-slatted cattle car, moved it in, opened up the ends, and what a bargain; and that mountain goat in the Great Northern logo somehow looks right at home.

The bridge is located at the Argyle Roadside Park on US 75, at the north end of town.

Big Fish Supper Club
Bena

It is the world's largest muskie, at sixty-five feet long and fifteen feet wide, and it has a huge wide-open mouth; Charles Kuralt called it his favorite building in the United States. It was originally built as the Big Muskie Drive-In; one of the builders was fifteen-year-old Butch Dahl, who now owns the wonderful red, white, and blue pagoda and service station three miles east, an attraction in itself. The fish is big enough that you can stand inside the mouth and have your photograph taken, an idea that seems to occur to a major portion of the passing public. All

Charles Kuralt called this his favorite building in the United States.

day long and every day, they lie in it as if about to be devoured, put a ladder up to it and ride it, tie a fishing line from it to their rod and reel; some back the car up to it as if they are all about to become lunch.

The big fiberglass teeth are removed in winter for safekeeping. There was at one time a hamburger stand inside the fish but that function has been incorporated into the adjacent Big Fish Supper Club, which is shaped like a building. There is a picture of the fish in the opening credits of *National Lampoon's Vacation Movie,* making it a Certified World Famous Landmark, or CWFL, as if it wasn't one already.

The Big Fish Supper Club is at 456 US Highway 2 (thirty-two miles east of Bemidji). Call (218) 665-2299 or visit http://bigfishsupperclub .com for more information.

Schott Stone Barn
Chokio

Two crisp stone structures and a windmill stand on the far west end of Stevens County, southwest of Chokio and very close to County Road 79; there is no house nearby, nor any trees. They are a large barn and a machine shed, beautifully designed in a style you cannot name. They are simultaneously Gothic and modern; religious, industrial, and agricultural. They are also deserted, windowless, and roofless.

The dramatic emptiness of the scene renders it more desolate than the usual abandoned dairy farm, which for most of us is brutal enough, and the overgrown broken-wood silence speaking only of the irretrievable. Here on this straight-line rural road, their visionary ambition suggests a loss of what might have been.

Construction began in 1923, a surprise to learn because the walls look like it could have been 1523. The builders were Frank Schott and his two sons, Bill and Tony, and it would be nineteen years before it was done. Frank was building other houses, including his own, and farming at the same time, and this construction was no simple nail-it-up barn. It has a hand-poured concrete frame and measures thirty-three by fifty feet, with walls two feet thick reaching five feet into the ground, to below the frost line. The framed double buttresses at each end rise to about thirty-six feet.

The floor of the loft is also concrete, eight inches thick, mixed on ground level, poured into wheelbarrows and pushed up a long ramp barefoot; the ramp was too slippery to walk in boots. The three of them poured straight through for thirty-six hours, because Frank

The unique vision of a determined man.

knew if the mix hardened it would leave a crack. He adjusted the cement slurry by tasting for the lime content.

The exterior walls are of stone, taken from theirs and the neighbors' fields, the universal curse of farming glacial land. In its working days the barn held the Schott's fourteen cattle and six Percheron horses.

Barns collapse when the cattle leave; their presence maintains a steady temperature and humidity, and without them the daily fluctuations cause a constant expansion and contraction, weakening every joint. Here the roof timbers are lying on the loft floor; the fact that the barn held up when the timbers fell says that Frank, in addition to his design genius, had good taste in cement.

Take Highway 28 three and a half miles west of Chokio to County 79 and turn left (south). The Schott Stone Barn stands on the east side of the road, five and a half miles south of the intersection.

The website is called Little of.This and a Little of That. The page address is http://cbm293.fotopages.com/?&page=6.

Paul Bunyan

There are Paul Bunyans in Canada and in nearly every state in the Union, except perhaps Hawaii; here in Minnesota we have the birthplace, the girlfriend, the ax, the ox, the anchor, the cradle and the grave, and five big statues of Paul himself, including the tallest in the world. Other places may claim to have his cap or his gloves or his rattle or his pacifier or his baby shoes; it's a free country and they can claim anything they want. Nobody's going to hassle anybody over the truth here. But we also have his rifle, razor, and CB radio; his tools, phone, coins,

He seems friendly but keep an eye on that axe.

harmonica, Zippo lighter, shovel, moccasins, his footprint, and his mailbox. There are places in Minnesota where there are no Paul Bunyan icons whatever, but in the northern part of the state odds are good that there's one down the road.

Akeley lays a rightful claim to having the birthplace, the cradle, and the world's largest P. B. statue. The stories were first published here by the Red River Lumber Company in 1914, about the time big lumbering was winding down. The statue kneels down and holds

a hand out for people to sit in and have their picture taken; if he were standing he'd be thirty-three feet tall. They hold Paul Bunyan Days here at the end of every June; among other things, it fills Yodelin' Swede's Bar for a few days. Bemidji claims the original Paul Bunyan because they built the first statue, back in 1937. They sent a statue of Babe the Blue Ox on a national tour that year and got attention from the *New York Times* (something Minnesotans seem to crave) and *Life* magazine.

Big and beautiful—and oh what a smile.

Brainerd jumped the claim in 1949 with a talking Paul Bunyan, who scares little kids by calling them by name and who holds forth in Paul Bunyan Land, where many of the icons are kept. They maintain theirs is the "most photographed statue in the world," another hard-to-disprove unlikely statement. A man in Hackensack built a huge statue of Paul's girlfriend in 1952 and gave her the melodious name of Lucette Diana Kensack, causing distress in Brainerd because they already had a Pauline they'd use in parades. Lucette, unconcerned,

(Continued on next page)

(Continued from previous page)
smiles all the time, and especially when she presides over the annual Sweetheart Days and the musical *Ballad of Lucette*, performed by the Hackensack Light Opera Company.

Ortonville, farther south, has a huge piece of rectangular stone held up off the ground billed as Paul's anchor; Kelliher has the grave, Isle has statues of Paul and Babe, and Chisholm has a Paul in the Museum of Mining. There are twenty-six statues of or pertaining to Paul Bunyan in this state and only one gopher, making a person wonder if Paul and Babe the Blue Ox shouldn't have been the university mascot. The Minnesota Bunyans has a nice ring to it, and the Minnesota Blue Oxen isn't bad either. Or just the Lumberjacks, if foot sores and slow dumb animals don't do it—but everyone's used to the rodent, so we're stuck with it. But it's not a gopher you see on the state map; it's a photo of that huge square-shouldered stiff-looking guy and that big wide-horned blue ox. People in Minnesota don't really like gophers. They like Paul Bunyan.

Bigger than a tractor and harder to hitch up.

Grasshopper Chapel

Cold Spring

Minnesota is regularly beset with what we like to call "natural disasters," generally related to the weather but not exclusively; natural as opposed to "unnatural disasters," which would cover train wrecks, arson, murder, and anything else brought on by our fellow humans through carelessness, inattention, or just plain wrong thinking.

In the springs of 1856, 1865, 1873, 1874, and 1876, the area around Cold Spring was chewed up by Rocky Mountain locusts, called choppers to differentiate them from your standard-model grasshopper. These guys were three inches long and had eyes round as shingle nails and heads the size of the last joint of your little finger. Mostly, though, they had big jaws and they ate everything. First the young green wheat and then everything else, including pastures, gardens, and the laundry off the clotheslines. They ate big holes in the hides of cattle, so that the animals had to be destroyed.

In the spring of 1877, farmers figured the months of thirty-below cold of the previous winter would have frozen whatever choppers might have been hiding around; it looked like it was going to be a good year, and it was, right up until the sunny April morning when the sky darkened and the choppers came back, this time much worse than ever before. Farmers were already far in debt and had fought back with oil fires, tar-covered sheets of metal dragged over fields, huge bulky nets; the Stearns County Board had offered bounties for choppers by the bushel, but nothing had dented the huge clouds of insects.

It was about the end of the line for most farmers, locusts for four out of five years. They were a solid Catholic community and turned to prayer, and with the help of a $10,000 donation from Governor John E. Pillsbury's own wallet they built the sixteen-by-twenty-six-foot wood-framed Locust Chapel, in Gothic Revival style, on a hill overlooking the town, as an offering in honor of the Assumption of the Blessed Virgin. A local farmer carved a wooden statue of the Mother and Child

A chapel dedicated to the departure of thousands of unwanted guests.

for the altar. And about four months later, on August 15, the choppers packed up and flew off and haven't been seen since.

In 1894 the building was hit by a tornado and reduced to fragments. The statue was salvaged and stored, and in 1952 they rebuilt the chapel, this time of granite. It's officially the Assumption Chapel but is more commonly known as Grasshopper Chapel, and every August 15 the bishop of St. Cloud conducts a Mass there. Over the entrance is a plaque depicting the Virgin ascending into heaven on a cloud, with two grasshoppers below.

To get to the chapel take Highway 23 out of Cold Spring toward St. Cloud to Chapel Street; take a right onto Pilgrimage Road, then a left. The chapel is at the top of the hill.

You can visit online at http://stboniface.com/parish/assumption-chapel.htm.

Saint Peregrine
Collegeville

It is remarkable that we should have here among us, in this wooded rolling agrarian place with blizzards and below zero temperatures, the actual bones of an Italian saint, a martyr from nearly two thousand years ago.

In the year 192 AD the Emperor Commodus appeared publicly on his birthday, when all of Rome was to pay him homage as the demi-god Hercules. He came out before a massive amphitheater crowd in nothing but a crown, a lion skin, and a club. He demanded adoration and he got it, even though the more cynical had to chew on laurel leaves to keep from laughing out loud. One little chuckle, they had learned, could be fatal.

Outside was a group of devout and tough young Christians; they included the leaders Eusibus, Vincent, Pontian, and the boy Peregrine, all willing to die for the cause. The emperor's fresh blasphemies in the amphitheater fired them to a holy fervor of street preaching. They converted not only commoners but also the Roman Senator Julius, who was moved to give his fortune to the poor.

So Commodus had Julius put in chains and thrown in prison. His choice was to worship the emperor or die and they say he didn't hesitate. Peregine and friends found his beaten body outside the amphitheater and buried him.

The emperor wanted Julius's fortune and figured the four Christians knew where it was. The dungeon would make them renounce their religion and reveal all. They were tortured for days on the rack, whipped, and burned with torches. They held fast and Commodus finally had them flogged to death with leaden scourges. Friends buried their bodies in the catacombs on August 25, 192 AD.

In 1731 Saints Peregrine and Aurelian were moved to an abbey church at Neustadt-am-Main in Germany. After a fire demolished that church in 1854 they came to the United States in 1895.

In 1928 St. Peregrine was moved from St. Anselm's Church in the Bronx to St. John's Abbey here in Minnesota, where the relic altars and crypt were consecrated in 1961.

What a story. A brave young boy stands up to torture and is killed by the boss of the entire Roman Empire and eighteen centuries later lies consecrated in the center of a nation a mere 236 years old. And they say he "is in an excellent state of preservation, covered with silk and silver filigree and brightly ornamented."

More detail can be found at the St. John's Abbey website, www .saintjohnsabbey.org/abbeychurch/shrine.html.

Red River Ox Cart
Crookston

The pioneer version of today's tractor-trailer rigs—the familiar ten-wheel tractor with the eight-wheel trailer—was a four-legged tractor and a two-wheel trailer. Pulled by an ox or horse, thousands of Red River carts moved furs, skins, meat, pemmican, salt, tools, and general freight from Manitoba, the Dakotas, and Montana down to St. Paul.

They were built and operated by the Metis, half Indian and half French or Scottish, who dominated the trade routes from 1801 until the advent of the western railroads. A settler reported in 1840 that 1,630 people were present at the departure of a cargo expedition from Pembina, North Dakota, with 1,210 Red River carts. In 1869, 2,500 carts passed through St. Cloud carrying six hundred tons of freight for the Hudson's Bay Company in St. Paul.

They were made entirely of wood and held together with pegs and leather straps. The absence of steel made them easy to repair and thrifty to build; they weighed five hundred pounds and could carry

Early version of the eighteen wheeler.

more than that, usually the dressed weight of nine or ten buffalo.

They were well suited to the terrain, but they were neither pretty nor quiet. They couldn't use grease because the dust on the trail would mix with it and quickly wear the axle down.

Once the weight was upon it the wood-on-wood friction of axle to wheel gave off a scream that would curdle a man's blood. It could be heard for miles, an instantly recognized unearthly screeching that must have been taken by some to be the painful keening of the lost buffalo herd they were hauling.

One wonders how anyone could stand such a trip across the plains, two miles an hour, twenty miles a day, crossing creeks and rivers with those tortured axles wailing every miserable step of the way.

An experienced drover could handle ten carts at once. Average drovers took six. They would run in trains, sometimes two miles long. They followed the buffalo hunters out, six or seven hundred carts with families and tents and supplies, cleaning and skinning carcasses and taking horn, hide, and skull back to the eastern market. Bones were left on the prairie.

There are two outsized models on display in Crookston. The one with an ox and a man is located on the north side of town along University Avenue/US Highway 75. The other is just the cart but claims to be the World's Largest Ox Cart. It is located on the south end of town on US Highway 2 next to the Polk County Museum.

The city's Ox Cart Day Celebration is held annually in Central Park at the crossing of US 2 and the Red Lake River on the third weekend of August.

Nordic Inn

Crosby

Well, here's something different: A Minnesotan gets a wacky idea and works at it like a madman and his neighbors think he's crazy and after a while it all seems to turn out okay. In this case it's a man who left northern Minnesota, joined the navy, got out, and ended up with a pretty decent job in a California biotech company; got sick of that and moved back to his hometown and opened a medieval B&B in an old Methodist church.

He was given the name Richard Edward Schmidthuber and it worked all right for him up until he became the builder of an ancient Viking castle. Now he goes by Steinarr Elmerson, has a full beard and long curly hair, and dresses in the kind of outfits that allow a person to walk around in public carrying a battle-ax without anyone becoming alarmed; the ax fits right in. (They might still give him a problem at the airline security gate, but no more than anyone else: Ax, nail clipper, it's all the same these days.)

Where you are encouraged to eat with your fingers.

You'd think they'd welcome new enterprise up there where the farms are shutting down and the mines are already closed, but it was like pulling teeth for him to get a license, even as a homeboy. All part of the Viking struggle, apparently; first crossing the North Atlantic in open single-mast rowboats, and, generations later, four months of public hearings trying to get a liquor license in Minnesota.

When you stay there you get the full treatment: soap cut from a big block with a hatchet (your choice of birch or cedar), a wake-up call from a big long curved horn, deer antlers for toilet paper holders. You dine in a marauder's outfit and eat with your fingers and a blunt knife, and you become part of an interactive mystery theater with local actors.

There are five rooms at the inn: the Look Out up on top in the steeple; Odin's Loft, with the bed in a longboat projecting over the Great Hall; the Jarl's Den and Freya's Boudoir, both done in appropriately medieval Scandinavian decor; and, down below, the Vikings Locker Room, with pennants on the walls, Astroturf carpet, yard markers, goalposts at the headboards, and a double-nozzle shower.

And if you happen to stop by on game day you might well miss the host; he's also informal mascot for the Minnesota Vikings football team. Been on television, too.

The Nordic Inn Medieval Brew & Bed is at 210 1st Avenue Northwest in Crosby. Call (218) 546-8299 or visit www.vikinginn.com for more information.

Wood Tick Racing

Cuyuna

Wood tick racing is all match racing. Two sprinters are placed in the center of a thirty-three-inch-diameter circle, on the bull's-eye; the crowd presses in, wagers are waged, and the arthropods are released under the expert eyes of seasoned judges—some seasoned to the point of pickled—and whichever arrives first at the outer circle lives to race again. The loser, having no clue as to what was at stake in his little trip across the plywood, is smashed flat, giving real meaning to the term *single elimination*. And at the end of the long day of matches, the final lone standing Supreme Champion Racing Wood Tick is celebrated with raised mugs and loud huzzahs, bets are paid off, and then, at his crowning triumphant tick moment, he's smashed flat, too.

Persons who live in city apartments and never walk the Minnesota woods might wince at this, but most of us who have hosted a wood tick for any length of time—behind the knee, say, or in the hair—generally find it most gratifying. No reading of the Miranda rights even, much less the appointment of an attorney; it's just lights-out,

Gentlemen, start your engines.
Professional racing at its highest level.
COURTESY OF WOODTICK INN, CUYUNA, MINNESOTA

you little bloodsucker: We know your intentions. You were lucky to make it this far.

The first wood tick races were held here in 1979, three guys sitting in the Cuyuna Bar after working on a pasture fence line, having a beer and picking the wood ticks off, putting them in an ashtray; they make a break for it and the bar's owner, Bill Simons, bets on which one will make it to the edge of the bar first. Inspiration hits, they make a circle

You don't know the players if you
don't have a scoreboard.
COURTESY OF WOODTICK INN, CUYUNA, MINNESOTA

on a piece of cardboard, and a new sport begins. The next year it
goes public, including printed rules and a plywood field. No spurs, no
supercharged ticks, and so forth. In 1982 the crowds get bigger, augmented by bikers, and in 1985 the Cuyuna Bar changes hands after
the passing of Bill Simons and becomes the Woodtick Inn, creating a
natural pun. (How far is the Woodtick Inn?) The race has grown every
year, drawing close to a thousand spectators and the attention of the
media, and is keeping the last remaining retail operation afloat in a
town of 165; it's a tick-based economy, sort of like the watch industry
in Switzerland.

The town was named after the miner who founded it, Cuyler Adams, who took the first half of his name and added to it his dog's name, Una. Appropriate for a town now famous for ticks to be named after a prospector and a dog.

To get to the Woodtick Inn, take Highway 210 to Crosby, then go north on County Road 31 for about three miles to Cuyuna. The inn is at 24916 Minnesota Avenue. For more information call (218) 546-5313 or visit http://cuyunalakes.com.

Restaurant Capital of the World

Dorset

Dorset lays claim to this title with the low resident-to-restaurant ratio of 5.5 to 1: They have four restaurants and twenty-two people. And it's not on a main road from one big place to another; it's up there in lake country between Nevis and Park Rapids, about a block long at the intersection of the Heartland Bicycle Trail and the two-lane "Interstate 226."

They have a few other stores—antiques, books, gifts, and bike rental—and a newspaper, the *Dorset Daily Bugle,* published once a year. It is a paper with such great respect for accuracy as to apply it very sparingly, even on its masthead. They inform us of such events as the upcoming Running of the Skunks: Eleven thousand men will run through the winding streets with two thousand skunks, a century-old event expected to draw a hundred thousand spectators. They are also anticipating a crowd of 55,000 at the X-treme Full-Contact Tag-Team Indoor Fishing Championship event, held in the big Dorset Bowl, which has been flooded up to the thirty-fourth row for year-round fishing ever since Dorset sold off both its pro football and pro baseball teams.

They report that a local biotech firm has developed a method of extracting blood from mosquitoes using a powerful vacuum chamber and is presently working on a giant hammer to recover blood from wood ticks; both processes would help reduce the shortage of emergency supplies. A local critic claims the investors are the ones being

(Continued on page 116)

Broken Down Dam

In 1909 Ben Snyder was the head dynamo man at the new city electrical dam on the Otter Tail River east of Fergus Falls. At 4:20 a.m. on September 24 he woke to the sound of water splashing. He jumped up, grabbed his clothes, looked out, and saw the river up at platform level. The lights were fading. He and coworker N. P. Johnson hit the door of the powerhouse at the same time the floor buckled and a ten-ton dynamo sank through it. They scrambled up the riverbank as the entire powerhouse disappeared in a torrent of black water, and after the building went down the dam itself burst apart at the center. Describing their run up the bank, Snyder said: "You could have played cards on my shirttail."

They climbed the hill above the railroad tracks and ran to the nearest farm, where Ed Burau hitched up his team and they headed into town. They met the city electrical superintendent on the way, coming out to find out why the lights had gone out. They all got to town in time to warn the citizens, as the whole reservoir of water came roaring down through the valley and took out four more dams, picking up force and debris with each one. The wreckage piled against the pier of the Mount Faith Avenue bridge and brought it down. Workers got to the Dayton Hollow dam at 6:15 a.m., just in time to open the floodgates, and it withstood the pounding.

It was the city's worst flood. Word had it that the dam had been built on a spring and that instead of providing an escape tube they simply plugged it over with concrete. The spring washed that new dam away from underneath, and once she started to go it was all over.

It's a beautiful and peaceful place, the Broken Down Dam site. Huge wedges of concrete sit strewn around like the ruins of a Roman fortress; you stand on the abutment and mentally try to reassemble the pieces. For years it was a favorite picnic spot.

Said the dam engineer: "Let's build it on a spring."

People would hike east along the track past the Hoot Lake Power Station carrying baskets. At night it was a place to party. Now it sits largely forgotten; there's a whole generation in town that never goes out there.

The river glides innocently through the wreckage, lapping at the big white blocks, widening itself in a shady relaxed pool just downstream. It looks too beautiful to be throwing concrete around; or, you figure, even if it could smash powerhouses and shove dams aside, it'd never do it. It's just not the type.

To get to the Broken Down Dam Park, take Interstate 94 to Highway 210; follow Highway 210 north then east. When you come to 229th Avenue take a left (north) and follow 229th until it turns into Main Street heading west. Watch for Broken Down Dam Road on your right. You may have to ask for directions, but the people are friendly.

★ ☆ ★ ☆ ☆ ☆ ★ ☆ ☆ ★ ★ ★ ★ ☆ ★ ☆ ★ ☆ ☆ ☆ ★ ☆ ★ ☆ ☆ ★ ☆ ★ ★

(Continued from page 113)

sucked dry, which the company rejects. Another story details the opening of the new Dorset Antique Rocks store; many of the rocks are said to be thousands of years old and are in "mint condition," according to the owner.

The restaurants have been reviewed by outside observers; a typical arugula-crazed Minneapolis food critic gave them passing marks, which is exactly what you want. Rave reviews from high-tone critics generally mean the food tastes weird and you don't get much of it, plus the service is slow. The restaurants are, from north to south on the boardwalks: the Dorset General Store & LaPasta Italian Eatery (family dining, Italian,

You Don't Need to Be Big to Be Funkley

If you ask Wikipedia for the smallest town in the country you will get Minowi, Nebraska, with a population of one; it was a married couple until the husband died, and now she is the mayor, librarian, and bartender.

And then Wiki says no. It takes more than one to be a town; a council must meet regularly, a levy must be certified each year, and public services must be provided. So at least as far as they were concerned, the smallest functioning city in the USA was Tenney, Minnesota, with four citizens.

wine, beer; 218-732-0275); the Dorset Cafe (chicken, steak, ribs, sea-food, drinks; 218-732-4072); Compañeros (Mexican food, drinks; 218-732-7624); and the Dorset House (family dining, evening buffet, soda fountain, beer and wine; 218-732-5556).

The reader is cautioned that with neither post office nor city government the precise population figure is subject to interpretation; locals say it "depends on who's around at the time."

Take Highway 34 for six miles east of Park Rapids or six miles west of Nevis, to Interstate 226; go north about a mile. Visit their website at www.dorsetmn.com.

But that's no longer true, either. Tenney dissolved itself in late June, 2011, leaving Funkley, with a population of five, as the state's smallest incorporated city. How it stands nationally is apparently in dispute, probably no surprise for a town named after a lawyer.

It's located in northwest Minnesota on state highway 71, about thirty-four miles north of Bemidji, and is home to the very successful Funkley Bar & Grill, a statewide magnet for anglers, hunters, and motorcycle riders. And they have live music.

There are memorable images of the town taken in the 1930s by the noted photographer Russell Lee. And although most of the original Funkley is gone, you can still find it on Facebook and the Library of Congress.

Kensington Runestone

Kensington and Alexandria

If it was a practical joke it backfired and caused more trouble than humor, but if it was a hoax it was a darn good one; and if it's the real thing like the supporters say it is, well, then it should be in the history books. It's a debate not likely to be settled soon, given the weight of experts on both sides. But at the museum in Alexandria of course the word *hoax* is like the invisible two-ton elephant in the room.

Still, without the suspicion there'd be no runestone industry. If everyone had said, "Okay, well, it looks good to me, and if you say so I guess there probably was a Norwegian in Minnesota 130 years before there was an Italian on the East Coast; okay, fine," the whole thing would have disappeared among the other boring historical facts we all forget about. But because of the skepticism, some twelve thousand people a year visit the Runestone Museum in Alexandria, and who visits where Columbus first set foot? Who even knows what state it's in? If you can prove it for sure—whatever it is—it's going to lose appeal; it's the third rule of show business. (The first one is well known, and the second one says, "Yes, there is one born every minute, and every ten minutes there's someone born to take advantage of him.")

The stone that caused all the ruckus is thirty-one inches high by sixteen inches wide by six inches thick, weighs 202 pounds, and now sits in the Runestone Museum in Alexandria. It was found in 1898 by Olof Ohman, who had been born in Sweden and farmed near Kensington. It wasn't until 1907 that the first complete translation from rune to English was made, by a graduate student from the University of Wisconsin named Hjalmer R. Holand:

8 Goths and 22 Norwegians on exploration journey from Vinland over the West We had camp by 2 skerries one days journey north from this stone We were and fished one day After we came home found 10 men red with blood and dead Ave Maria Save from evil.

Linguists, archaeologists, runologists, geochemists, historians, and just about everyone with an opinion has jumped in on one side or the

The cornerstone of the great controversy.

other. But whatever your own take on it is, there is a large and fine statue of Big Ole, representing Scandinavians in general, standing in the main street of Alexandria just in front of the museum.

The original stone rests at the Runestone Museum, 206 Broadway in Alexandria. Phone (320) 763-3160 or visit the website www.runestone museum.org.

Fishing Museum
Little Falls

So, you are thinking, a fishing museum in Minnesota? What's so curious about that? That's like a rodeo in Wyoming, or a library at Princeton. A steakhouse in Texas. Would it not be more curious if there wasn't a fishing museum?

And that's the point. This museum is nearly new. It opened in 1998; it's curious that this state of obsessive fisherfolk was 140 years old before it had a fishing museum. On the other hand, there is a lot of competition—half the bars in northern Minnesota are fishing museums of one sort or another.

Al Baert got the idea in 1990 and lured his pal Morry Sauve into helping him spread the word, and five years later Al had his basement crammed full of fishing stuff. They went to the city of Little Falls for official approval, and with some help from the city, the chamber of commerce, and a few other organizations, opened on Broadway in June 1998.

There are thousands of items on display, more every week, and the place touches people in ways they don't expect. Fishing is one of the few things that people still do with their kids, now that we no longer watch the same programs or listen to the same music, or even raise chickens together. This by itself explains why the highways from the cities to the lakes are bumper-to-bumper on Friday afternoons, and why the museum stirs people:

"My dad had a motor exactly like this old Evinrude here; we fished with that thing for thirty years."

No beer coolers in here but a lot of churchkeys.

"We had a sixteen-foot wood Larson boat exactly like this one. The outboard special . . . wow."

"The Lazy Ike. Grandpa swore by that thing . . . said he caught more fish on a Lazy Ike than anything else he tried."

Displays group individual collections together, along with a picture of the donor and a short history. To see a person's own gear all in one place gives it a reality that would be lost if the pieces were all thrown together and lined up in scientific groupings, like orders of insects.

The star of the show, among all the record fish and the old knuck-lebuster motors, the bat lures and the thousand-dollar lures, and the fishing art of Minnesota's legendary Les Kouba (the world's most-viewed artist; he designed the Coke and Greyhound logos), is a nickel-plated 1902 Submersible Electric Trolling Motor, made in Menomonie, Wisconsin, and donated by Leonard Dzieweczynski. (This choice may be influenced by a lifelong appreciation of folks with two Z's in their name.)

Baert and Suave publish a great little newsletter, the *O'fish-L News,* and have expanded into larger showrooms. Local artist Frank Gosiak recently painted a mural on their front wall, an event that drew spectators on folding chairs. Donations could cause them to move to even larger quarters, although they'd want to bring the mural if they did. It's a museum whose time has arrived; apparently already overdue. They are open 9 to 5, winter and summer, Tuesday through Saturday, and in the summer open on Sunday, noon to 4.

The museum is located at 304 West Broadway in Little Falls. For more information call (320) 616-2011, e-mail mnfm@mnfishing museum.com, or visit www.mnfishingmuseum.com.

Turtle Races
Longville

Longville sits at the junction of Highway 84 and County Road 54; or you can drive up to Hackensack and take County Road 5 east for eighteen scenic miles. It's on Girl Lake, within easy reach of about fifty other lakes. With apologies to Canterbury Downs, Longville is to Minnesota what Louisville is to Kentucky: the longtime racing center. It's been declared by the state legislature as the Turtle Racing Capital of the World so you know it's authentic.

There is a lot of racing in this state, primarily staged with critters that not only can't run but also won't walk a straight line. We generally avoid contests between trained mammals, preferring wood ticks, frogs, box elder bugs, turtles, turkeys, and the like. They do race Dachshunds down there in the Cities, but speedy and graceful mammalian racing is pretty much confined to Canterbury and the county

Some are just born with racing in their blood.
COURTESY OF LONGVILLE CHAMBER OF COMMERCE

fairs. And the state prefers the circular field to the racing oval; it places greater demands on the judges, because the athletes all start in the middle and the first one to clear the outside circle is the winner and it's a tough call for a judge if they're on opposite sides.

Wednesday is Race Day. They've had afternoon racing on Main Street here since the mid-1960s, June through August, a tradition that draws throngs of children as well as seasoned race fans. The street is closed at 12:30 and the Turtle Mobile is trundled out near the track—a fifteen-foot circle painted on the pavement. The racing is done in heats of eight to ten turtles, where the winner gets a white ribbon and moves on to the finals; a green ribbon goes to the winner in the Slow-poke category, for the turtle that ends up nearest the starting point. They go to the Slowpoke final, where the grand winner is the one that moved the least. There are twenty-two volunteers who help run the event; we assume one is a veterinarian who determines that no dead, drugged, moribund, or chronically depressed turtles are registered into the competition.

If you don't own a mud turtle at least four inches in diameter, for a buck or two you can rent one at any number of vendors' kiosks, set up along with the registration kiosk and the memorabilia kiosk and all the other kiosks. There are peripheral games and contests going on— Turtle Golf and Turtle Hoops, Fishing for Fun, and so forth. The town population doubles on Race Day, to about four hundred, and there are about as many turtles in town as people. A local woman has a rac-ing stable of a hundred, mostly rescued from the roads around there, where they nightly risk their all just to get to some other lake.

Racing starts with the first heat at 2 p.m. sharp; the racers are held in the center circle by their handlers until the starter hollers "Go!" and then they're off. And the screaming and shouting start, and kids get down there along the finish circle with ice cream and call to their turtles by name.

After a hard day's racing, they award the prizes and pack it all up until the following week, just like at any other racetrack.

The races take place every Wednesday from June through August. Call the Longville Lakes Area Chamber of Commerce at (218) 363-2630 or (800) 756-7583 or visit http://longville.com/turtleraces.html for information.

St. Urho

Menahga

It's pronounced with rolling *O's, Oooorho,* and in some versions with a little *L* in there, *Oooorlho,* and from there the story gets a little murkier. It's apparently a combination of the folktales of Sulo Havumaki, a psychologist at Bemidji State, and the imagination of Richard Mattson of Virginia, Minnesota.

Mr. Mattson was the manager of Ketola's Department Store there, a Finn with a number of Irish employees. He claimed the Finns had a hero even greater than the Irish St. Patrick, St. Urho, who drove the frogs out of Finland. On his chosen Feast Day of St. Urho, May 24, 1956, the employees gave him a hand-carved nutcracker in the image of a saint and a frog, along with a scroll describing Urho's deeds in pidgin Finnish. A humorous little prank, except there happened to be a reporter in the room and the story hit the front page of the *Mesaba Daily News.* Local Finns jumped at the chance to celebrate for any reason, and it took off from there.

In Mr. Havumaki's version, Urho drove out the grasshoppers who threatened the Finnish wild grape crop and its wine industry. He had a big voice and he chanted: *"Heinasirkka, heinasirkka, menetaalta hiiteen,"* meaning "Grasshopper, grasshopper, go away." This is the public translation; the street version is either "Grasshopper, grasshopper, go to hell" or "Get the hell out." Less saint-like, but with more oomph. (The name Menahga, incidentally, was derived from an Indian word for the wild blueberries that grew there. Not exactly grapes but close enough.)

Either way, in 1975 Finns in the town of Menahga, halfway across the state, commissioned a Minneapolis sculptor to carve a statue of the saint from a one-ton block of laminated oak. The guy grabbed the money and produced nothing, but in 1982 a traveling chainsaw sculptor named Jerry Ward took the block and cut away everything that didn't look like a twelve-foot-tall Finnish saint with a giant locust impaled on a pitchfork. The statue stands near US Highway 71, a

The Finnish answer to all those Italians.

fiberglass replica of the original, which is stashed in a mausoleum in a local cemetery. (The town is apparently a bit more cautious about strangers these days.)

St. Urho's Day was changed to March 16—the day before St. Patrick's, to give its celebrants a head start at the beer—and is recognized in all fifty states. The big celebrations are held in Finnish settlements across the country, like Butte, Montana; Houghton, Michigan; Naselle, Washington; Hood River, Oregon, and quite a few others.

In Minnesota there are a number of them, in Palo, Finlayson, and in Finland (where there is a good sculpture of his head), and of course in Menahga. Guys lumber around in green costumes for awhile, looking like grasshoppers, and there's a parade and a buffet and a dance, and somewhere along the way they change into purple costumes. They say they have wine there and it's a lot of fun.

The statue is located at the south end of town, on the east side of the Palms to Pines Highway, US 71, which runs from Louisiana to Canada. Call Menahga Commerce and Civic at (218) 732-4111 or (800) 2470054; the city website is http:/menahga.com.

Viking Ship
Moorhead

The exhibition hall at the *Hjemkomst* Center is of a goodly size, larger than a typical church, and the big wooden sailing ship fills it right up. One wonders, diving immediately into the trivial, if this is a ship-in-the-bottle trick here or did they build ship first and hall second.

It began in 1971 when a junior high guidance counselor named Robert Asp began talking with his brother Bjarne about building a Viking ship and sailing it to Norway; a year in research and planning followed, and then Bob went searching for trees. He found white oak up by East Grand Forks and hauled it to Harvey Enden's sawmill north of Viking, where it was cut into planks, or strakes, eight inches wide and an inch or two thick. The ends were sealed and it was sorted and left to dry for two years.

The brothers converted the old Leslie Welter potato warehouse in Hawley into a shipyard; they tore out the first floor and built the boat in the basement, six feet down from street level. The eleven thousand board feet of lumber and the shipyard were ready in 1974 and construction began on the keel and hull, and the work became a tourist attraction. The hull is different from modern ships in that the ribs are not rigid: strakes are riveted first to the keel and then one upon another and the ribs are fastened later, through waterproof rope connections, so that the shell is flexible, able to ride the roughest seas without breaking up. It's seventy-six feet long, seventeen feet across, and seven feet high at the low point. The mast can be raised and lowered so the boat can be rowed up rivers. It is a truly amazing piece of engineering from 890 AD.

Six years later the front wall of the Hawley Shipyard was torn down and the sidewalk ripped out, and they began hauling gravel in for the ramp. A week later, July 17, 1980, they winched the hull up on its rollers and out into daylight; a photo from the opposite roof shows a gigantic canoe with high dramatic prows at either end, stretching all the way across the street, surrounded by figures the size of gophers.

They staged a three-day celebration, Viking Ship Days, and raised $35,000 for a voyage to Norway; Bob's mother-in-law, Hannah Foldoe, christened the ship the *Hjemkomst* on July 20. The word means "welcome" in Norwegian, pronounced *yem-komst*. It left for Duluth on August 5 and they hoisted sail for her maiden voyage on August 9; Bob took his last voyage on September 27 and died two days after Christmas, of leukemia. The family was committed to sail her to Norway.

And they did that, leaving in May 1982 with a crew of twelve including three sons and a daughter, under a mainsail of thirty by forty feet and a topsail measuring ten by thirty, out the Great Lakes and around the Statue of Liberty and on across the stormy Atlantic, a fabulous adventure noted around the world, landing six thousand miles later, on August 9, to a heroes' welcome in Bergen. They were greeted by the king of Norway himself.

To Norway and back in a ship designed
a thousand years ago.

They proved it could be done; their ancestors could have, and did, come across the Atlantic five hundred years before the Spaniards. And you can see that same beautiful ship in Moorhead, where they built the hall first, rolled the hull in, and then hoisted the sails.

Bachelormania

In 1992 a survey of twenty young women in Herman found that not one of them planned to stay in town after high school graduation, and just before that a young couple had moved away simply because the wife couldn't find a job. Herman had an eligibility ratio of 6 to 1—seventy-eight bachelors and twelve single women, out of a total of 458 citizens. The odds were bad for the men and they weren't getting better, and then in 1994 they surprised even themselves and actually did something about it.

What they did was so shocking it drew national attention: They just came right out and asked. They went public in February, said they wanted women to come to the Grant County Fair in July for a big Bachelormania. Television, radio, newspaper people picked up on it. The town's economic development coordinator, a farmer named Dan Ellison, appeared on the *Today* show. The word was that they wanted women to come to town not only to meet the bachelors but also to stay and start businesses, and by May Dan was so busy with all the publicity he had to hire help for the crops.

They drew something like twenty thousand to the event; the Prairie Cafe was selling T-shirts that read BACHELORTOWN, USA. YOU CATCH 'EM, WE FEED 'EM. Bachelors from outlying towns drove in, and hundreds of women arrived from California, Florida, Oklahoma; all over the country. And for every Herman bachelor there was a camera crew and a microphone; one showed his driver's license to verify he was for real, and said he'd met about twenty women. "Most of 'em

The *Hjemkomst* Interpretive Center is at 202 1st Avenue North in Moorhead. Call (218) 299-5511 or visit www.hjemkomstcenter.com for more information.

are pretty nice people. I would say I'm kinda inexperienced. Single women don't seem to like me for some reason. I'm not quite their type."

There were singles dances and bachelor bingo—twenty-five women playing bingo for a date with one of five men—all four nights of the fair. By Friday and Saturday things were moving along fairly well, to the point that the manager of the only bar in town, a woman named Sally, was using a police escort to take the bar's money to the nearby bank. Nobody just up and got married on the spot, but a few couples met and corresponded. The organizers made plans to repeat it in 1995. Dan Ellison himself proposed in December 1995 and the lady accepted; the national media haven't reported if they are yet married. And a few new businesses were started in the town. The population jumped by sixty.

A movie was made about the event, *Herman USA*, although it wasn't filmed in Herman—it was cheaper closer to the Twin Cities, so they shot it in New Germany. And they released it nationally on September 20, 2001, at a time when nobody was in the mood to go to movies.

So Bachelormania faded, replaced by an annual Iron Pour wherein they heat scrap iron to 2,700 degrees and pour it into sand molds to make sculpture, and they have a parade and a liars' contest. It draws enough artists from out of town that some people lock their doors, so you know it's probably a pretty good time. A good place to meet people.

★ ★

Great American Think-Off
New York Mills

It's not exactly made-for-TV drama, even though it's been broadcast on C-SPAN; they debate the great late-night issues that have been debated by country philosophers for decades, only without all the beer. Beer lends a passion and urgency to such questions as "Does God Exist?" that is often missing in the cold crystal light of logical discussion, set before a polite audience; still, people who've watched the Think-Off say it's quite the deal. It's drawn attention from NBC, *Smithsonian* magazine, the *Baltimore Sun,* the *New York Times,* and the *Christian Science Monitor.*

New York Mills is a town of 1,158 sitting on the old main road between Fargo and the Twin Cities, US Highway 10; it's forty-five miles north of the new main road, Interstate 94. They have a good-sized Lund Boat factory there, and they have the New York Mills Regional Cultural Center, which figured they were in as good a place as any for this sort of thing. In 1993 they hosted the first Great American Think-Off, the subject of which was "The Nature of Humankind: Inherently Good or Inherently Evil?" The finalists were a priest, a newspaper editor, a fifteen-year-old cheerleader, and a tribal police officer. They debated so well the audience couldn't decide; it was a hung audience. The issue is unresolved to this day.

Four finalists are picked from hundreds of entries, from all fifty states and some foreign countries; you send in a 750-word essay and you state your opinion and back it up with personal experience, and you come prepared to debate. The Final Four get five hundred dollars plus travel and lodging. Gold, silver, and bronze medals are awarded; with the gold goes the title of America's Greatest Thinker, at least until next year.

They address burning questions long discussed by amateurs in tavern booths, such as "Does Life Have Meaning?" (the 1994 audience found that it does) and "Is Honesty Always the Best Policy?" (the 1998 audience judged not). Definitive answers to questions like these are seldom settled in the presence of pitchers of lager—where no winners are declared nor medals handed out—but in any venue healthy debate is considered a good thing, and the bedrock of a functioning democracy. Which was itself the subject of the 2000 debate, where the question was "Is Democracy Fair?" and the audiences, both in the arena and online, voted that it is. In 2006 the question was, "Which Is More Valuable to Society: Safety or Freedom?" Freedom won in a landside. Check the website for other years and other winners. And for your entry blank.

The Think-Off is held every June. For more information write Think-Off, 24 North Main Avenue, PO Box 246, New York Mills 56567; call (218) 385-3339; or visit www.think-off.org.

The Last One-Room Schoolhouse
Northwest Angle

The last one-room schoolhouse in Minnesota sits on the northernmost piece of land in the contiguous forty-eight states, connected to us only by water; geographically it's a peninsula but politically it's an island, and how odd for a state locked in the center of the continent to have an offshore island up in Canada.

We've always understood the reason for this was a surveying error by a crew waking up hung over and setting off ninety degrees out of whack. The truth is, as usual, more complex, having to do with border negotiations in the Treaty of Paris with the British in 1783. The British said the boundary was to follow the Rainy River to the northwest point of Lake of the Woods and then west to the Mississippi, not knowing at the time that the Mississippi doesn't start in Canada. It was eighty-nine years before they settled on a vertical stretch of border lopping off the Angle and some outlying islands and putting them in Minnesota.

The school has seven grades available; kindergarten through sixth. In 2012 there were five students, ranging from a kindergartener to a sixth grader. Linda Kastl, their teacher, says, "Five students and five

(Continued on page 136)

Cordwood Pete

Cordwood Pete was a real man, a short and fearless lumberjack who literally did become a legend in his own time. His name was Peter DeLang. He stood four feet, nine inches according-ing to most estimates and weighed something around a hundred pounds, but he could work alongside men twice his size and more. He held his own in the taverns after work, the places that made it possible to do that North Country kind of labor day after day, and would challenge anyone who looked at him the wrong way. Fosston was a rough spot in those days, the jumping-off place from the prairie into the forest, a town full of saloons, hotels, and all the rest of it; it's hard to picture that now on the quiet main street with the grain elevators in the background, but it was no place for the faint of heart back in the early 1900s.

Pete built such a reputation that when the Paul Bunyan legend arose near the end of the boom days in the logging business, people began to promote Cordwood as Paul's younger brother, from back there in Bangor, Maine. He had a donkey named Tamarack, and his personality and build made him a natural counterbalance to the giant with the blue ox. Not everyone was pleased to go along with the idea of turning this real person into the brother of a fictional character. To some it just didn't sit right, but legends are legends, no matter how they get started, and most think old Pete wouldn't mind.

Pete lived to be eighty-four years old, spending his last years in a small cabin in Hill River Township. He is buried in Rose Hill Cemetery in east Fosston; the cabin and furnishings were recently donated to the Heritage Center by the Lowell Sundeen family. The East Polk Heritage Center is easily found on the main street of

Arvid Clementson with a carved likeness of Peter DeLang.

Fosston. The center is open May 31 through Labor Day, Friday through Sunday, 1 to 4 p.m. For more information call (218) 435-6594 or visit www.fosston.com.

(Continued from page 133)

different grades. You should see how many manuals I teach from! Just think: reading, math, English, social studies, science, etc. When other teachers get prep time for their class, I have to teach that class, too (phys ed, music, library). I'm continually looking for new art ideas because I don't want to keep making the same paper jack-o-lanterns every year!"

There's a computer for each student, class size is real small, and nobody comes up short on their learning. Some ride snowmobiles to school in winter and take boats in spring and fall. When the ice is unsafe, they'll put in at one of the local resorts, and Kastl will sometimes sleep on the floor of the school.

The Angle is 150 square miles of mostly national forest, accessible by air or water or by a road cut through 45 miles of Manitoba swamps and woods; one uses a videophone in a shack by the road to clear Canadian customs. Life there is peaceful but not without complexities, especially as regards conflicts in US and Canadian fishing and hunting laws. And in 1945 the feds gave up on homesteading the place out and put it all under the care of the Red Lake Indian Band.

So you need Canadian approval to drive to it but it's part of the Red Lake Indian Reservation and is also under US Forest Service jurisdiction; plus it's in the Warroad School District. Most residents think it's worth that to live in such a pristine wilderness, on a huge lake with fourteen thousand islands, with great fishing, great birding, plentiful wildlife, and historic Fort St. Charles nearby. A lot of kids have less interesting places to go to school.

Visit Angle Inlet School at http://warroad.k12.mn.us/angleinlet school or www.yahooey.com/angleschool. For visitor information write Northwest Angle & Island Chamber, PO Box 54, Oak Island, MN 56741 or call (218) 223-4161.

Lake Wobegon

It's far and away the best-known small town in the state and many claim to have seen it, though no one seems to have found anything there interesting enough to photograph. The railroad quit its line into the place years ago, and a surveying error combined with an unfortunate position in the exact corner in a crease of the map have made it tough for travelers to locate.

It's somewhere in corn and dairy country and the residents, as near as we can tell, are pretty much like rural people in the rest of the state: stubborn, resistant to change, and given to the occasional practical joke but perhaps not quite so much as their ancestors were. And of course churchgoing and practical, at least most of the time. It's a place best read and heard about from a distance; if you were actually to find yourself there you'd face the possibility of a letdown, disappointed by its everyday nature and by how closely the residents resemble your own relatives. You might be so struck by it all as to forget even how to give directions to the place.

Lake Wobegon is best explored through the works of the distinguished American writer Garrison Keillor, who claims to have been a resident—although he also once claimed to be "a professional liar." Few would challenge either claim.

Treasure City

Royalton

It sits behind a tall sign and a large pirate knee-deep in lawn ornaments, on the north side of Highway 10 in Royalton. It's on the way up to lake country and is an institution to generations of fisherfolk; a good place to stop and take a break, exactly the right distance from

Minneapolis. It was built in 1926, one of four in a chain of that name—the other three were in Michigan and only one of them survives, as a clothing store in Manistique. This one was bought by the present owner, Robert Janski, in 1977, as an unwanted throw-in parcel in a land deal.

Janski was busy with Granite City Construction and a real estate company, and he somehow found himself stuck with a roadside shop and $35,000 worth of souvenirs; they eventually multiplied by ten and took over his entire career.

Sin City

The Fargo-Moorhead visitor bureau says their metropolis has one of the lowest crime rates in the nation, but it wasn't always that way, especially from 1878 to 1915. Will Rogers once called Moorhead "the wickedest city in the world." He was a humorist and given to embellishment of course and it's hard to imagine Moorhead in a league with Tangiers, Tijuana, Rio de Janeiro, or Singapore, or even London at that time; but Moorhead did pretty darn good for a little town way out there on the frozen plain.

The Law of Unintended Consequences was partly in play there, and so was the Law of Intended Consequences: Fargo, North Dakota, allowed easy divorce—ten minutes—because they were generally hardworking practical folks who felt that being in a bad marriage was miserable enough without having to go through a big rigmarole to get out of it, and they also were a dry state at the time so you couldn't go out and drink afterward. You were supposed to go right back to work. Folks across the river in Moorhead knew an opportunity when they saw it, and saloon-keeping became a big industry in a hurry.

There were dozens of them, and they didn't go at it in a halfhearted way, either. One, the Higgins-Aske Co., had three

To browse the narrow aisles of this store is like your first stroll through a major Vegas casino: an experience in extreme sensory overload. Thousands of glittering doodads, so many as to become a texture rather than a collection, gleam overhead; the counters are overflowing with great ideas, this for Duane and that for Edna, and this over here for little Tyler and that for little Ashley. What a bonanza.

The hottest items last season were the glass crystals, solid glass cubes with laser figurines cut inside somehow. Mounted on a slow-turning base

eight-drawer cash registers, an enormously long bar, and tile floors; another boasted of four hundred electric lights; Rustad's had inlaid brass footsteps in the sidewalk leading to their door, and the White House had an outdoor summer garden and a functioning electric fountain inside.

And they didn't just sit and wait for clients. They'd send out wagons; some would go over to Fargo and bring patrons back free, while others would actually go out into farm fields and sell shots of whiskey to the hands working there. Farmers' hearts would sink in the middle of a harvest afternoon to see that wagon show up.

But when you stay up late and you've got gambling and all those women dressed in silk coming in there, and there's all kinds of money floating around—in other words, when you start having too much fun—you just know it can't last. The whole thing got run underground by do-gooders in 1915 when they voted Clay County dry. Moonshine was made there in basements through Prohibition, just as it was in every city in the nation; but at least for a while Moorhead had style and opulence, and the honor of being a famously wicked place.

and lit from beneath, they were nearly irresistible. Some were bought as night-lights.

Wind chimes are another bestseller. He'll have a thousand of them in the store in the spring, and some people will buy eight or ten at a time. And Minnesota souvenirs are always big, whether it's shot glasses, Uffta mugs, or anything at all with Ole and Lena or Paul Bunyan on it; plus collectible state spoons, thimbles, bells, and refrigerator magnets, and three hundred different postcards. Books about the state sell, and it doesn't matter if they're about mannerisms, fish, critters, history, or hotdish.

The fireworks department is fairly new, a direct result of Jesse Ventura's governorship, and the staff actually knows what's in the

There is not room for all of it in your house.

package and what it does, unlike the tent vendors who set up two weeks before the Fourth of July. They'll even shoot them off if you ask for a demonstration. Fireworks buyers are a repeat business here.

There's a huge pirate section in the back for the kids and new joke items every year, including fake traffic tickets, cigarette loads (now back in style), and jackalopes—a rabbit with antlers (mounted ones go for $129, and the replicas for a lot less). Alligator skulls, baby sharks in a bottle, a fantastic variety of seashells; bumper stickers, ballpoint pens, license plate holders, and lots of T-shirts, caps, moccasins, and sandals. A broad variety of knives and jewelry, from common to collectible. It takes four people a whole month to take inventory and the paper stack is two and a half inches thick when it's done. Two-thirds of the people in the state live in the Twin Cities, Janski says, and a third of those two-thirds want to get out of town on the weekend: 80 percent of his business comes from there. It's a hard place to pass up.

Treasure City is located at 308 North Highway 10 in Royalton (320-584-5140).

House of Big Steam
Sabin

If it should ever occur to you to keep a steam-powered farm tractor in your living room, perhaps as a handsome conversation piece, perhaps as a good place to mount your new flat-screen television, you could go ahead and do that, but you couldn't do it to be the first or to be the largest. Because it's pretty much been done.

Jim and Lynette Briden have beaten you to it. A legendary 110 HP Case sits in their well-furnished family room in Sabin and it's been there for over eight years now.

Jim spent years before that restoring the big fellow, originally manufactured by Case in 1910 and one of a famous series of heavy power from that company. The 110 HP is 110 horsepower, about four times the average farm tractor even into the modern age. He hauled it and fired it up every year at the four-day Western Minnesota Steam

Threshers Reunion in Rollag, about twenty miles to the west, and the rest of the year it sat in the shed.

For as beautiful as it is and for all the work he has in it, it didn't seem unreasonable to have it sitting a little closer, like maybe inside the house. Lynette agreed on the condition that it be kept spiffy and the house not become a big garage.

No problem. He added a family room with a thirteen-foot ceiling and a big door and a strong floor, all nicely decorated with leather couches, stained glass windows, and antique furniture.

Adding a room like that would be child's play, one might think, to a fellow who had rebuilt one of the largest steam tractors ever manufactured.

A Case Steam Engine. They look even better in the house.
PHOTO COURTESY OF JIM DACHTERA

Threshers Reunion

On the surface it's a nostalgic celebration of times past, a time for family get-togethers, with a merry-go-round and parades and dances and bands big and small, and long-tabled church dinners. Train rides, shows, wagons, souvenirs, fashion shows and a queen coronation.

The modern combine we see in the fields at harvest is a combination swather and threshing machine; back in the steam era the grain was cut and brought to the thresher, a stationary machine powered by a long belt that ran back to the flywheel of a steam tractor. It required a family crew to get the wheat from the stalk into the bin. In 1940 the Nelson boys thought it might be ceremonial fun to fire up the old steamer and bring back some of the drama now missing in the modern harvest, where one person on a combine, along with a couple of grain trucks, can cover the whole process.

They made it an annual event and in 1954 the Western Minnesota Steam Threshers Reunion had their first meeting; it has grown from that simple beginning into a Labor Day festival featuring hundreds of events and exhibits. It takes over a square mile of land to hold it and the crowds number into the many thousands.

What really makes it the big deal it has become is sort of a guy thing, and it's not the historical or the carnival or the festival atmosphere but of something much louder and more immediate: raw horsepower. And especially steam power. Large steam power. Part of the reunion at Rollag includes a steam school and one can experience large tractor pulls, plowing contests, engine demonstrations, lumber sawing, and blacksmith shops. Some of the old steam tractors are nearly as big as early locomotives.

It's on every Labor Day weekend in Rollag. Join the thousands. For information visit www.rollag.com/index.php.

Molehill

Sauk Rapids

If you dream about temples rising out of rock and rubble—and who doesn't—there is a place at 601 3rd Avenue North in Sauk Rapids that might look familiar to you; if it's not exactly what you dreamed of, it probably comes close in some places.

It was built by a retired railroad man named Louis Wippich, whose parents had come over from East Prussia in 1879. He was born on a farm near Gilman; they moved to a vegetable farm in Sauk Rapids in 1913. Louis left school in the fifth grade to help his father, joined the navy in 1916, was discharged in 1919, and worked as a carpenter and cement finisher until he hired on at the railroad, from which he retired twenty-four years later. Kind of standard upbringing for the time. Nothing in there to suggest he would one day lose himself in theosophical teachings of Madame H. P. Blavatsky and in 1932 begin writing and building a gigantic fantasy in stone on four city lots.

It's a memorial to the imagination of man, the freedom of the spirit, and the lost art of heavy lifting; even the smallest stones weigh 1,200 pounds. Louis moved them into place with cables and levers and the thirty-five-cents-an-hour labor of teenagers. He built a pair of angular towers, the tallest forty-five feet high, plus a Grecian temple, a reflecting pool, a Romanesque stairway, and a wall with seven Doric pillars standing on it, most from leftover stone from local quarries and demolition sites. But there are a few special pieces, like the blue granite quarried from the bottom of a Swedish lake. There are labyrinthine passageways underneath the fantastic stone structures. He called it the Molehill, and himself the Clown of the Molehill.

Water, of course, is always at war with stone, and water brings green things in to move stone and break it down, and when Louis got too old to work it became overgrown, and eventually the people in the rental house he'd built there began to use the garden for a landfill. When he died in 1973, at the age of seventy-eight, he left no will; his

A railroad man tries his hand at building a temple.

estate was put up for sale to the highest bidder and in 1974 a grand-nephew named Donald Manea, who had played in the garden as a boy, bought it.

Donald and his wife, Alina, have worked for a long time now, first the years cleaning out all the garbage, next the years restoring the old stonework, then the years building a new stone home integral with the structures already in place. You can't describe it, and they don't offer tours. You just have to go and see it, even if you can't get inside; it's plenty dramatic from the sidewalk.

The Molehill Rock Garden is on the corner of 3rd Avenue North and 6th Street in Sauk Rapids. Take the Sauk Rapids exit off US 10, then turn left up 6th before the downtown. The Manea residence is at 601 3rd Avenue North.

World's Largest Lefse
Starbuck

It was a big year, 1983, when they celebrated the centennial of the founding of Starbuck, and they wanted to do it right. They put on a ten-day extravaganza in late June and early July, including an all-class reunion attended by Bertha Metlie Lilienthal from the first graduating class, class of 1910, along with 1,200 others who followed; and vocal concerts and band concerts, and the Pope County Dairy Princess was there to serve ice cream to the public, and an open house was held at the fire department so you could climb on the fire engines. Those who had airplanes flew in to the annual Pope County Fly-In.

They staged a Centennial Historical Pageant, a Water Fun Carnival, and a Medallion Hunt. Scandinavian crafts and food booths lined the main street. The Snoose Street Singers sang and there was Norwegian dancing and then the Swedish Singers sang, and it was quite the deal.

The highlight of the whole thing was the baking of the World's Largest Lefse. Lefse is a delicate flat potato pastry—at least my grandmother's was delicate—best served warm with butter, powdered sugar, and morning coffee. It measured nine feet, eight inches by nine feet, one inch when it was done, larger than they had expected and a grand success. Eight men baked it using thirty-two pounds of potatoes, thirty pounds of flour, four pounds of shortening, two pounds of sugar, and twelve ounces of salt. A hay rack was used as a counter for the pastry board where they rolled the dough, using a six-foot binder roller. A slatted roller was built to roll the flattened dough around to move it onto the griddle.

The griddle was made of two five-by-ten-foot flat plates of steel, each weighing six hundred pounds, welded together to make a ten-foot square. Parallel rails were set, fifteen bags of charcoal were spread between the rails and lit, and then with log chains and pry bars they slid the griddle onto the rails. The dough was unrolled over the griddle and they stood around and judged its progress, and then eight guys in unison, using boat paddles, turned the dough over on its other side. An official measurement was taken and verified.

Getting the pastry off the hot plate was tricky but they managed, with minimal damage, and it was cut up and buttered and sugared, like it's supposed to be, and served warm to the crowd. They saved a piece for Governor Perpich and another for King Olav of Norway. We don't know if it ever reached His Majesty or not, but it did make it into the *Shipstead Book of Records*, the Norwegian equivalent to the *Guinness Book of World Records* (which didn't even have a category for giant lefse). The city still celebrates the event every summer.

Starbuck is twenty miles east of Morris on County Highway 28. For information on Lefse Dagen in Starbuck, call the chamber of commerce at (320) 239-4220 or visit www.starbuckmn.org.

Prairie Chicken

Prairie chickens were once as common in Minnesota as blackbirds, of which there were millions. They were hunted, of course, but it was all that farming that really put them out of business. There's a strip of bluestem prairie out west of Barnesville and Rothsay where they're making a comeback these days, though, and for the few dozen folks who get out there to the mating grounds around April 20 at dawn, they put on a spectacular show. The males gather in crowds of about forty, stake out territories, square off, and bully each other, dancing and hopping and inflating big orange sacs on each side of their necks, making a three-note booming sound; females walk around among these wild guys and act disinterested. Eventually some get interested enough, which is why there are now 2,700 prairie chickens in the state.

They weigh about two pounds apiece and are considered tasty by those who remember the days when they were hunted; of course those people are thinking back to 1941, the last time it was legal. These days the meat is a secondary consideration; it's show business that draws the fans now. Prairie chicken is almost too honest a name for such a feisty and dramatic bird. It sounds like a derogatory term someone might use for a Midwesterner, out of his element in a bar full of longshoremen.

Rothsay was roughly the center of the prairie chicken population in its heyday, and there is a grand statue of a male in full formal mating dress there. It was built of cement and steel in a big garage by a man named Art Fosse, who spent most of his life in the trucking business; he says he's not really a sculptor but he's got quite a shop and he's handy with a torch and that sort of thing. It's "one of my hobbies," he adds, and the bird was built at his suggestion. Using a mounted bird from the university as a model, he made a steel frame and subframe, covered it with cement and plaster, and painted it. He makes it sound like there was nothing to it, but it weighs nine

A nine-thousand-pound bird looking for a date.

thousand pounds. It was covered with a World War II parachute and hauled to the site; at the big dedication in June 1976, Art says, they removed the parachute and "there was all kinds of fanfare . . . radio stations and so forth." It was pictured on the front page of the *Minneapolis Tribune*.

It's close to the road and very photogenic, and the nearby little truck stop is not that bad of a place to get some pie and coffee.

The World's Largest Prairie Chicken stands near the eastbound exit ramp on Interstate 94 at Rothsay.

Pottyville
Villard

There are eleven buildings in the collection, with two more in waiting. They are a young village of old houses. Old outhouses, specifically, each wrapped in a new theme and most looking a lot better than the main house they once served. They are also no doubt in much better condition than most of their original owners, if you get the drift there. The irony becomes part of the charm.

The community began when Nell Riccatone of Villard and Gary Hoover of Glenwood were driving to Clara City in the summer of 2010 and spotted an old outhouse about to fall over. They thought about restoring it, or one like it. Nell thought she might be able to use it as a potting shed.

They found the first available one not far down the road at a place called Ring Recycling. They began the restoration at Hoover's farm and then went looking for more neglected little structures, most not that easy to spot from the road. An ad in the *Senior Perspective* brought forth candidates in abundance.

Once all dedicated to the same specialty, they are now each shacks of different themes: Winter, Spring, Summer, Fall, Wild Wild West, Huntin' Fishin' Shack, the Throne Room. Plus a Trading Post shack where people bring things to trade. A Road Kill Grill behind it offers specialties such as Chuck of Skunk, Rack of Raccoon, and Smidgeon of Pigeon.

Their neighbors jumped into the project with enthusiasm and hard work, giving what seemed like an odd notion a remarkable feel of purpose and reality. They are colorful, full of whimsy and country humor, and all sitting on solid foundations.

And the Little Village of Retired Outhouses has grown into one of those things where the "reality is greater than the sum of the parts."

You are free to drop in and if no one is around just go ahead and check it out on your own. Pottyville is located a few miles west of Villard. From County Road 28, go north on County Road 25 and then

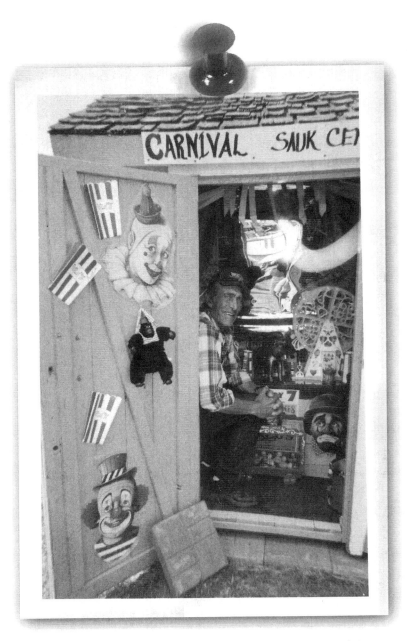

Not as glamorous as it looks being an outhouse model.

west on 165th Street. When the road comes to a T, take a left on Amelia Drive. Pottyville is on the left-hand side and visible from the road. If you have an outhouse you'd like to donate you can call Nell at (320) 554-3100 or (719) 248-1739. You can view the "Gallery" at www.srperspective.com.

Big Foot in Vining

Vining

If asked to name the city with the most outdoor sculpture relative to its population, one would think quickly of Florence or Paris, or perhaps Rome or Venice; but with a population of eighty-four persons and seventeen monumental outdoor metal sculptures, Vining surely has more civic art per person—one piece for every five citizens—than any city in the world. But these aren't the kind of folks to go around making claims and tooting their horn. It's there and if you want to stop in and see it, well, that's fine with them but no one seems to think it's a big deal; least of all the artist himself, a modest ex-construction welder named Kenny Nyberg.

He's reluctant to consider himself an artist at all, and when he was forming his signature piece, the ten-gauge twelve-foot Big Foot, he kept it out in his shed and didn't tell anyone about it for a year. It ended up taking more than two years to complete and it's not just that it's a big foot, but that it has an oversized big toe that's big even for a big foot. The toe has a place for weary travelers to sit upon, although most travelers aren't all that weary anymore; most just stop their air-conditioned car long enough to get out and be photographed sitting on the Big Toenail.

He began with a Tree, which still sits in his backyard; then he did a Dog, a likeness of his own dog, but not a Dog relating to the Tree in the familiar way. He then built the ambitious and difficult Square Knot and realized he could weld about anything he could imagine. He uses scraps of fourteen- to ten-gauge steel from grain elevators and other agricultural buildings he's worked on over the years; now that he's

The nation's most sat-upon toe.

retired, his son, also a welder, keeps him supplied. He said, "If you make a shirt, when you cut the pattern there's a lot of scrap pieces left over. Same thing with a grain elevator."

He has quickened his output since retiring, building a Lion for the Henning Lions Club, a Giant Stethoscope for the Henning Health Care Center, and an Otter for Ottertail. Vining itself is nearly full. Besides Big Foot and Square Knot there is a big midair Coffee Cup pouring a stream of coffee on the ground; a pair of giant Pliers standing upright with an unlucky cockroach in its jaws; a very large—it's all large—Clothes Pin standing on its legs; an Astronaut, representing his own daughter Karen who is a real-life NASA astronaut; a Cowboy next to a Saddle on a fence; an Indian on a Horse; a Hummingbird midair at a flower; a Flower Pot growing a cactus; an Electrical Plug raised on a coil of wire; a Blue Heron; an Alien; and an Elk. His latest works are a Spartan, a Bulldog, a Viking, an Elephant (from lawnmower blades),

Fabulous Bob

It would be interesting enough to live in Motley—or Fertile, or any other place with an adjective name—just to read the newspaper headlines (MOTLEY FARMER MARRIES FERTILE WOMAN; MOTLEY POLICEMAN PROMOTED; MOTLEY TEACHERS TO STRIKE; et cetera) without someone coming along and making outrageous news on their own. In this case it's a local man known as Fabulous Bob who says he "went to New York and graduated from Columbia University with a double PhD in psychology and theology," and became an ordained minister in the Church of Christ.

He had disagreements with his church, feeling that they were too conservative in some ways, and when he was "somewhere between thirty-five and forty-five" he moved to New Orleans, visited the hall of the High Priestess of Voodoo, Marie LaVieux, and suddenly, as he says, "felt comfortable." He followed through with these feelings and became a High Priest of Voodoo himself, however one goes about doing that, and he ultimately moved back to his hometown where he got a regular job and then set up an altar and developed a small clientele . . . and seems to be doing just fine. He says, "People think voodoo involves the sacrifice of chickens. We do not. That is a Hollywood myth."

He's also a member of a conservative think tank and is a flamboyant dresser and doesn't see any of it as contradiction, and goes to and a Bighorn Sheep. He's working on a lawnmower-blade Rhino.

It is a beautiful collection. Asked what his fellow citizens think of it all, he said, "Well, they don't seem to say anything too bad about it."

Kenny's shop is located "one and a quarter mile straight north of the Foot." The Foot is at Highway 210. Call (218) 769-4343 or visit http://nybergsculptures.com.

meetings wearing whatever seems right at the moment, whether it be furs, jewelry, knickers, or sweatpants. At first people had problems with some of this, he says, but they adapt. " 'It's just Bob,' they say, 'don't worry about it. It's just the way he is.' "

Fabulous Bob, bringing comfort to voodoo-deprived Motley citizens.

None of this finds its way into the local headlines and he doesn't advertise, but it's not exactly a secret, either; if we could find him, anybody else in town could as well. He says, "You can do this in rural Minnesota, and people will adapt."

And there you have it. Motley residents adapt to voodoo priest.

Bob Jenkins lives at 281 1st Avenue South, Motley. His phone number is (218) 352-6629.

Eelpout Festival
Walker

The dictionary says this about the eelpout: "1. any fish of the family Zoarcidae, esp. *Zoarces viviparus*, of Europe." It could also have said: "2. one of the world's unique and truly ugly creatures, bringing shock, disgust, and revulsion into any boat unlucky enough to catch one." The eelpout and his family may or may not be named after Zoar, the city in the Old Testament where Lot is said to have sought refuge during the destruction of Sodom and Gomorrah, but at any rate it ranks low on most people's social ladder of fishes. It has a blunt face, bulging eyes, no scales, and smooth slimy skin like a catfish except in a splotchy brown-and-black instead of a sleek all-black. But as the name suggests, its worst aspect is a double-flex backbone that gives it the same menacing moves as a snake; all this plus a creepy little barbel on its chin. It gives some fisher-folk nightmares.

In Walker they are buying none of this silly fearmongering; up there, they claim the eelpout to be "the only true game fish" and celebrate it every February with a three-day festival, the high point of which is an Eelpout Fishing Contest where elite teams of crack fishermen compete for prizes. Ken Bresly, the organizer, says that there are strict mental and physical examinations for the entrants before they're actually allowed to enter the contest; for instance, one of the questions on the mental exam is "What is your name?" You don't necessarily have to know your last name, but you have to at least remember your first name, or one of your names. For the physical, you have to be able to stand erect for more than thirty seconds ("we eliminate a big pile of them right there"); another requirement, for example, is that you have to be able to find your car keys. Or at least, somebody's keys ("and that's another toughie").

He notes that contestants aren't encouraged to bring an ordinary fish to the judges: ". . . If they catch a walleye, or somethin' like that, and they bring those into the headquarters, we won't even allow that to be hung on the same rack that the eelpout are on. Because we

A face only a mother could love
COURTESY OF THE *PILOT-INDEPENDENT*

don't want to contaminate the eelpout. We're real concerned about that." Asked whether, if you were to by chance catch a record walleye while you were fishing for eelpout, you'd have to not say anything about it and toss it back, Ken says, "Either that or hide it. Sneak it home and have it ground into pet food . . . in fact, you're not allowed to bring anything like that in. We have a number of people arrested each year for that very thing. Because again, they might contaminate the eelpout. We just can't take a chance on that."

We allowed as how the festival sounded like a good time and Ken said that it's possible, if you force yourself, to have a good time, but of course that's not the point of it. The point is the sport of it, the *art* of the eelpout, and to get out and become one with nature. And all that sort of thing. A person is permitted one glass of sherry before dinner, which often features Eelpout Nuggets; any more than that might blur one's palate, so as to obscure the amazing flavors of the deep-fried eelpout.

You fish for eelpout exactly as you fish for walleye, but certain people have their little secret baits and so forth. World-class eelpout anglers are on hand at the tournament, going from fish house to fish house, apparently to offer tips and encouragement. The world record, as far as Ken knows, is seventeen pounds. A seventeen-pound eelpout, we thought, would be well over two feet long, and he says, "Yes indeed; I think it's closer to three feet, or maybe four." We couldn't help but wonder if whoever caught that thing was able to sleep that night. Or even now.

The Eelpout Festival is held the third weekend of February. For more information call the Leech Lake Area Chamber of Commerce at (800) 833-1118 or (218) 547-1313 or visit www.eelpoutfestival.com.

UFO Collides with Sheriff's Patrol Car

Warren

All the elements are here: the lone eyewitness; an honest, well-respected small-town deputy sheriff whose credibility had never been questioned, knocked cold at the scene; the actual damage on the patrol car caused by an unknown object; the bright flash of light so intense it injured the deputy's retinas for a time; and the mysterious simultaneous stopping of two clocks, one mechanical and one electrical, for fourteen minutes. All this followed by a visit from an investigator sent by UFO headquarters in Indiana.

At 1:30 a.m. on August 27, 1979, Marshall County Deputy Val Johnson was headed west from Stephen on County Road 5. Approaching

Highway 220 he saw a light to the south that looked like it might be a light plane in trouble about two miles away. He turned south onto Highway 220; the light seemed to hang there and then suddenly came right down the road at him, he said, fast and bright. There was a crash. He was knocked cold and came to forty minutes later, remembering the sound of breaking glass and nothing more. He called for help on the radio, saying he'd been hit by something but it wasn't a vehicle. He didn't know what it was.

The car traveled 854 feet from the point of impact to the place where the brakes were applied, and then it skidded 99 feet and ended up crosswise on the road. It had a broken headlight, a dent on the hood, a broken windshield, and a damaged red light on the roof. Two spring-mounted antennae were bent sharply backward, and the clock was running fourteen minutes slow. There was no evidence of another vehicle anywhere within a mile. Deputy Johnson had a bump on his head, apparently from hitting the steering wheel, and his eyes hurt from "welder's burn." And his watch was fourteen minutes slow.

When it hit the paper, a number of other people came forward to report similar incidents in that area but none had made actual contact with a bright object; investigations looked into the case but no solid conclusions were drawn. Johnson himself still says he doesn't know what it was; it's a mystery to this day. The sheriff at the time, Dennis Brekke, said, "We've had something here and we really don't know what it is. I'm not reporting that we believe in flying saucers or don't believe in flying saucers. What he's [Johnson] seen, he's seen. None of us are trained to explain things we're not used to seeing."

But because it drew national attention at the time, the patrol car was never repaired; it sits now on display in the Marshall County Museum in Warren. People around the area still wonder about it. There are many theories.

Warren is located thirty-one miles north of Crookston on US 75. To see the UFO Car, call the Marshall County Historical Society at (218) 745-4803 or visit www.mnhistoricnw.org.

The Wadsworth Trail

In the years following the Civil War, the Wadsworth Trail ran west from St. Cloud through Sauk Center and Glenwood and on to Fort Wadsworth in the Dakota Territory. There was a stop along the way called Gager's Station, just north of Morris, where in an unknown year between 1864 and 1871 a gentleman from the East arrived driving a team of oxen. He was a musician and had played in "a famous orchestra in the East," and had come out here for adventure. Seems like kind of a joke now, that someone would come to Minnesota from Philadelphia or New York for adventure.

His name was Albert Hawkes, his clothes were always clean and pressed, and he didn't smoke, drink, swear, or gamble; stood out like a bride in a pigsty. His sense of humor was all that saved him from being run out of town, that and his team of oxen. When he had shopped for them, he didn't care for the ordinary animals that answered only to hish, gee, and haw; he thought that far too crude. So he bought a young pair and trained them himself, teaching them to respond to square dancing commands. It became a real treat for the town when Albert would drive that team down the street and around the block, singing out "Forward all," "Gents to the right," and "Allemande left." They'd do more than just start and turn, too; they could "Promenade" and "Swing your partners" and do "Ladies forward and back."

Albert took a job driving the stagecoach from Gager's Station to Bismarck, described as a teamster's nightmare, through sinkholes and mud and along easily ambushed high ground. He made it to Bismarck and then was sent out on a newly laid trail to the Black Hills in South Dakota, where he became "one of the first drivers to be shot by Indians on that trail." They didn't say what happened to the team of oxen, but without the manual it would have been hard for anyone else to drive it.

Seems unfair, doesn't it? A clever guy, a musician, a free spirit in clean clothes out there on the muddy frontier, gunned down by people who just didn't give him a chance to show them his talent or his humorous side. If there's a moral to the story it would be something like this: In hostile territory, wit is less valuable than having someone along to ride shotgun.

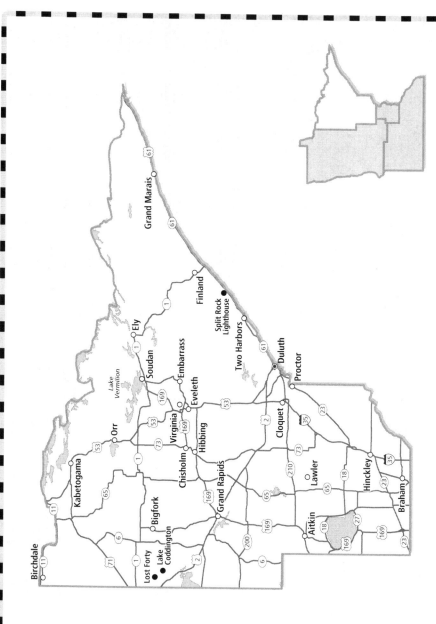

3

Northeast

From the evergreens on the hill at Cloquet, the freeway glides 677 feet down into metro Duluth, a most scenic arrival, overlooking the tracks curling out onto the high timber trestles, the hopper cars unloading down chutes into improbably long ore boats, all deep iron-ore red. You see out at the eastern end of the big sheltered bay a high lift bridge, and beyond that the largest lake in the world, holding a full 10 percent of the planet's fresh water. A glorious scene.

Lake Superior is known to throw up twenty and even thirty-foot waves, a fact that generates pride and respect but doesn't encourage folks to go out there in fourteen-foot aluminum trailer boats.

And, of course, no one needs to, with the Voyageurs National Park and the Boundary Waters Canoe Area covering nearly the entire Arrowhead area. Rainy Lake and the Vermillion, the Kabetogama, the Namakan, the Pelican, and a few thousand others are perfect for those Minnesotans who prefer their lakes a bit smaller and smoother.

The lodging at the resorts is comfortable, the food home style; there are docks and boats and gear, and beauty and serenity all around.

And if you find it just a bit quiet after a week or two on the lake or hiking and camping—and if your timing is right, say the second week in August—you can slip down to Duluth and have a fine time at the big-time Bayfront Blues Festival, with national acts there every summer.

Fish Houses on Parade
Aitkin

They hold the parade on the Friday after Thanksgiving, someone said, "to not distract everybody away from Macy's." Someone else said, "There's not many in northern Minnesota who much care about Macy's—it's just that we don't have a mall, so why not watch fish houses go by? Gotta be more fun than shopping anyway."

And it seems to be. The annual event draws thousands of spectators as well as its fair share of media attention. Another one of those cold celebrations that the media seem drawn to like mosquitoes to a baby, or more like frost to a windshield. They've been in *USA Today*

(Continued on page 168)

Hollywood in the North Woods.
PHOTO BY ANN M. SCHWARTZ

The world's draftiest igloo.
PHOTO BY ANN M. SCHWARTZ

A fish finder,
finding fish.
PHOTO BY
ANN M. SCHWARTZ

Cuyuna Range

Minnesota is variously translated as "stands in canoe," "falls into water," or "drops things in lake." Bill Matthies has been diving in the North Country for more than forty years; the lake and river bottoms yield a steady twenty snowmobiles and three cars every winter, plus a broad range of other valuables, from wedding rings—they slip off cold fingers—up to D7 Caterpillar tractors, two of which sank in twenty feet of mud near Randall. Bill uses an underwater metal detector if the bottom is soft, but is generally able to see what he's looking for down there. He's pulled up boats, fishing tackle, guns, airplanes, trucks, slot machines, and ninety-nine unfortunate persons.

Last year a man was ice fishing on Mille Lacs Lake as part of an American Legion steak fry; somehow his upper plate fell out and dropped through the hole. He wore a ski mask the rest of the day so people couldn't see what he looked like without his teeth. They called Bill and he put a float in the hole with a weight set to ride a foot off the bottom. Then he sawed a bigger hole nearby, went down, and found the teeth right where they were supposed to be, under the weight, and the man had steak that night. It's not uncommon to find teeth, Bill says; one pictures lakebeds strewn with upper plates.

Besides the recovery business he also teaches; he says the first tool of ice divers is a snow shovel. They clear a patch of ice and then shovel pathways radiating out from the center. They cut a triangular hole with a chain saw and from below the pathways create a bright illumination, "like a big fluorescent light up there." They lower themselves into a blue-green world, cold and wet and luminous, with this amazing brilliance streaming down.

The favorite waters of the recreational diver are the old mine pits of the Cuyuna Range, where the water is crystal pure and you can see for a hundred feet. The terraced landscape is a fantasy of steep cliffs, old shacks, tunnels, power lines, and railroad beds. Fish move in the trees down there, and in spring eelpout wrap themselves around branches and lay eggs. Loons come down to cruise among the divers; an odd symbiosis, human and bird, swimming underwater. One pit is more ghostly yet; swimming near a bare-branch woods, you make out what looks like a far-off pale skeleton hanging from a tree and find to your horror that it is. Farther on another sits grinning in a chair, legs crossed, and yet another slumps against a power pole, bone fingers gripping two bare wires from a fusebox. A gigantic Jurassic turtle, eight feet across, lies on the bottom like a musty sunken UFO. This lake draws crowds of divers.

Thin ice is one of nature's ways to cull the herd.

If being underwater in a freezing cold mine-pit lake with two feet of solid ice between yourself and the real world is your idea of a good time, you will find yourself in good company on the Cuyuna Range. And you'd better bring your sense of humor, because there are jokers among them.

Minnesota School of Diving is located at 712 Washington Street in Brainerd. Call (800) OK-SCUBA or (218) 829-5953 for information or visit www.mndiving.com.

(Continued from page 164)

and a number of newspapers from the warmer latitudes, like Dallas; one year Comedy Central brought its own float, along with a camera crew.

There are prizes: Most Creative, Most Humorous, Noisiest (lots of racket before that long winter silence sets in), Best Fish House, and Best Youth Entry. Some have bands, some have boom boxes, some have walkers alongside tossing candy; they all have a fish house, or a suggestion of one. We figured if we entered a fish house we'd build it invisible: all mirrors, inside and out, and set diagonally on the trailer. (Go ahead and win a prize with our idea, somebody; we just don't have the time.)

The floats gather at the fairgrounds at noon and the parade starts at 1 p.m., goes for eight blocks, and then the awards are given out at City Hall. Bathroom humor was a popular theme when the event began in the early 1990s—a guy fishing out of a toilet was big hit— but they've moved onward and upward to wacky costumes, igloos, Jaws, hot tubs, fish finders, a dog with antlers, the Crappie Queen, celebrities and athletes, plus every fire engine the town ever owned. All this and an American Legion Chili Cook-Off, the bank's Fish House Stew at the Moose Lodge, and pancake breakfasts and sloppy joe lunches.

You don't see the skin you see at Mardi Gras, and Aitkin isn't quite the French Quarter, but they do have a party spirit up here.

Call the Aitkin Chamber of Commerce at (218) 927-2316 or (800) 526-8342 or visit www.aitken.com for more information.

The True Canoe
Bigfork

In an age when cheap quartz watches are more accurate than anything ever made by hand, there are still certain instruments of which the best can be built only by ancient methods. Violins, for instance. And canoes.

Ray Boessel Jr. and a rack of future national treasures.

Canoeists generally agree that birch bark is superior to aluminum and fiberglass: it's lighter, stronger, more flexible, easier to repair; most importantly, it's easier to paddle, quieter in the water, and it *feels* better. It has spirit. But they aren't manufactured; they're hand-made and lashed together without fasteners. One of the few places in the world where they take the time to do this is the Hafeman Boat Works in Bigfork, now run by Ray Boessel Jr.

Bill Hafeman and his wife, Violet, homesteaded here in 1920 and faced a seven-mile weekly hike to town for supplies; the river offered an easier way. Bill learned how to build canoes using age-old Indian methods, built from the outside in, with bark from birch trees, white cedar strips for the ribs, black spruce roots for the binding, pitch and bear grease for sealant. Canoes like this were used by the Natives and by French traders to travel the Great Lakes. The big ones, thirty-seven feet long and five feet wide, could carry more than three tons of cargo and fourteen men. They were called the *canot du maître,* the Montreal canoe, and they were the mainstay of the fur trade in the North in the 1700s. Not a single old one survives today, because nobody ever thought of putting one in a museum. Most of the few in existence were built by Hafeman Boat Works.

Bill became a legend as a woodsman and boatbuilder; he built about six a year for sixty years. His canoes were of all sizes and became known worldwide, and famous people like Lady Bird Johnson bought them. Two of his apprentices are still helping to keep the tradition alive; one of these is Ray Boessel Jr., married to Bill Hafeman's granddaughter Christie.

Ray makes ten to fifteen canoes a year; each begins as a long search through the woods, and most are spoken for before they're built. He builds them in the various styles; the shape of the ends identifies the tribe of origin. He's made more than 250 canoes since the early 1980s, including the big ones, and he's not optimistic about the future of the birch canoe, mostly because of the difficulty of finding large enough birch trees and the recent efforts to stop the taking of even small amounts of cedar.

So if you've always wanted to own a Stradivarius but can't quite afford it, you might consider a canoe with five hundred years of history, made by Ray Boessel Jr.

Hafeman Boat Works is located thirty miles straight north of Deer River on County Road 6 where it intersects with the Big Fork River. Call (218) 743-3709 if you get lost.

Basshenge
Birchdale

It began as one of those "Why not?" moments between couples. In the summer of 1999 Joe Gaustefeste, who has been with the Chicago Symphony forty-one years and is their principal bassist, was sitting with his wife, writer Yvette Journeau, watching a National Geographic special on TV about Stonehenge. She turned to him and said, "Why not a Basshenge?"

An innocent question he couldn't answer, and on the Fourth of July 2001, set in a clef-shaped walkway near the Rainy River, twenty-one

Seven sins and seven virtues—in ⅜-inch steel plate.

steel basses stood tall on twenty-one concrete pedestals. To a passerby they imply there could be more here than meets the eye, and there is.

They already had the land, eighty acres and a cabin west of International Falls, near Birchdale. (Chicago used to stash gangsters in the North Country but now they're sending classical musicians; considered an improvement, in many ways.) Joe was born in Brooklyn, where they raise people who like to get things done, and through his work he had

The Lost Forty

The first requirement of a legend is that it has to have a cool name, as in Big Foot or the Bermuda Triangle. If this place were called the Erroneously Marked Remote Hundred-Forty-Four you wouldn't hear much about it, and neither, of course, would we. So the fact that it's not actually lost and that it is 104 acres more than forty is unimportant. Truth in advertising can be overrated.

It actually was lost, but not in the sense that it couldn't be found; it was lost to the thirty thousand loggers up there sawing down all the trees around the turn of the last century. A survey completed in late 1882 called the tract Coddington Lake, which in reality lies a half mile to the southeast. As a lake it couldn't be bought and couldn't be logged; it stood untouched and primeval while all around it the land was cleared of its old growth red and white pines.

A tough-looking surveyor with the grand name of Josiah A. King led his crew of three rodmen to map out three townships in the forest forty miles north of Grand Rapids. The combination of freezing rain and snow, swampy ground, a bitter wind, and a month in the boonies living on pork and beans and dried apples had apparently taken its toll; some have speculated they didn't bother to go out that day. They may have done the survey from inside a canvas tent. And connections to artists and sculptors. He decided on ⅜-inch ordinary plate steel as the medium; they would be of three different styles abstracted from the three clefs in which the bass is played—bass, tenor, and treble—designed by himself, sculptor Richard Hunt, and puppet maker Mathew Owens. Ten lintels would span between the eighteen six-foot basses, and three ten-foot basses would stand in the center, all on five-foot pedestals.

for that we can give thanks to the cold wet misery in November in the north.

The mile-long little trail through these fabulous two-hundred-foot pines, some five hundred years old and holding enough board feet to build a small barn, is serene and beautiful in an almost spooky way, especially after surviving because of nothing more than a lucky blunder. Surveyors are a precise and proud lot, and no one has suggested that Josiah King decided to spare this small tract of utterly pristine woodland on purpose. But it's not impossible. It could have been a love of natural forests, or perhaps his little prank to play on the timber interests. We'd like to think, naively, that he meant to leave his mark one way or another. Even knowing he'd someday be found out.

From Grand Rapids take US Highway 2 west; one mile west of Deer River take Highway 46 northwest approximately thirty-two miles to Itasca County Road 34. Turn right (north) twenty miles to County Road 29 and turn right (east) one mile to Dora Lake. Turn left on County Road 26 for two miles to Forest Road 2240 on the left. A sign for the Lost Forty stands about one and a half miles down this road.

It's possible the tract got its name because that's how many people get confused trying to follow the directions every year, becoming themselves the Lost Forty.

The lintels were designed from images by painter Sam Agres of the seven virtues—prudence, temperance, justice, fortitude, faith, hope, and charity—overlaid on images of the seven deadly sins—covetousness, pride, lust, anger, gluttony, sloth, and greed. Three other lintels represent arcane musical concepts, like harmony, conflict, and brotherhood.

The pedestals are sixteen inches in diameter and fourteen feet tall—nine of these feet are below ground—and because the soft ground couldn't support a cement truck they all had to be hand-poured. Leland Nelson cut the steel, his brother Ralph did the surveying, and Eugene Molberg poured the concrete.

People stand and wonder, "Will future anthropologists decipher the imagery? Will they figure out it was built by a bass player from Chicago who bought a shack from a woman hunter up here in this town of only nine people?"

Take Highway 11 west of International Falls about forty miles, through the towns of Loman and Indus, and continue eight more miles past the INDUS sign; Basshenge is on your right, north of the highway. If you reach Birchdale you've gone two miles too far.

Pie Day
Braham

Braham claims to be the Homemade Pie Capital of Minnesota, and they've done a lot to seal that claim with their annual Pie Day celebration.

Traditional events on Pie Day include the pie baking contest and, following naturally, the pie eating contest (two, in fact: junior and senior); the pie race; the art show; the small-quilt show; the artisans; and the homemade pie in the park. A popular booth outside the post office will even cancel your stamps with an official Pie Day logo, and send your mail from there.

A newcomer to the festivities is the Pie Medallion Hunt, which awards a cash prize to whoever finds the medallion. Organizers openly

Lighthouses

A lot of states have soybean fields and quite a few others have light-houses but Minnesota is one of the rare places that have both; it's not a significant relationship—the lights never burned soybean oil—but it's an oddity relating to this deep-water seaport we have here in the middle of the continent.

The stretch of Lake Superior shoreline between Two Harbors and Split Rock was considered one of the most dangerous waters in the world. A storm in 1905 wrecked twenty-nine ships in two days, most of them belonging to US Steel, and they pressured Congress for some warning lights and foghorns, and they got them. The fundamental problem was the huge deposits of iron ore beneath the lake, which mess up navigational compasses; being caught in a winter storm at night with no compass was many a sailor's nightmare finish.

The lighthouses are no longer needed in the age of radar, depth finders, and global positioning, but they make excellent tourist attractions; the one in Two Harbors is a bed-and-breakfast and the one at Split Rock is just a beautifully proportioned and dramatically situated famous building.

Contact Lighthouse Bed & Breakfast, 1 Lighthouse Point in Two Harbors, (888) 832-5606, or visit http://lighthousebb.org.

Split Rock Lighthouse is roughly twenty miles north of Two Harbors on Highway 61; there are signs. The phone number is (218) 226-6372. It's open only in summer.

admit, in a refreshing bit of frankness, that the purpose of the hunt is to get people not to spend all their time at Freedom Park, where the main event is staged, and to go snoop around the downtown.

Pie Day is a lot more than just the highlights: There's a pancake breakfast and a spaghetti supper, a pie auction, the Pie-Alluia Chorus singing "songs that have to do with pies . . . or songs that have been altered to have words that have to do with pies." There's the Sweet as Pie Collector's Car Show, and the Sweetie Pie Street Dance. Throughout the day visitors visit crafters' booths and see entries in the Small Quilt Show, where quilts entered are about the size of a bath towel.

Braham was named the Pie Capital of Minnesota by former governor Rudy Perpich, who was from the Iron Range; before the freeway went in, the town was on the main route between the Twin Cities and Duluth and people would stop for pie at the halfway point. Friday was the big day, with all the traffic of folks going up north to their lake cabins, so when Pie Day was begun it was natural to place it on a Friday in August.

Actually, it's a combination of two events: The Isanti County Historical Society used to hold an annual ice cream social around that same time. Ice cream and pie was a natural merger and gave rise to the famous Minnesota battle cry: "Remember the Alamode."

Braham Pie Day is held the first weekend of August. Braham is located north of Cambridge on Highway 65 and County Road 107. For more information call (320) 396-4956 or visit www.pieday.com.

Iron Man
Chisholm

On the website for the World's Largest Things, by state, Texas comes in third with thirty-five, mostly items like the world's largest rattlesnake, largest killer bee, largest crab, watermelon, horse shoe, mule shoe, and so forth. They claim the world's largest cowboy boot, but it's tiny compared to the world's largest shoe, period, in Minnesota. California is second with forty-three pieces, things like the largest olive, the largest box of raisins, the largest can of fruit cocktail, largest paper cup, biggest skateboard, biggest champagne glass, largest yo-yo. The world's largest wind chimes were taken down because they were too loud, leaving California with forty-two items.

* *

Minnesota is the champ with forty-nine listed biggies, including such significant and essential pieces as the famous ball of twine, the largest pelican, otter, prairie chicken, eagle, loon, polar bear, and tiger muskie. The list goes on to include the boot, the ear of corn, the anchor, and the clothes pin; but it doesn't include the Iron Man Statue in Chisholm, which is bigger than anything on the list and is the third largest free-standing sculpture in the United States. It could be the world's largest miner but they don't call it that.

The Statue of Liberty and the St. Louis Arch are larger, but this work is still huge. Tall as an eight-story building, it's a memorial to the people who worked in the mines on all three iron ranges: Mesabe, Cuyuna, and the Vermillion. The miner is made of copper coated with brass, standing on a base of steel I-beams, rods, rails, plates, and bars. Under the base is a mound of taconite ore from the three ranges.

The miner's face is six feet tall and his shoulders are eleven feet wide. His helmet is four feet long and two feet tall; the boots are six feet long and two feet wide and his shovel weighs four hundred pounds; the memorial itself weighs three hundred thousand pounds. It was forty years in the making, conceived in 1947 and dedicated on July 4, 1987. It was designed by a sculptor from Lake Linden, Michigan, named Jack Anderson. Visit online at http://ironrange.org/communities/chisholm.

A Gas Station Extraordinaire

Cloquet

There is a story that Frank Lloyd Wright was once called to testify in a court case; he took his seat on the witness stand and an attorney asked him his name and then his occupation. "I am the world's greatest living architect," he answered. Chided later by his wife for his lack of modesty, he said: "I had no choice; I was under oath."

There are two of Wright's buildings in the Cloquet area, a house and a gas station, both owned by the same family. The house was one of the Prairie series, built in 1954 of concrete block, a material more

Wright's flying gas station foretold the era of midair refueling.

closely representing the client's bank account than the architect's preference in masonry. Making the best of the situation, Wright had the
horizontal joints, which he called the heart lines, raked deeply back for
the shadow, and he kept the vertical joints flush with the face of the
material. It is a graceful structure, at peace with its surroundings, and
the grandson of the client still lives there.

During the budget negotiations, Wright, who wanted it done in
stone and if not that then brick, and who was famous for his own
monetary problems, asked his client: "Lindholm, don't you know some
banker you can corrupt for the money to do it?"

The R. W. Lindholm Service Station was begun in 1956, a year that the Guggenheim Museum and eighteen other Wright projects were under way. In 1958, during the course of the construction, his son-in-law Darrell had reason to visit him at his office in Taliesen, in Spring Green, Wisconsin, where he asked Wright if he might take his photo; the architect struck a relaxed pose. The photo was printed back in Minnesota and Darrell asked Wright's apprentice if he'd take it back and have it signed; he came back and said the man had torn the picture up because he looked "too old" and had sent an earlier portrait back instead, signed. He was ninety years old at the time, and died the following year, proud to the end. Darrell had his negative printed again of course with the image of the signature on it.

The station is famous for its soaring canopy, flying optimistically unsupported out over the pumps, as well as the upstairs glass waiting lounge, built back when cars actually needed tune-ups. It is a most dramatic building and reflects Wright's enthusiasm for all things automobilian, and for the horizon; it was an integral part of his concept for the Broadacre City, as he named it, and the only component of such that was ever built.

Lindholm Service Station is found at the corner of Highways 33 and 45 in Cloquet. For more information call (218) 879-2279.

The Geek Prom
Duluth

Let's face it: It had to happen. Once the computer began its takeover, geeks would become gods as surely as caterpillars become butterflies. The inaugural Geek Prom took place at the NorShor Theater in Duluth in 2002 and was such a success that it has become an annual event. Over the years, prom activities have included a spaz-dancing contest, cow eye dissection, video game tournament, and a "Geek Streak" (a group of nude nerds running through the crowd and out into the night). A panel of celebrity geeks selects a king and queen at each one of course, and trophies are handed out and a lot of flash pictures are taken.

Naturally no one can be turned away from a Geek Prom, no matter how cool or beautiful or how big a jock you are, because to be rejected admission to any prom at all is to become a geek right there, and therefore instantly eligible. But once inside if you don't truly let out your inner nerd and if you don't look geeky enough and act weird enough you might be shunned. And then you'll try to act cool about it but the word will get out that you went to the prom and even the geeks wouldn't have anything to do with you and . . . well, you get the drift. The other contradiction is that when it becomes way cool to go to the Geek Prom then being cool wins again, despite the triumph of the geeks.

It was organized by Paul Lundgren as a celebration of clumsy social skills and obsessive-compulsive behavior, for people who were too geeky to attend their high school prom and also for those who did go but who were too cool to properly enjoy it. They expected, and got, a "night filled with awkward romance, cheesy music and spastic fits of clumsy dancing." Paul says we're all susceptible to geekiness; he himself was jock enough to play high school football but geek enough to also be on the audiovisual squad. He told a writer of his latest geek moment, which had happened that very day as he exited his car, walked behind a pickup, saw a lovely woman, and simultaneously banged his shin on the trailer hitch. He could have acted cool but he took the Geek Choice, as he called it, and let out a loud and uncool shriek of pain.

His partner in the prom endeavor is Scott Lunt, who says a bartender named Lefty developed special geek drinks for the ball, with names like the Pocket Protector and the Leonard Nimoy. He said the Pocket Protector "actually tastes like a Pocket Protector."

For more information visit www.geekprom.com or contact Paul Lundgren at (218) 624-6087, paul@geekprom.com, or Crystal Pelkey at (218) 336-1416. If the website is not operating, try again. They are geeks, after all.

All geeked up and ready to rumble.

Ship of Ghouls

The *William A. Irvin* was a big ship in her day, 610 feet long and 60 feet across the beam. She (you wouldn't say "he," even if her name is William) was built in 1938 and was at the time the flagship of US Steel, named after the president of the company. She had a crew of thirty-two and carried fourteen thousand tons of iron ore at about eleven miles an hour across the Great Lakes, powered by DeLaval cross compound steam turbines with two thousand shaft horsepower; her forty years on the Great Lakes were called "uneventful," meaning just the usual bitterly ferocious storms and the blazing heat and all. When she retired in 1978, she had carried 1,292 loads—an average of thirty-two trips a year. At eleven miles an hour, you wonder how she did it.

The flagship of the fleet also served as the hospitality center for executives; they'd come aboard in Conneaut, Ohio, and ride along for a round, wining and dining, hitting golf balls, playing cards and shuffleboard, flying kites, that sort of thing. But not fishing or swimming. Being the flagship is what saved her from the cutting torch on retirement and earned her this easy duty in port.

Her job now consists of scaring the cookies out of people in the Halloween season, and if you think an old house is scary, wait until you take this tour; the fear factor rises in direct proportion to size of the menace, and this thing is immense. The gigantic steel hull screaking and echoing in the darkness, the high catwalks and narrow passageways, the ominous piping and valves and hatches . . . in blackness, all of it would be terror on a grand scale even without any help at all from the shrieks and screams and the blood and swinging ax and the monsters and the near certainty of sudden dismemberment and all the rest of it; the gore, the eyeballs, the severed limbs—we can't go into it here, save to say it is a trip that a lot of folks are not able to finish. It is a professional-level nightmare, with help from the University of Minnesota–Duluth's Theater Department.

Children under twelve aren't allowed to enjoy the experience, for their own good and for the good of their parents. Some say extra underwear for the parents is not a bad idea either.

The last entry in her log, penned by Captain John J. McDonough in 1986, reads: "She was the Queen of the Lakes and so shall she remain for the rest of her days." He had no idea it would come to this.

The *William A. Irvin* is moored near Duluth's Aerial Lift Bridge. To get to the ship from Interstate 35, take Canal Park Drive, then take a right onto Railroad Street. The ship is moored at Railroad Street and Harbor Drive. For details call (218) 727-0022, ext. 234, or visit www .williamairvin.com.

Graffiti Graveyard
Duluth

It took years of wrangling, a lot of hard work, and a ton of money to build the extension of Interstate 35 through downtown Duluth. There was an enclosed void left beneath a quarter mile of it, and in that grand and hidden substructure artists have slathered nearly every wall, beam, and column in bright graphics.

It is art performed without benefit of an art director, new imagery often laid upon the old, dynamic stylized messages mingled with Felix the Cat and Betty Boop.

It's not easy to get in there, and it's not family entertainment, but any adult in good physical condition and hiking clothes can get through the opening at the west end, where a shallow drainage canal exists, and climb up to the compacted earth on the roadbed level. You stand and find yourself in a enormous space—a colorful, conflicted world of order and anarchy, engineered concrete covered with flamboyant spray paint.

The great structure has the ritual feel of an ancient underground palace, one that may have been overrun by a large tribe of artists. A long and wide slot overhead—the gap between the traffic lanes—runs straight down the middle of thirty huge bays, each as big as a hotel ballroom and decorated in a cacophony of color. You are struck by the sheer vigor and volume of art. Bright light and a loud freeway roar come from above, like a nonstop tempest from Mount Olympus.

The roadway stays level, but the framework slopes down to the east; you hike past progressively lower and darker rooms, the back walls of which become indistinct in the deep shadows. The place could use some picking up, and it would not be difficult for the city to seal the place with chain-link gate. You sense that what you see writ so wild and bright in that big free art gallery is an implied contract, a deal between the artists and the city, and you can't help but notice, after you leave, that there is not much other graffiti in Duluth.

Large art for a small audience.

But the real value of the place comes from simply knowing, as you cruise the freeway between the downtown buildings and the harbor, that you are driving on the roof of one of the world's largest art galleries.

From the west on Interstate 35 take the downtown Michigan Avenue exit and turn right on Lake Avenue, crossing the freeway. Take the immediate right on Railroad Street and follow the retaining wall to its western end. There is an opening the height of a garage door around the corner, underneath the roadway. Visit online at www.youtube .com/watch?v=kAnghwJorvo.

Aerial Lift Bridge

Duluth

It is one of the grandest harbor entries a ship can make anywhere in the world—to traverse the entire St. Lawrence Seaway and Lakes Erie, Ontario, Huron, and Superior, then arrive with the Glensheen Mansion and downtown Duluth to starboard and a lacy steel structure as distinctive as the Eiffel Tower a mile dead ahead. You whistle the traditional "long-short, long-short" and see road traffic come to a halt and the great lift rise for your precise and majestic approach. And of course your departure is equally huge. Ships don't just sneak in and out of the Port of Duluth without anyone noticing.

The first edition wasn't even a bridge; built in 1905, the twin towers held a trestle across the top from which a gondola was hung just above the water. It traversed back and forth by a system of cables and pulleys, a suspended ferry, and carried sixty-two tons of horses, wagons, automobiles, and people. By 1929 they needed something faster and so began building the lift bridge, raising new towers right inside the old ones, lifting the fixed span 42 feet up to a clear height of 172 feet; the lift span was 386 feet long and weighed nine hundred tons, balanced by weights inside the towers.

They were lucky to get it built when they did. Nowadays, of course, the uncontrolled tyranny that is the highway department would simply condemn miles of the city on both ends for a long and wide approach and build a huge rising causeway, cap it in the middle with Ugly Concrete Bridge Design No. 2, and call it a job well done. But the City of Duluth owns this graceful landmark, built to fit into the city as it was and still is, and the US Army Corps of Engineers owns the land around it. These are a couple of large bureaucracies not easily kicked around by the highway department, so, luckily for us, they've had to keep their clumsy mitts off.

They paint the bridge every fifteen years, which adds enough weight that they have to recalibrate the counterweights. It was given a total redo in 1986, with four new hundred-horsepower electric motors and a new operator's cabin in the center of the lift span with new radios, radar, emergency, and navigation equipment; new cables, structural repairs, and a good sandblasting. And, of course, more paint.

Ships have the right-of-way over road traffic, but they have been known to wait for the passage of fire trucks; outbound ships have the right-of-way over inbound because they have less room to maneuver in the harbor. The bridge is raised an average of 5,500 times each season—the port is frozen over in winter—meaning that if you spend a summer afternoon in Duluth, you are likely to be able to watch the bridge lift and then have the giant steel side of a ship pass so close it seems you can almost, but not quite, touch it.

To view the bridge, take Interstate 35 to Duluth and turn onto Canal Park Drive. You can't miss it.

Flat Irons

Duluth

It's a subject one would expect to be curious but not necessarily stunning, this collection of old irons, but stunning is precisely the right word for it.

It began when Ken Broman was at an auction some years back and on impulse bought some old irons in a box. After more auctions and more irons, the collection grew with one year even leading to a blue ribbon show winner: a stunning model from World War II built of brilliant white glass, a direct result of the steel rationing in the war effort. An iron that helped win the war, one could say, and beautiful as well.

This blue ribbon show winner sits on one of many sturdy shelves now holding a vast and varied steel and copper fleet, prows forward like an international navy in dry dock. Nearly a thousand irons from around the world, in a wide variety of styles and moods: some aggressive, some elegant, some just solid worker irons; some small for cuffs and collars, some curved to iron the inside of a man's felt hat and some huge for commercial laundry ironing. One has a dragon's head at the prow. They feel like artworks in the shape of tools.

"We never expected to fill the basement with 'em."

The big ones were called "sad irons": hefting a sad iron makes you think whoever it was that used one of these every day might develop the upper body of a gorilla, and probably not a real happy gorilla either.

They have suitcase irons for the traveling salesman, where the handle of the case becomes the handle of a folded iron contained cleverly within.

They are heated by a variety of fuels. Early ones are solid iron castings with wood handles that would sit on a fire or a stovetop; when it cooled you would put it back and grab the next one. Some were large bins themselves, heated by taking coal or briquettes from a fire and placing them directly in the iron and then locking the top back on.

The problem was that the handle of the hot iron would itself get hot. Irons with removable handles were a big hit. They'd come in a set of two or three sleds with one handle that would clip into place. Sometimes the metal body is hollow with a door at the back into which an iron slug fits. One slug in the iron and two more on the stove, and now the handle stays cool. The next step put the heat source back into the iron by hooking into the gas lines that preceded electricity, or by having an onboard tank holding kerosene.

There are dozens of miniatures on display, some of which were actually used to iron trim and some that were purely decorative. It's a hard place to leave; you keep seeing something you missed on the first pass.

The collection is not as unusual as one might think: Broman belongs to an international club of iron collectors with more than four hundred members.

You can contact Ken Broman at (218) 724-0676 or kenmary@ cpinternet.com.

Life at 60 Below
Embarrass

The mean annual temperature here is 34.4 degrees, a full degree colder than anyplace else in the state. In 1996 they had a stretch of twenty-five straight days below zero; a plaque at the Timber Hall in Embarrass states that on February 2, 1996, the temperature reached sixty-four below, Fahrenheit. It had been an exciting day because the official electronic thermometer had quit at fifty-three below—a power failure caused by all the television crews—and nearby Tower hit an official sixty below, a new record. Men were pounding nails into wood boards with bananas, just for the sport.

(Continued on page 192)

189

The Glensheen Mansion

Crime is no curiosity in any state. Minnesota has had its share of attention, going back to the kidnap and murder of the Lindbergh baby, the assassination of anticrime editor Walter Liggett, attorney T. Eugene Thompson's wife's murder, the Piper kidnapping, the Brom ax murders, the disappearance of Jacob Wetterling, and many others; books have been written about St. Paul's safe haven for John Dillinger, Ma Barker, Baby Face Nelson, Machine Gun Kelly, Alvin Karpis, and Kid Cann.

On the other end of the range of human endeavor stands the Glensheen Mansion in Duluth, a fabulously beautiful house, one of the finest in the country, now owned and maintained by the University of Minnesota. It was built by a very nice couple, Chester and Clara Congdon, both children of Methodist pastors who met at Syracuse University in New York. Chester found himself practicing law in St. Paul in 1880, five years out of college and still too poor to marry Clara; he had $9.67 in cash. But he caught a break when he met Henry Oliver of the Oliver Iron Mining Company in Duluth and became his legal counsel; US Steel bought the mine in 1901 and Chester, then forty-eight, opened his own mining company. In five years he was the second richest man in Minnesota.

Clara had a degree in art and architecture and she put it to good use. The Congdons became a great asset to the city, giving it, among other things, nineteen miles of Lake Superior shoreline, a landmark house, and a legacy of seven children who have now become three hundred. About forty descendants still live in Duluth.

It's tough to have such a great family dragged into sensational headlines by one person, but the youngest daughter of Chester and Clara, the kindhearted Elisabeth—who had never married, staying home to care for the parents—had adopted two girls. One of these was Marjorie, whose second husband was Roger Caldwell. In 1977, when Elisabeth was eighty-three, the Caldwells came to Duluth to ask for an $800,000 advance on Marjorie's inheritance and were refused. Shortly afterward Elisabeth and her nurse were found murdered in the mansion. The whole nation heard about it.

Marjorie and Roger were tried separately and things got confused and in the end both were freed. She remarried while still married to Roger, and then her new husband and his ex-wife both died of suspicious causes; the details of it all are far too dreary for a book of curiosities, save to say that Roger committed suicide and Marjorie now lives in Arizona. Lives in a prison there. Finally. Locked up for arson when sheriff's deputies caught her in the act. By coincidence, a long string of fires in her and her neighbors' properties immediately ended.

But the Glensheen Mansion in Duluth is a sweet place to visit; eighty-five thousand people do so every year, and they go home and tell their friends about it. It is so magnificent as to make folks forget about crime for a while.

The Glensheen Mansion is located five miles northeast of downtown Duluth on Highway 61 at 3300 London Road. The mansion is open extended summer hours, 9 a.m. to 5:30 p.m. daily. November through April it is open Friday through Sunday only, 11 a.m. to 2 p.m. For tour information call (218) 726-8910 or (888) 454-GLEN, or visit www.d.umn.edu/glen.

(Continued from page 189)

There was a party of weather masochists up from the Twin Cities who slept under the snow outside the Timber Hall that night and had four thermometers with them, all reading sixty-two to sixty-four below. A Taylor recorded the minus sixty-four degrees and was sent to a testing laboratory, where it was certified dead accurate. So the record isn't a National Weather Service record, but it's the real record.

Embarrass is more a township than a town; no church, no bar, and you can't drive around the block there. It's stretched along County Road 21 between Highway 135 and County Road 362. The town hall is at Salo Corner, along with the Corner Cafe and the visitor center, and the post office is a couple of miles east, near the gas station, the bottle shop, and the Timber Hall (incidentally, the nation's second largest freestanding log structure), and there isn't that much in between them. The 814 residents live scattered through the adjacent timberland and open country; it sits in a beautiful valley on the Laurentian Divide, between two rivers flowing in opposite directions. The Pike flows north to Lake Vermilion and the Rainy River, the Embarrass south to the St. Louis River and Lake Superior.

The French named it the Rivières des Embarras, meaning "river with barriers or obstructions," because of frequent logjams in spring. It has nothing to do with being embarrassed about cold weather, and in fact the residents are proud of getting themselves regular national bylines. People have moved here from Arizona, Alabama, and the Marshall Islands, just for the cold.

Roland Fowler is the township foreman/coordinator and longtime community leader—a veteran, one of the last of the army's muleskinners—and also the keeper of the weather station at Embarrass, which means he's been on national television. He talks slowly and directly. "There's no way the Falls can keep up with us," he says about International Falls, the so-called Icebox of the Nation. "Even in July we have had the lowest temperatures. We have had overnight killing frosts in July." Asked in an interview how cold it was in Embarrass—it was between fifty and sixty below at the time—he said: "Well, let me put it this way . . . we don't have a lot of dope dealers hanging out on the corners today."

Embarrass is located east on Country Road 21 off Highway 135 between Tower and Virginia. Town tours are conducted daily at 10 a.m. and 2 p.m. from Memorial Day through Labor Day. For more information call (218) 984-2084 or visit www.embarrass.org.

Hockey Hall of Fame

Eveleth

The town calls itself the Hockey Capital of the United States. A certain country to the north has a Hockey Hall of Fame in Toronto, but Eveleth has their own Hall of Fame, with a Great Hall featuring the 1960 and 1980 Olympic gold medal teams. They claim that no other town of their size has done more for the sport in this country than Eveleth. And in fact four of their players were on the 1956 US Olympic team and two local players, John Mariucci and John Brimseth, are enshrined in the Toronto version.

But, of course, what gets them into this book is yet another outlandishly overdone sculpture, this one the World's Largest Hockey Stick. And it's huge, 107 feet long, which is about twice as long as the Jolly Green Giant is tall. It was laminated at the Christian Brothers factory down the road in Warroad and hauled over on a traffic-stopping big rig in 1995; it's mounted as if about to slap a seven-hundred-pound hockey puck across the street at the big goalie mural over there. And as over-the-top as it all sounds, it's actually pretty doggone tasteful. The wood is beautiful and the whole thing is more art than road cheese. In fact, we'd just flat say that it's art. We take back the part about outlandish. It's pretty cool.

The US Hockey Hall of Fame is at 801 Hat Trick Avenue in Eveleth. Phone (800) 443-7825 or (218) 744-5167 or visit online at www.us hockeyhall.com.

The Cabin of the Root Beer Lady

Her name was Dorothy Molter, born in 1907 in Arnold, Pennsylvania, one of six children of Mattie and Cap Molter. Mattie died when Dorothy was seven; the children found themselves in an orphanage in Cincinnati until Cap remarried, moved to Chicago, and brought them all back together.

She graduated from the Chicago Nursing School in 1930, just in time for the Great Depression. With employment opportunities slim, she went fishing with her father and stepmother that summer at a small resort on Knife Lake near the Canadian border: four rough cabins on three islands called the Isle of Pines, connected by log bridges and all built by a retired logger named Bill Berglund. He needed someone to help run the camp. She figured it beat waiting by a phone in Chicago, and moved to the resort. "It was a real adventure for a young woman," she said in 1980. "I've been here ever since and I have no intention of leaving."

Bill died in 1948 and left the islands to her, and she returned to Chicago only long enough to keep her nurse's certificate current. In winter she lived in a cabin on the largest island, and in summer she'd move into the tent cabin and rent the other four out. She made good root beer and sold it to campers, hikers, fishermen, and snowmobilers. There were about six to seven thousand visitors a year, for whom she made eleven to twelve thousand bottles of root beer, a remarkable accomplishment for a lone person fifteen miles from the nearest road. In 1952 the *Saturday Evening Post* ran an article about her, billing her as "the Loneliest Woman in America." She would later say that even though in midwinter she yearned for summer and in midsummer she missed the quiet times, "I've never been lonely in my life . . . I have an extensive library of books to read. I snowshoe over the frozen lakes and through the forest each day for several miles. I fish through the ice and shoot partridge and other game birds for food. My animal friends visit me every day. I cut wood from fallen trees and carry the logs back on a sled pulled by my snowmobile. I don't have time to get lonely."

She died in her cabin in 1986, at age seventy-nine, after living fifty-six years in what became the Boundary Waters Canoe Area, a million acres, the largest wilderness preserve east of the Rockies. Two of the cabins were moved to Ely, log by log, to become a museum; it took fifty-seven air flights, plus an uncounted number of dogsled and snowmobile runs, to bring the logs and furniture out. A brewery is now making a Dorothy Molter Root Beer from her recipe, with part of the proceeds going to maintain the museum.

In her last years she was the only permanent resident in the BWCA; everyone else had died or been evicted and every structure, including her rental cabins, had been bought by the US government. Impossible to imagine what it would be like to be the only resident in a million acres of forest. She wasn't even allowed to sell her root beer, but if you stopped by in your canoe she'd give you one, and you were allowed to put something in the donation jar.

The Dorothy Molter Museum is open 10 a.m. to 5:30 p.m. Monday through Saturday, Sunday noon to 5:30 p.m., Memorial Day until September. It is located at 2002 Sheridan Street in Ely. Call (218) 365-4451 for information or visit http://rootbeerlady.com.

The Reverse Road at Finland

Finland

North of Finland there is a road that leads up the high hill to the old air base, where a radar installation was built as part of the early warning line to track incoming Soviet bombers. The base was closed in 1980 but some folks still live up there and the road is maintained.

If you stop at one of the restaurant/taverns in town and ask about the uphill road that goes downhill, someone will direct you to County Road 7, where you turn and go some short distance to the old Air Base Road. You take it and drive uphill, level off, climb again, level again, and then finish the climb up to the top of the hill, where you turn around and head back down.

Ahead of you now are the crests you felt going up. They've likely told you that at a certain point on the guardrail, after the road has leveled off and begun to climb up again, you stop and put the car in neutral, and then you wait. You do that. You are at that point looking uphill as the road rises to that last crest you felt on the way up. If you found the right place, the car, instead of rolling backwards, will now begin, miraculously, to move forward. Uphill. It will climb the hill and then begin rolling faster on the other side.

It's a strange feeling. We talked to a young man named Joe who lives up there and he said it always works, rain or shine. He gets the same sensation of rolling uphill every time he tries it. "It's a world phenomenon," he said, "I saw it one time on TV and I said, 'Hey, I live right by that place.' Works every day of the week, doesn't matter, nighttime or daytime. A world phenomenon, right here in this little town."

There's no sign, no admission fee, no stamp, no brochure, no reservations taken. No guest book to sign. No website. No gift shop. Not even a bumper sticker. If you go there and feel it, you will become part of a nationwide secret society, mostly unknown even to each other.

From Duluth, take the North Shore Drive (Highway 61) northeast sixty-two miles to Highway 1. Turn left to Finland, six miles in. Take a right on Country Road 7, and then a left onto Air Base Road.

Polka Mass

On May 5, 1973, in the Resurrection Catholic Church of Eveleth, Minnesota, Father Frank Perkovich held the first Polka Mass known to the modern world. He took to heart the freeing spirit of Vatican II and had hymns adapted to traditional Slovenian and Croatian folk music, as performed by Joe Cvek and the Variables and a men's singing group, the Choraleers.

In 1975 a Chicago newspaper reporter wrote about the Polka Mass and the national wire services picked up on the story, leading to the good father's performing at churches and festivals around the world, and ultimately to an invitation in 1983 from the pope himself to do a Polka Mass at the Vatican. Quite the deal for a humble working polka band to play under the high painted domes and arches of the fabulous ancient Basilica of St. Peter.

When Father Perk, as he's known to his parishioners, moved to St. Joseph's Catholic Church in Gilbert in 1987, he brought his polka tradition with him. The musicians are now called Joe Cvek and the Polka Massters—the singers are now the Perkatones—and the Mass is performed only on special occasions such as the Fourth of July and Labor Day weekends. Father Perk is now in his seventies; he was inducted into the Ironwood USA Polka Hall of Fame in 1991 and into the Cleveland Style Polka Hall of Fame in 1992.

But the priest and the Polka Massters do keep up a schedule of guest appearances, and if you go they'd just as soon that you leave your dancing shoes at home. The idea has spread some, and certain of the imitators get a little wild; Father Perk prefers Mass without fancy costumes and without drums. He told a magazine writer: "There have been some variations. Some, to my regret, have too much oompah-pah."

To contact Father Perk for future schedules, his website is www .polkas.nl/fatherfrankperkovich~home.html.

★ ★

Build Your Own Casket
Grand Marais

In the beautiful land where the Boundary Waters Canoe Area meets the Superior shoreline in Grand Marais, there sits an institution of learning called the North House Folk School. For very reasonable tuition fees you can discover processes you've always taken for granted, like how to make soap or twine, or how to hook a rag rug. Learn how to build using stones, logs, straw bales, or fabric; learn timber framing or compound joinery. Build Thoreau's cabin or a yurt or a wood-fired brick bread oven. Learn how to homestead and to find medicinal herbs in the woods. Make a basket out of sweetgrass. Grow, cut, clean, and make a lid and sheath for your own gourd. You can cook three kinds of hearty chili, bake Italian flatbreads, make stew or chowder for the trail, cook wild game, or make Swedish sausage.

They offer courses in blacksmithing, knifemaking, and stone tool-making. You can learn fly casting and fly making, or how to make your own snow goggles or your own snowshoes, or a pair of skis. Even a toboggan. Six courses deal with using birch bark, and even more teach you how to make your own clothes, including moosehide mukluks, a felt hat, and an anorak. One wonders if some students might be escaped fugitives.

They have a fifty-foot gaff-rigged schooner named the *Hjørdis* and summer courses ranging from two hours to nine days are available, teaching seamanship, sailing, rigging, biology, geology, astronomy, and navigation.

Not only that, but they have a number of courses in woodworking. Which leads naturally to courses in boatbuilding. And if you can build your own boat, you can build your own casket. In four days you can learn proper sizing, joinery, handle construction, hardware, and design options. They also cover cemetery policies and legal questions.

About the class's origin the instructor said: "There was an old Norwegian fisherman who lived up the shore, an old friend of mine, Helmer . . . who wanted a coffin before he . . . before he took the big

dirt nap of course and he was an old-timey Norwegian fisherman who
. . . wanted to get it all taken care of. And he had it in his boathouse.
And he would, from time to time, drink a little too much, and he
had some old straw and an army blanket in there . . . and he was in
there sleeping off a good white port drunk. So that was how that got
going."

He said they look great at a funeral. "People like 'em. They like
that look." And they have other uses: Between the time you finish
your casket and the time you move in, it can be used as a bookcase,
a bunk, a coffee table, or an entertainment center. Or a storage con-
tainer. Perhaps for recyclables.

For more information on the North House Folk School, call (888)
387-9762 or (218) 387-9762 or visit www.northhouse.org. The school
is located at 500 West Highway 61.

Rock Carvings
Grand Marais

*"Those who have never seen Superior get an inadequate idea by hear-
ing it spoken of as a lake. Superior is a sea. It breeds storms and rain
and fog like a sea. It is cold, masterful, and dreaded."*

—REVEREND GEORGE GRANT, 1872

If you take Highway 61 east from Duluth and cruise along the North
Shore of Lake Superior—a shoreline so beautiful that it's always
capitalized—you will, in less than two hours, find yourself in Grand
Marais. It's a great drive along that rocky coast, and it's a sweet small
town out there near the Canadian border. It gets even better when
you drive down the main street to the small forest, park in the clear-
ing, step over the low breaker wall, and walk out onto Artist's Point,
where spreading rock a billion years old holds that most amazing lake,
still young at twelve thousand years.

Out there in the breeze—assuming you're not there in a storm—
you stand quiet in the great tranquil reach of it all: the inky water,

Graffiti before the spray can.

the breakers, the birds, the lighthouse, the flowing dark stone with its small captured pools. You gradually become aware of the carvings, and then see that they are sewn all along the shoreline, dozens of names and dates from a century ago, when this was a new and active seaport.

Harvey Demore and W. J. Jones from 1909, and Dean Fortin from July of 1908. J. McGuire, Port Huron, 1899, and J. G. Scott, May 10, 1898. Most names have already blurred in the weathering rock, like John Hector, 1898, but J. D. Hoskin carved his letters deep; he didn't put a date there, but his name will take Superior's pounding longer than most.

The women, like Mary McDonald from 1902, favored a script writing style, while the men favored block letters. These were seafaring people and there are a couple of ships; Sam S. cut a good-sized fishing boat in the stone in 1902. There is a sense here of art driven by fatalism; 550 known ships have gone down in Reverend Grant's cold and dreaded sea.

It is a more direct monument than a graveyard. These folks all were once here, kneeling on the very spot of their own remembrance, where they patiently chipped notes to future strangers. Strangers who would someday stoop to read and to wonder for a moment of what life that name had led.

We are less interested in permanence these days; our images are stored in electric impulses and our graffiti is sprayed upon, not carved into, the rock. The chance that any of it might be appreciated by strangers four generations hence seems mighty slim.

Naniboujou Lodge

Grand Marais

In 1928 Babe Ruth, Jack Dempsey, Ring Lardner, and a circle of lesser notables got together and built a fabulous lodge on the beautiful North Shore of Lake Superior—easy to sling the superlatives around when you're talking about this place—which is operating to this day, offering great rooms and wonderful meals, all at reasonable prices. And for a little extra you can even get a room with a fireplace, but you won't get one with a telephone or a television. You are supposed to get away from all that up here.

The food is good enough to write a 125-page book about and they have, titled *Dining in the Spirit of Naniboujou,* with full-color photos of the lodge and eighty succulent recipes. It would be near understatement to call the high-ceilinged main dining room "stunning," richly decorated as it is in Cree Indian motifs, hung with intricate paper chandeliers, and containing the largest native stone fireplace in the state. Two hundred tons, that fireplace weighs.

The lodge is on the National Register of Historic Places and is located near the Gunflint Trail, the Boundary Waters Canoe Area, and the Superior National Forest. We can't think of anything else you'd need. Certainly not a television.

They are located at 20 Naniboujou Trail; the mailing address of the Naniboujou Lodge and Restaurant is HC-1, Box 505, Grand Marais 55604. Call (218) 387-2688 or visit www.naniboujou.com for more information.

Greyhound Bus Museum
Hibbing

The bus industry began right up there on the Iron Range, the direct result of one man's shortcomings as a salesman; its story is told in the angular red, white, and blue bus museum, brought into existence by another man's enthusiasm and persistence.

In the spring of 1914, a Swedish immigrant named Carl Erick Wickman got tired of being an iron miner—hard to believe, but true—and he put his savings into a Hupmobile agency; he had one car to sell. A lot of miners wanted to ride and test drives would usually end up at the Hull-Rust Mine, but miners weren't really the Hupmobile's natural clientele. Carl got frustrated after a few months and started charging fifteen cents for a ride.

A good part of Hibbing sat directly over iron ore deposits; buildings in the direct path of progress were put on rollers and moved south to a settlement called Alice. Over time, a substantial part of the town had been carted off and was sitting two miles down the road; a test ride in the Hupmobile down to Alice would save forty minutes of walking, and the car was full almost from the minute it went into operation. They offered a round trip for twenty-five cents and were making ten bucks a day right from the get-go.

It quickly wasn't big enough and Wickman's partner, ex-miner Andrew Anderson—who became known as Bus Anderson—took a cutting torch to the frame, welded in an extension, and installed more

A Swede quits his day job and starts America's bus industry.

seats; the weight of the extra passengers put the fenders right down on the tires and it wouldn't budge. Stiffer springs cured that, and the flame of Anderson's torch had lit two American core industries, the bus line and the stretch limo.

Fifteen people would be riding at once, hanging all over the thing. They recruited partners and stretched their cars and soon had a line to Nashwauk, and they became the Hibbing Transportation Company, dubbed the Snoose Line by the tobacco-chewing riders. In December 1915 they grew into the Mesabi Transportation Company and in a few

Judy Garland Museum

"It's a swell state, Minnesota. We had a lovely house . . . we lived in a white house with a garden. Grand Rapids is surrounded by lakes. . . . It's a beautiful, beautiful town." It's true that Dorothy talks about Kansas in L. Frank Baum's *The Wonderful Wizard of Oz*, but when Judy Garland talked about home, she talked about Grand Rapids.

Wizard was her seventh film; she was seventeen when she put her hand and shoe prints in the forecourt of Grauman's Chinese Theatre in Hollywood, an international star. She was born on June 10, 1922, in the Itasca Hospital in Grand Rapids, and christened Frances Ethel Gumm. Her father, Frank, owned the New Grand Theater in town; he was also a journalist and a piano player and singer who thought he would someday become a star. He was pretty much alone in this view, but his stage became the launching pad for the careers of his three daughters. The youngest, Baby Gumm, as she was called then, walked out there when she was two and a half years old and sang "Jingle Bells," and the roar of that crowd rang in her ears from then on.

They traveled northern Minnesota as a show for two years—knocking the socks off Bemidji, Cohasset, Deer Park, Hibbing, Coleraine, et al.—and they would have stayed here longer except Baby had so much talent. When she was four they took a trip to Hollywood, visited studios, and got a whiff of the big time; by now they were billing themselves as Jack and Virginia Lee and the Three Little Lees, who were "fully competent to render the very latest musical numbers and the Charleston, plus black face and impersonations if desired." At three years old, Baby had done a stunning little Al Jolson routine.

They became the Gumm Sisters and made money. On a show with George Jessel in Chicago during the 1934 World's Fair, he looked down at Frances and said, "You're as pretty as a whole garland of flowers, young lady," and they instantly became the Garland Sisters. And later, as she stood ready in the wings listening to Hoagy Carmichael sing "Judy," Frances turned to her sisters and said, "That's it! That's the name I want." The next year, at thirteen, Judy Garland signed her first movie contract with MGM.

Before she died in 1969, she would appear in thirty-two feature films; win an Oscar for *Wizard of Oz*; record almost a hundred singles and twenty-four albums, winning five Grammys; appear 1,100 times in concert; star in her own television show and guest on thirty others; do hundreds of radio broadcasts and military benefits; and marry five times and bear three children.

Her town hosts a world-famous Judy Jubilee here every June, where you can mingle with the Munchkins and visit the Gumm residence; and you can also walk up the Yellow Brick Road to the fabulous old Central School at 10 Northwest 5th Street, now the Itasca County Historical Society, where on the second floor you will find the largest collection of Judy Garland memorabilia in the world. And if that isn't enough there is also the Judy Garland Children's Museum at 19 Northeast 4th Street, where, among other *Oz* artifacts, they have the actual Emerald City Carriage, once owned by Abraham Lincoln. It's an amazing story, all of it.

The museum is located on US Highway 169S and the hours are Monday through Saturday 10 a.m. to 5 p.m., April through Memorial Day; Monday through Sunday 10 a.m. to 5 p.m., Memorial Day through September 30; and Friday and Saturday 10 a.m. to 5 p.m., October through March. For more information call (800) 664-5839 or visit www.judygarlandmuseum.com.

months had eighteen vehicles on the road. They hooked up with the Great Northern Railroad and by 1925 had 150 buses. Headquarters moved to Chicago and the name changed to Greyhound; today it's in Dallas and nineteen million annual passengers take eighteen thousand daily departures to 2,600 destinations. And not one of them is named Hibbing, Minnesota.

Sometime around 1974, in Hibbing's sadly abandoned bus depot, a grocer named Gene Nicolleli found a dusty old sign that read BIRTHPLACE OF THE BUS INDUSTRY IN THE UNITED STATES. He did some research and found a remarkable story, and he thought someone should build a museum in his town and he should be that person. He lobbied governors and legislators for fifteen years for backing and finally in 1989 a small museum opened. In 1999 the dynamic new building was finished; it holds seven historically significant buses and a ton of surprising bus paraphernalia. Another of those things you take for granted that turn out to be far more interesting than you thought they would.

To get to the Greyhound Bus Origin Center at 1201 Greyhound Boulevard, take 13th Street off US 169 going northeast out of Hibbing. The center is open mid-May through September from 9 a.m. to 5 p.m. and Sunday 1 to 5 p.m. For more information call (218) 263-5814, or visit www.greyhoundbusmuseum.org.

World's Largest Pit
Hibbing

The Hull-Rust-Mahoning Mine is called the Grand Canyon of the North, a misnomer given by an enthusiast at the chamber of commerce who believed it was dug by employees of the state tourism board to attract Iowans to northeastern Minnesota. The unpainted truth is that it was dug by great gangs of mercenaries, some of them foreign nationals from Finland and Italy; their descendants still populate the Iron Range, three generations later, and are proud to be called Rangers. They don't move into other parts of Minnesota, because life is too soft in those places.

Iron mining is cleaner than coal mining but it's similar in that the miners don't have to be searched at the end of a shift, the way they do in gold and diamond mines. You couldn't carry a dollar's worth of iron ore away in a wheelbarrow, and even if you could you'd have a hard time selling it on the street. And pawnshops won't touch iron ore.

It is the world's largest open ore pit, three miles long, one and a half miles wide, and six hundred feet deep. From it has come some 30 percent of the nation's iron ore in the last century, more than eight hundred million tons of it. The mines are quiet now, but when blasting used to shake the town of Hibbing three times a day, nobody ever minded; it sounded to them like the rumble of money. There were more than fifty mining companies here at one time, some open pit and some vertical shaft, and as the endeavor grew most of them merged into this one large canyon, today filled three hundred feet deep with spring-fed water and looking like a pristine mountain lake. They had to move 1.4 billion tons of earth to get at all that ore; each bucketful of the loader held thirty-three cubic yards, more than three large ready-mix cement trucks can carry, and their 240-ton trucks—nine times the capacity of the average highway semi trucks—have engines with sixteen cylinders, four turbochargers, and 1,600 horsepower. Tires tall as a basketball rim.

Hibbing itself is unusual in that it used to sit right over what is now the pit. Only a few streets and some foundations remain along the edge from 1919, when they had to move off the iron; it's now a town of 17,071 people sitting a couple of miles away. It was like moving the dog off the couch.

To reach the Hull-Rust-Mahoning Mine, follow signs from US 169 through a residential neighborhood in north Hibbing. The mine is open to the public from mid-May through September, 9 a.m. to 5 p.m. Monday through Saturday and 1 to 5 p.m. on Sunday. Admission is free. Call the Hull-Rust-Mahoning Mine at (218) 262-4166 or the Iron Range Tourism Bureau at (800) 777-8497 or visit www.ironrange.org.

The Hinckley Fire Museum

In 1860 eastern Minnesota and western Wisconsin were covered by a vast forest. When it was opened to logging they found white pines 120 feet tall; logging towns sprang up throughout the forest, and Hinckley sawmills kept two rail lines busy to St. Paul. In the drought years of the early 1890s, fires in the underbrush and slash were so common the sky rarely cleared.

September 1, 1894, was blazing hot and dry; outlying fires and a breeze brought smoke so thick that payroll clerks lit lanterns to see their work. A wind whipped up about 1 p.m. and a telegraph came from Pokegama, to the south, saying the town was burning furiously and could not be saved. The gray smoke in Hinckley turned suddenly black; the local priest set out running through the streets, shouting for all to get out of the path of the fire.

It didn't take much urging. People ran to the Grindstone River and some ran out to the gravel pit; seventy-five ran to the Eastern Minnesota Railroad station where two trains sat, a passenger and a freight, waiting to leave. The engineers coupled the two together and people piled into empty boxcars. They cleared the trestle south of town as the timbers burned beneath them and paint blistered on the cars. The depot agent sent out a telegraph warning to the next station in Barnum, adding "I think I've stayed too long" as fire took the depot.

To the north of town people found barely three inches of water in the river and gravel pit; they headed up the tracks and met a crowded southbound St. Paul & Duluth passenger train under the throttle of Jim Root. He braked and a hundred people crammed on board. As he backed up, the forest erupted in flames. The first water would be Skunk Lake, six miles up; the worst six miles any engineer ever held a throttle to. Winds were whipping the fire around them so hard the glass blew out of the cab, set the curtain on fire, set the very coal in the tender behind them on fire. When they finally reached the lake they dragged Root out of the cab; he left the skin and the meat of his right hand sizzling on the throttle. His shirt was burned, he was blistered and unconscious and not expected to live.

The other train made Sandstone, eight miles to the south, and stopped briefly, but they'd heard so many fire warnings there that not one person would get on; they wouldn't even put their children aboard. Twenty minutes later fire leveled the village.

The smoke could be seen in central Wisconsin and in Iowa. In all, 418 people perished and six towns burned. Thirty miles north and twenty-four years later it happened again, in Moose Lake, when 450 died in a fire that nearly reached Duluth.

Hinckley Fire Museum is located at 106 Old Highway 61. Take the Hinckley exit off Interstate 35N then west on County Road 48 to Old Highway 61 and turn right. The museum is open May 1 through mid-October, Tuesday through Saturday from 10 a.m. to 5 p.m., and open seven days a week in July and August. For information call (800) 996-4566 or (320) 384-7338 or visit http://hinckleyfiremuseum.com.

Ellsworth Rock Gardens

Kabetogama

Lake Kabetogama translates roughly from the Ojibwe as a lake parallel to another lake, in this case the fabled Rainy Lake on the Canadian border. A cabinet-maker and contractor from Chicago named Jack Ellsworth started coming here back in the 1940s. The big lake has an island with a dramatic forest outcropping; it cast a spell upon him so strong that he came back year after year to move rocks and soil into a huge tiered fantasy garden.

From 1944 through 1965 he hauled stone and dirt, plants and timbers, and shaped them into walkways, stairs, benches, and even

He left no stone unturned.

tables, set in the tall forest among stone towers and odd creatures. He created a mysterious and wonderful place nearly as wide as the island and sixty feet above the water.

Walking through it, one pictures him moving a two-ton boulder onto a chosen ledge up there, and you think the man had to have at least a mule and a crew and a lot of rope to make that happen. The story says he did all on his own energy, including mowing the meadow at the base, wider than a football field, with a little hand-pushed reel lawnmower.

The Rock Garden fell into neglect for a time after his passing but has been restored by volunteers and workers since it became part of the Voyageurs National Park. It doesn't have all the exotic plants and flowers that Jack once planted there but it does have an abundance of mystery and magic.

It's not real famous. It's more the kind of place you only hear about from someone who lives up there or has been there, and you are grateful to that person after they talk you into going there. You can find information online at www.nps.gov/voya/planyourvisit/ellsworth-showplace.htm.

Mailboat
Lake Vermilion

Lake Vermilion would be on the Top Three Lakes list of almost everyone in Minnesota for its beauty, its size, the water, the perfect campsites, and the amazing tranquility of its bays. It's a lake with 365 islands, so you could visit a different one every day of the year. It is also the locale of one of only two water mail routes in the state, the other being a mailboat that circles Isle Royale in Lake Superior and makes fewer than ten stops.

The mailboat on Vermilion covers 110 miles and delivers to some fifty to seventy-five island cabins, leaving its dock at the Aronson Boat Works six days a week at 9 a.m. and returning sometime after 1 p.m.; the twenty-one-foot Lund boat will take up to six passengers for a fee, and they recommend that you call ahead for reservations. The season runs from the first of June through the first week in September.

The pilots, who double as tour guides, change every year or two, but they maintain a tradition that goes back to 1923, when John Aronson's father contracted with the Postal Service to deliver mail. In those days the boat was bigger and was mainly a water taxi, delivering everything from groceries to construction materials; most of the older cabins here were built with lumber delivered by mailboat.

It's a different world up there. Dogs come out to the end of the dock to greet the mailman, tails wagging, running around, excited to see him; the mailman's different, too, because he carries two pouches of mail and a pouch of dog biscuits. A pooch pouch. They go through five pounds of dog biscuits a month, donated by a couple of longtime lake families. If there's no mail for an address the carrier will pull in there anyway and flip the dog a biscuit; in one stretch there are three mailbox docks in a row and a pair of dogs run out to the end of each of them and score each time, figuring they've got the guy fooled into thinking there are six dogs.

The arrival of the mailman is a big deal to people, too; a lot of folks don't even have a television set, by preference, and to many he's the only daily contact with the outside world. He's got a cell phone for emergencies, so if you're going to have one it's best to try to hold off until just before the mailboat arrives.

Call the Aronson Boat Works in Tower at (218) 753-4190 or visit www.aronsonboatworks.com for more information.

Carved Barstools
Lawler

A person might walk into Jackson's Hole, the only commercial enter-prise still running in Lawler, to order a beverage and perhaps some-thing from the hand-lettered list of new appetizers, like the Battered Corn Nuggets or Battered Green Beans, or Breaded Pickle Chips or even the Pepper Jack Chz Shotz; they might enjoy the warmth of the mellowed wood and neon interior and the elegant old nickel and steel wood stove in the center of the room, and they could easily miss the art down there at their knees.

They could check out the dance hall in back of the bar, where live music still lives, and leave completely unaware that they had been sitting on the city's sculpture gallery.

The padded stools are a small solid population of mischievous short folk, some jolly, some cranky, all carved by a local legend named Cliff Letty. He cut the figures as well as the bar surface itself, a large and long relief of the Minnesota outdoors.

It's a whole different world down under the beer drinkers.

He was a baker by profession, a carpenter by trade, and a sculptor by choice. He carved the bar top first, a serious work, and once it was set in place he moved on to the exuberance of trolls. He worked in his own garage over near Sandstone and Finland and brought them in as they were finished.

The town has an interesting past. The tavern was originally a co-op store and creamery selling groceries, feed and seed, supplies, and tools; farming and logging were main businesses. The old meat cooler is still in there, a great piece on its own. They closed the store in the mid-1970s and it became a bar in 1980, one of the three downtown buildings that had survived the fire and now the only one left.

Lawler was devastated by the always-capitalized Great Hinckley Fire, as were five other towns, in September of 1894. The casualty toll was variously listed from 418 to 800. Among the notables who perished was a man named Thomas Corbett, widely thought to be Thomas P. "Boston" Corbett, the soldier who shot John Wilkes Booth. They say he lived "in a forest settlement near Hinckley."

One could make a case that without the fire Lawler might be as it was and the bar might still be a general store, and so would not be home to the barstool people, so their existence is directly tied to the calamity that claimed the life of the man who killed the man who killed Abraham Lincoln.

The barstools are highly prized. "You wouldn't believe how many people want them bar stools," said the owner.

Jackson's Hole is located at 26232 Kestrel Avenue (County Highway 16) in Lawler and their phone number is (218) 768-2162.

The Bog Walk
Orr

If the Orr City Hall isn't enough for a curiosities glutton there is a good bog behind it, easily traversed by a floating wooden walkway. One like a person might have running out to their luxury yacht hidden in the Florida Everglades, only without the alligators or the Burmese pythons.

When a tree falls in the forest . . . take a picture.

To see the oldest bog body in the known world one must go to the Fyns Oldtid-Holufgard museum in Denmark and check out the Koelberg Woman from around 8000 BC. She was discovered in a bog in 1941 and has been the object of a good deal of study, along with about twenty other complete remains from the ancient peat marshes of northern Europe; one of the latest is Boris Lazarev, a Soviet fighter pilot shot down in 1943. Bog bodies are usually assumed to be castaways, thrown into a bog rather than being given a proper burial, and many show evidence of being crime or accident victims. Most have been given names, like Grauballe Man or the Windeby Girl.

Bogs are unique in their makeup, sometimes called a tamarack swamp surviving in a pickle jar—a high-acid low-oxygen stew that will preserve animal and human remains for centuries (generally until a peat cutter comes along digging up stove fuel). This means that a lot of organic material is stored away as peat and that plants have to get creative in finding nutrients; meat-eaters like the pitcher plant have evolved, trapping insects in tubular flowers and then soaking them in enzymes.

Northern Minnesota holds more bog acreage than all the other lower forty-eight states combined: six million acres, a much under-appreciated benefit. The Orr Bog has all the same ingredients as the European bogs

Orr City Hall

We would not be going out on too thin a limb to flatly state that this is the nation's only city hall located in a highway rest area with a stuffed albino beaver on a glass cabinet and with a wooden walkway through a swamp behind it.

And as funky as that may sound it is an extraordinarily handsome structure. It's not exactly rustic but it has rather a natural and comfortable dignity to it, so much so we'd also say it could be the best small city hall in Minnesota. Or most anyplace. At the same time it's also the best rest area in the state.

It's a spacious wood and stone structure, high and wide enough that a large canoe floats under the big wooden timbers and that a bear stands in a corner and great horned owls wing it along a wall.

Over and alongside the official city filing cabinets and desks stand a great grey wolf, a moose calf, a bobcat, and a fox. A full bear pelt graces one high wood wall; a large moose skull is featured on another.

There's a lot more. It's worth getting a parking ticket just to have to go the Orr City Hall, located on Highway 53 just south of Orr.

but, so far, without the human bog bodies. This doesn't stop locals and visitors from hanging jack-o-lanterns and telling frightening tales along its length at Halloween.

The walk is an easy half-mile through a cattail marsh by Pelican Lake and a prehistoric ash swamp, plus a spruce bog with ten-foot-tall beaver dams. It's well marked with illustrated signs about the local ospreys, eagles, otters, and muskrat.

Given that it's an ideal environment for summertime bugs, there is little walking traffic until things cool down in the fall. It's usually just real quiet in there.

"I believe it's birch," said the albino beaver. "White birch."

The Famous Lounge Chair
Proctor

We aren't sure of the timeline that led to this international story because the police don't give out a lot of detail to incidental strangers, but it appears that Mr. Dennis Anderson lost his automobile driver's license some time ago and set to building a powered lounge chair for short trips around Proctor. He likely didn't expect that it would bring him international fame, no matter how stylish and well constructed, but few would do that much work for such a slim chance at celebrity.

But fame found him anyway. An evening trip downtown led to his consuming a considerable amount of beer and as he left his parking space he said a woman tried to get in the chair with him. He momentarily lost control of it and hit a parked car, causing a minor ding, and the cops came and booked him. He ultimately pled guilty to a DUI but before that the story hit the news media: *New York Daily News,* the BBC, the *UK Daily Telegraph,* LeMonde, NPR, Wired News, Fox, *the Oakland Daily Tribune,* the *Columbus Dispatch, The Smoking Gun,* and a slew of others. It was worldwide news.

We tried to contact him but the police said he's not talking to anyone anymore so don't bother him. We called anyway because that's what pseudo-journalists are expected to do, to rudely call folks who want to be left alone, and the police were right. He's had the "phone disconnected at the customer's request."

The now famous chair was powered by an eight-horse Kohler lawnmower engine; it had a stereo system and cup holder built into the wide armrests and the emblem of the National Hot Rod Association on the seat back. It had a rear bumper sticker that read HELL YEAH IT'S FAST. It was artfully done in brown leather with blue and red trim.

After the collision, the police confiscated the vehicle and put it up for auction on eBay as a motorized La-Z-Boy lounge chair. The bidding went all the way up to $43,700 when La-Z-Boy jumped in and said it wasn't their chair. It had been listed that way because the media had

★ ★

It even looks fast.
PHOTO COURTESY OF THE PROCTOR POLICE DEPARTMENT

called it that. The bidding on eBay was stopped and had to start over. They did it twice more and it ended up selling for $3,700 to a local resident.

So after building and losing a cool vehicle like that and then having half the world cackling about it, who wouldn't have their phone shut off?

You Can Lead a Bear to Doughnuts, but You Don't Really Need To

There are about thirty thousand black bears in Minnesota, mostly in the north, and it only takes one three-thousandth of 1 percent of the bear population—one—to break into your cabin, eat all your food, and trash the place. They aren't mean by nature, but they'll eat anything—and they generally weigh between 250 and 500 pounds, and they can run thirty-five miles an hour, and they have pitchfork claws and ice-tong teeth, and a truck-tire hide, and they climb trees.

Vince Shute grew up as a logger on his grandfather's homestead, moved to a nearby spot in the woods in 1944, and pretty much stayed put from then on. He ran a logging company, meaning he had to pay and feed and look out for a big crew of loggers. When he'd leave his shack for any length of time, he'd sometimes come back to find the subtle signs of bear: the smashed-in front door, the broken-down empty cupboards, the busted furniture, and the total absence of edibles. He'd take his rifle and find the culprit, who would not be offered much in the way of due process; certainly not bail or parole.

But Vince was a big guy and he wasn't mean by nature either, any more than the bears were, and he concluded they weren't wrecking his place out of malice but just from hunger, something he himself had grown up with, so he began to set out leftovers from the T. Patton Cafe in Orr as protection money. And he had a legendary rapport with animals—so much so that a friend of his said when he was growing up their family dog would run around and bark and wag his tail about ten minutes before Vince dropped in; he could feel his presence out there. He said, "Vince was the most thoroughly good person I've ever met, and animals can sense that."

The bears not only quit trashing the shack, they brought in relatives and they all became Vince's pals. He gave them names and they started a syndicate, with a few of them getting very large, especially Duffy, who hit 816 pounds and became the world's largest black bear; the Don Corleone of Minnesota, who would share giant Patton doughnuts with Vince and keep lesser bears in line.

Before Vince passed on he realized that without him his bears would become vulnerable to hunters, so in 1995 his friends formed the ABA, the American Bear Association (the more famous ABA is known as an association of sharks), taking his 40 acres and adding 320 more and creating the Vince Shute Wildlife Sanctuary. They built a viewing platform that is now the best place in North America to view black bears in their natural habitat.

The Vince Shute Wildlife Refuge is one mile south of Orr on US Highway 53. Turn left onto County Road 23 and continue on for thirteen miles, just past County Road 514. It's on your right. The sanctuary is open Memorial Day through Labor Day, 5 p.m. to 8 p.m., Tuesday through Sunday. Closed Monday. Call the American Bear Association at (800) 357-9255 or (218) 757-0172, e-mail bears@americanbear.org, or visit www.americanbear.org for more information.

★ ★

Neutrinos
Soudan

You wouldn't think that a fun family outing in a creaky cage dropping you half a mile down into the deepest mineshaft in Minnesota would put you face to face with stuff like neutrinos, muons, wimps, taus, proton decay, and quantum physics, but there they are. There are scientists down there to measure neutrinos to be sent up from Batavia, Illinois, near Chicago; sent straight through the ground, so as to avoid the Illinois Tollway. Doing basic research, to determine things like the ultimate fate of the universe. (Expanding Forever? . . . Or Heading for the Big Crunch? . . . The answer when we come back from a break. . . .)

We know all about this stuff, no problem, but when you're on a mine trip and you run into dark matter—matter even darker than the walls of the shaft—it's best not to go into explanations. A time like that is a time to relax and enjoy your neutrinos. Take 'em as they come, and don't worry about the end of the universe. It'll be here soon enough, and no point hurrying it along, either.

Iron ore was discovered on the Vermilion Range at Soudan during the Minnesota Gold Rush of 1865—sounds like a joke, doesn't it?— but they didn't start mining it until 1882, waiting for technology to catch up with them. The first ore was shipped from the Soudan Mine to Two Harbors on July 31, 1884, which was the very first day of the Iron Range. Seems odd; we've assumed it was always called the Iron Range, even before they found iron there; that maybe even the Indians called it that.

They brought 15.5 million tons of iron ore up this narrow shaft, this one and the Alaska shaft, before they ceased operations in 1962. US Steel donated the mine and 1,300 acres to the state as a park in 1965; it's visited annually by 39,298 people and by some 24,000 bats. The bats don't go down to the lowest level; they kind of stay out of the way somewhere up near the entrance. There are twenty-seven levels and fifty horizontal miles of mine tunnels down there, and they take you down 2,341 feet to the bottom. There is a new mural there in the big main room, a brilliant portrait of the sun, and it's not only beautiful but also the world's deepest mural.

The temperature in the mine is fifty degrees year-round, except inside the Cryogenic Dark Matter Search detector, where it's minus 459.69—a slim hundredth of a degree above Absolute Zero. Which makes it colder than Embarrass by 396 degrees, and the coldest place in Minnesota.

The town of Soudan is located on Highway 169 between Virginia and Ely. The Soudan Underground Mine State Park conducts underground tours seven days a week on the hour, 10 a.m. to 4 p.m. Labor Day through the end of September. There is a tour fee. Bring warm clothing. For information call (218) 753-2245, e-mail soudanmine@dnr .state.mn.us, or visit www.dnr.state.mn.us/state_parks/soudan_under ground_mine/index.html.

Army Worm Wine
Virginia

In the famous Paris Tasting of 1976, nine French experts blind-tasted twenty fine wines, ten white and ten red, from California and France, to select the two best. To their shock and horror they put a Stag's Leap cabernet and a Chateau Montelena chardonnay, both from the Napa Valley, handily at the top of the list. Had there not been an American reporter on the scene we might never have heard about it. The news jolted the wine world.

Now America has taken another proud step forward in the realm of oenology, with Minnesota leading the way this time. The leafy bounty of the northern forest has yielded up the world's finest army worm wine. The French don't even have a second-rate army worm wine. Caught flat-footed again, they have no army worm wine at all. (Some say we shouldn't gloat about this.)

A man named Ray Reigstad is the viticulturist for the wine, although *ento*culturist might be a better term here. He has been making wine for fifteen years and is a veteran of two alternative rock bands,

The helmets and goggles are filtered out.
ILLUSTRATION BY JOHN REIPAS/ARMY WORM WINE CONCEPT BY RAY REIGSTAD

Stepchild and Static Taxi, so he has some idea of suffering. Suffering has always been an ingredient in Minnesota wines, with the grapevines getting punished every winter; same thing of course for the army worms.

The little leaf-gorged wrigglers, once they've stripped the forest of every green living thing, are gathered with a whisk broom into six-gallon sanitary buckets. Boiling water is poured in, bringing their greedy little existence to a sudden end, and the mix is allowed to settle out and is then filtered. Other things are added, like champagne yeast, Campden tablets, pectic enzyme, and of course sugar, since army worms, like most worms, have a low sugar content. This ferments and ages, and in time magically becomes drinkable; drinkable enough to get a grade of 7 (out of 10) from three local wine experts, who were not told of the basic source until after they gave the grades. It's hard to speculate about the French response; they may ignore it, or they might already be at work on a French garden slug wine.

You can't legally buy this delicacy from Ray, and he can't mail it to you, but he'll give you a glass if you show up at his Virginia home, and he'll sell you a most attractive T-shirt. His website is full of entertaining information, including the full recipe. Army worms, also called tent caterpillars, are thankfully not around every summer, so ye must gather them when ye may.

This is not accompanied by a "don't try this at home" warning because at home is the only place you *can* try it. It's legal at home for now, but you never know.

Ray has been interviewed twice on the excellent WineMaking Radio Show. You can find Ray's recipe at www.winemakingradio.com/rw/army wormwine.html, or visit Ray's website at www.armywormwine.com.

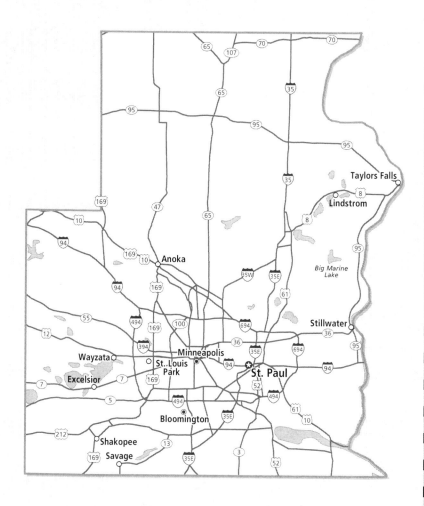

Twin Cities

4

Twin Cities

This region is *called the Twin Cities because St. Paul and Minneapolis are both in here, but it also includes a lot of non-urbanity. It's roughly three thousand square miles of mostly rural and suburban real estate, wherein a citizen might go into an actual urban place to shop or dine or catch a band at a night club. Or a major league sporting event.*

It's more an area of influence; very few residents of Taylors Falls, for example, would say they are from the Twin Cities. Many rarely go into the heart of it, dismissing it as if they are just too sophisticated to put up with a mess like that. Generally that's a sign of someone who went there once and got lost and is still embarrassed about it.

And if you try to find out how many lakes there are in the two cities you will find sentences like this: "Scattered about the city are more than twenty sparkling lakes of glacial origin." So we'll just say there quite a few lakes in this Twin Cities area. As in, dozens and dozens.

As far as urban places go, they are more than good enough; less crime than most cities and plenty of art and parks and not as packed with traffic as your average megalopolis; probably just enough to irritate an old guy from a small town but tolerable for the residents.

Big time sports championships, not so much. Two gigantic World Series wins and that's about it. Otherwise it's been season after season of "not even close," or "close but no cigar." The women's teams seem to have the killer instinct it takes to bring back national championships, and what a very endearing quality that can be.

Halloween Capital of the World

Anoka

After the end of World War I, on a late autumn night in 1919, a herd of cows was driven from nearby farms by masked and hooded young people right down the main street of Anoka, and store windows were soaped and outhouses tipped on their sides in citizens' backyards; this wasn't the first time, and the town elders reached their own tipping point and resolved that enough was enough and they must act.

Which they did in 1920 with the nation's first such celebration and ultimately turned Anoka into the Halloween Capitol of the World, verified even in Washington, DC, and well deserving the honor. It is a real prize considering Halloween has roots from two thousand years ago when the Celts in Ireland and northern France marked the end of summer and celebrated the new year on November 1. The night of October 31 was Samhain, when the dead returned to earth. People built huge bonfires and wore masks and costumes against the possibility of being identified by unfriendly spirits.

The Romans moved in about that time and parked for four hundred years. They combined the local festival with a couple of their own: Feralia, the day of the passing of the dead, and Pomona, for the Roman goddess of fruits and trees. Which we now suppose is the reason for bobbing for apples on Halloween.

By the ninth century the influence of Christianity had spread into the Celtic realm and November 2 became All Souls' Day to honor the dead. Big bonfires, parades, costumes of saints and angels and devils. The night before that was All Hallows' Eve.

Naturally the holiday came to America and ultimately to tipping outhouses and running cattle in downtown Anoka. That part has been set aside now in favor of big legal fireworks, celebrity appearances, a kangaroo court, royalty coronations, concerts, window painting, a pillow fight, costume contests, style shows, marching bands, and the police and fire departments; groups from all over come in.

And, of course, the grand finale, the Big Parade of Little People, where nearly every kid in town is in mask and costume and marching down that same street the cows did more than ninety years ago.

A person really should go there and see it. For more information call (763) 421-7130 or visit http://anokahalloween.com/pages/welcome.

Mall of America
Bloomington

Here's a collection of miscellaneous superlatives: Seven Yankee Stadiums would fit inside its volume; it was built using 13,300 short tons of steel, twice as much as in the Eiffel Tower in Paris; it holds 4 major department stores, 525 specialty shops, 50 restaurants, 7 nightclubs, and 14 movie theaters; and it draws 42 million people a year, nine times the population of the whole state and more than Disney World, Yellowstone Park, and the Grand Canyon put together.

It has a most direct parking ramp, which makes the experience much easier than you would expect—you drive straight up the ramp and straight down the other side; pick your floor as you see it. No spirals. It sits on the old Metropolitan Stadium ground, former home of the Twins and Vikings. Home plate is marked in Camp Snoopy, the entertainment park in the center, which also has thirty thousand plants and four hundred live trees. On a good day there are twice as many people in the Mall as there are in the entire city of Bloomington, where it sits, the state's third largest city, with ninety thousand residents.

When it was opened in August 1992, the experts said the market was saturated and the megamall combination would never work. A Chicago wizard was quoted: "The whole project flies in the face of this high-stressed, need-focused consumer of today. . . . Entertainment and retailing, it will not work. They are in direct conflict with one another. They couldn't have designed it worse in terms of creating a consumer nightmare." As one ages, one begins to realize that folks who make statements like this are seldom taken to task years later when they are proven dead wrong. A person can pretty much get everything backward and still get away with it; this is perhaps useful information to pass on to one's grandchildren.

Anyway, more than five thousand couples have been married here, an average of five a week. Hard to say if that proves anything.

To get to the Mall of America, take Interstate 494, then exit at Highway 77 or 24th Avenue; head south to 81st Street or Killebrew Drive. You won't miss it. For more information, visit www.mallof america.com.

The Killebrew Chair
Bloomington

On June 3, 1967, Harmon Clayton Killebrew hit the longest of his 573 major league home runs, a 520-foot shot into the second deck of the old Metropolitan Stadium. It didn't actually travel that far on the ground but it would have if the bleachers hadn't been there; it was the longest ball ever hit at the stadium.

The Met was torn down in January of 1985 and was ultimately replaced by the very large Mall of America. At the third level of the southeast wall of the public space there is mounted a red stadium chair. It's placed in the exact same location in the universe—elevation, longitude, and latitude—as the spot where Harmon pasted that mighty home run. (It's not the actual chair struck because that was a bench in the bleachers, but it is a chair from Met Stadium.)

There is also a plaque on the mall floor where the home plate of Met Stadium sat, so a person can stand there and visualize hitting a baseball so hard as to loft it high into the sky and to land it in that chair way up there. This also gives some idea of just how big that mall is. The street outside is naturally named Killebrew Drive.

It was not surprising that Killebrew did well. His father was a painter and a sheriff and part of an undefeated Milliken College football team; his grandfather was known as the strongest man in the Union Army, winning "every available heavyweight wrestling championship."

"No Honey, he didn't *sit* there—he hit it with a baseball."

Harmon was a teenager playing for a semi-professional baseball team and batting .847(!) when Idaho Senator Herman Walker saw him play and told the owner of the Washington Senators, Clark Griffith, about him. He signed for $30,000 in June of 1954 and hit his first home run when he was still seventeen years old.

The Senators became the Twins and Harmon became one of baseball's great longball hitters; he retired in 1975 as the league's career leader in home runs as a right-handed batter and second overall only to lefty Babe Ruth. He was the American League's MVP in 1969, the home run leader six times, an All-Star eleven times, and inducted into the Hall of Fame in 1984. He also had a reputation as a true gentleman.

His Twins jersey, #3, was retired in 1975. It was his second jersey retirement; the first was after his graduation as an All-American quarterback at Payette High School in Idaho.

It's widely believed but not officially acknowledged that Killebrew is the hitter in the Major League Baseball logo. He was in the commissioner's office when the logoist, Jerry Dior, was marking up his photo with a grease pencil. Dior later said he didn't know whose photo he used. And of course he would say that to avoid trouble. But we pretty much all know it was our guy.

"Killebrew can knock the ball out of any park, including Yellowstone."

—PAUL RICHARDS, BALTIMORE ORIOLES MANAGER, 1959.

Coffeepot Water Tower
Lindstrom

Well, the big thing about it is that steam comes out of the spout. You see the classic tower with that coffeepot up there with the WELCOME on it, and it looks good, but if you happen to look up and catch it when the steam is on, it's really quite the deal.

It's not their real water tower anymore, not since they got the new one in 1992, but a couple of community-minded citizens stepped forward to keep the old 1908 version standing and to turn it into a Swedish symbol, because of local cultural ties to the old country, and of course the coffeepot would be the ultimate Swedish symbol. A company was hired to take the ladder off, build an access door, add the button on the top, the handle, and the spout; and then to paint it white with the hand-lettered VELKOMMEN TILL LINDSTROM, and the Swedish rosemaling on the two sides.

It all went over so well that a city employee got to work on the idea of having steam come out of the spout, using the fire department's practice smoke generator, the same type of gear used for smoke at rock concerts. In 1994 they rigged the piping to get the smoke up to the spout so they could have fifteen minutes of steam four times a day, although they only fire it up during the summer months. There are lights at the base to highlight the coffeepot at night.

They are quick to point out that not a bit of the expense for any of this came from tax dollars. This is private enterprise at work here, and private charity in the best sense of the word. It is definitely not a case of public-funded frivolity, so please bear that in mind when you see it.

The water tower is located on the main street of Lindstrom. Watch for the steam. Call the City of Lindstrom at (651) 257-0620 or visit www.lindstrom.org for information on times.

Art Shanties

Minneapolis

There is a new freeze ritual here in the state of eleven-thousand-plus lakes. It's an annual clustering of home-built structures hauled onto one of them, Medicine Lake, and according to the organizers' home page, *"It is an artist driven temporary community, exploring the ways in which the relatively unregulated public space of the frozen lake can be used as a new and challenging artistic environment to expand notions of what art can be."*

People are encouraged to design shanties for the fun of it, like float designs for parades. Whimsy rules. Shanty names include the Robot Reprise, Solar Ark, Nordic Village Bridge, Sit-and-Spin, Reflection, Shanty of Wonder, Camera Head, Ice-Cycle, Monsters Under the Bed, Capitol Hill, Naughty Shanty, and Dance Shanty. There are twenty-four projects out there this year, including a full-size Basketball Shanty.

Fustian prose aside, the crowd is growing every year and people are enjoying it. There is hot white chocolate there, hot dogs, live music, free style dancing, Norse traditional song, bicycle competitions and events, found object musical instrument making, croquet on the ice, and an ArtCar parade as well as pretend marriage ceremonies in various Nordic languages, blanket making, and a soup served at noon in the One Room School.

The shanties are the stars of the show, there to stretch one's ideas on what a structure can be and they are, no pun intended, very cool.

Of course there are plenty of uncool examples of winter shelters all over Minnesota lakes, but they are inevitably dark and set above a hole in the ice and most are stocked with winter-resistant beverages. And the occupants don't consider themselves artists. One wouldn't call them athletes either, but they are ostensibly out there as agents from the Top of the Food Chain. And they have to buy a fishing license.

Visit http://artshantyprojects.org for more information.

Bell bottom blues.

It's fun city until the ice melts.

Stopping by Grandma's for cocoa.

Shoefiti

Minneapolis

There are at least seventy-six shoe trees in the US, according to Wikipedia, and many times that worldwide. This seems to be the only general fact we know about throwing shoes into trees. And while the shoe tree was not invented in the state, the author of the term *shoefiti* is a fellow named Ed Kohler who lives in Minneapolis and has the main website, Shoefiti.com; it's a source of photos and videos from everywhere and is very likely the world's best shoe-tossing website.

So Minnesota has some bragging rights and it also has one of the better shoe trees in the nation, mainly because the tree grows from a riverbank on the Mississippi; a high bridge connecting two parts of the university campus runs right by it and the passersby can look directly into the shoe gallery in the upper branches. No need to crane the neck to view the art.

The origin of hurling tied shoes over a tree limb seems to be lost in speculation, but it likely goes back to nearly the invention of the shoelace. "Shoe tree" has an older meaning of course, referring to the wooden insert one would place inside to keep a pair of good polished shoes smooth and elegant, uncurled and uncracked from a life spent pounding pavements and floors.

Which is the kind of life spent by most sneakers, unpolished, rarely cleaned, never enjoying the cozy feel of being wrapped around a friendly shoe tree. These are the type mostly hanging on branches and wires. Very few throw their Florsheims up there.

There is also speculation as to the symbology; various reasons are offered but there aren't many shoe-throwers who come forward to bear witness. There are a number of theories, e.g., a sign of a nearby drug house, a notification to one's peers about the loss of virginity, or a graduation. Or perhaps just the simple desire to become part of a great mystery.

The shoe tree can be viewed on the U of M Campus from where the Washington Avenue bridge intersects with the West Bank of the Mississippi River.

Birds of a feather.

★ ★

Nye's Polonaise—the Best Bar in America
Minneapolis

For some of us, this place has everything. It has a real history, it's posh, it's funky, the food is great, the prices are reasonable, the service is good, and there's live music both in the bar and the dining room.

The building on the corner of Hennepin and Prince was built in the 1880s and for years was a workingman's bar named Hefron's; Al Nye bought it in 1950 and kept it close to its roots. He was a machine shop foreman himself and he knew his crowd and he did well at hosting them, well enough that in 1964 he was able to acquire the place next door for a dining addition, which he named the Polonaise Room. It's all still there just as he designed it: curved piano bar with a Chopin portrait hanging above it, red carpeting, dark wood paneling, gold-flecked over-stuffed booths. The specialties are prime rib, lobster, and Polish food, including Al's own recipes for cabbage rolls, sausage, and short ribs.

All of which went over so well that in a few years he annexed the next building in the block, a former harness shop listed on the National Register of Historic Places, which became the Chopin Dining Room; and in 1974 he added the diner next door, Jon's Cafe, into the mix. Redecorated the place and hung pictures of military officers and called it the Pulaski Room, after the Polish-born general who helped us win the Revolutionary War.

It isn't just the food and the ambience that brings the crowds; in the original corner bar, unchanged in more than fifty years, there is a tiny stage between the cigarette machine and the men's room with a worn dance floor in front of it, and pressed onto the stage is the band that calls themselves the World's Most Dangerous Polka Band but whom the bartender smilingly calls the Wax Museum Trio. They played on national television in 1995 from New York and were a big hit.

In the more elegant Polonaise Room another veteran entertainer holds forth. Lou Snider's been at the piano bar for thirty years, from well before karaoke, and she can cover whatever tunes the Dangerous Polka Band doesn't. She's dealt with a lot of situations there and still enjoys the scene, and still makes folks feel good; lately both she and the band have become popular among the twenties set. Employees say the average age in the bar has dropped from fifty to thirty in the last five years.

The October 2006 issue of *Esquire* magazine named Nye's as the best bar in America, saying, "There are times when every person in the room is smiling."

Nye's is at 112 East Hennepin in Minneapolis. The World's Most Dangerous Polka Band plays Friday and Saturday nights. Call (612) 379-2021 or visit www.nyespolonaise.com for more information.

The World's Most Dangerous Polka Band.

In the Hall of Fame

Minneapolis

It would be natural in a state this size that some few would find themselves inducted into various halls of fame, and this of itself isn't likely to qualify them as curiosities.

But if one were to gain such an honor for his staging of a Valentine's dinner in a famous budget burger joint that might well get a person not only into a hall of fame but also into a book about curiosities.

White Castle Hall of Famer.

Roy Holdren is a Minneapolis professional singer-guitarist-songwriter who is lucky enough to be married to a woman who shares his passion for White Castle cuisine.

The company's headquarters is in Columbus, Ohio. It's a state with a lot of halls of fame, including the pro baseball and football ones in Canton, the rock and roll and the polka ones in Cleveland, the inventors in Akron, the classical music one in Cincinnati, and the Ohio Harness Racing Hall of Fame in Columbus.

But to some folks, the big one in Columbus is the Craver's Hall of Fame, also known as the White Castle Hall of Fame. Here is the letter of application Holdren sent to the hall:

My wife and I have been spending Valentine's Day at White Castle since shortly after we married in 1993. It has become a tradition we enjoy very much as the restaurants go out of their way to make it memorable with candlelight, tablecloths, and even waiters. Often we dress in our best outfits and, though I have yet to do it, I intend to rent a limo at some point.

In 2001 I hired a wonderful harp player to serenade us at the Bloomington, MN, restaurant while we enjoyed our White Castles. I had to pull a few strings as the harpist had another Valentine's Day booking that night and could only play early in the evening.

I called the WC manager and moved our reservation up to 5:30, earlier than they were even making reservations. I told my wife it was the only reservation I could get and enjoyed the look on her face when they seated us at the table next to the harpist. As a musician I have to say the acoustics were great! The manager even contacted a local TV station and we ended up on the news that evening. It was an enjoyable and unforgettable night.

They were guests of honor the night he was inducted at an elegant feast at the Ohio Historical Society, along with the other new inductees. It was a lavish event that even included a hired clown. He found out that his was the shortest entry letter.

His own favorite Castle meal is two cheeseburgers with mustard and ketchup, one turkey and cheese sandwich, and an order of onion chips well done. The Turkeycheese sandwich is now gone, missed by many, and a Turkeycheese Facebook page has so far failed to bring it back. So Roy is coping without it and says the onion chips are still to die for.

The Craver's Hall of Fame has had 6,629 applicants since 2001 and of those only sixty-seven have been chosen, making it harder to get into than the Country Music Hall of Fame in Nashville. Ron now thinks he might have a chance at the latter.

House of Balls
Minneapolis

In a big yellow brick building in the warehouse district on the edge of downtown there is a narrow shop window, into which is mounted a box with six push buttons; inside the window are strange skeletal figures, each with something set into motion by a different button. A finger moves, an arm, a head; a light goes on in the eyes. Over the door is a sign: HOUSE OF BALLS.

You open the shop door cautiously and find yourself in what could be a medieval craftsman's shop in a heavy wooden structure; muted colors, low lighting, and an incredible profusion of unfamiliar objects. The place is crammed with startling constructions. Life-sized transparent steel figures stand in various attitudes: One is welded entirely from drill bits. Percussive music comes from the next room, music you never hear on the radio, music of late-night bacchanalias, music of lost inhibitions. A wild-looking green-and-yellow human head seems to have been carved somewhere in the South American jungles by a lost culture.

On a stand you see another very human head made entirely of flatware, a startled look on its face that is somehow menacing and comic at the same time. There are other exotic heads, some on figures and

A violin finds itself in an uncomfortable situation.

some on platters, with eloquent eyes and expressive mouths, this one bizarre and vaguely threatening, that one with a great sense of peace, all rich in color and shaped from some indestructible colored stone, to all appearances more durable than marble, and you're told that they're carved from bowling balls.

You would never know it. Bowling balls are layered—like the planet—different in the core from the mantle. Carving into them in a flowing way creates unexpected and powerful color contrasts.

Allen Christian says that the idea of the shop and gallery is to show that art doesn't come from waving a magic wand—you sit and you work at it, and it is a lot of work. He uses the same shaped drill bits they use on stone and a six-inch flexible vacuum hose propped close to the work to draw off the hard plastic dust. He tells about the evolution of the bowling ball and why the older ones are better for carving, and which are the rarest and best.

The nationally known House of Balls 1984 pickup truck—with the ranks of bowling pins on the topper, the billiard balls on the fenders, the big green and red lights on the hood, the angel wings on the door, and the 230,000 miles on the odometer—fell victim to a broadside hit from a partygoer at 1:30 a.m. one night while it was parked, smashing it into a second vehicle. The crash awoke Allen and he caught up with the perpetrator, who left a trail of oil and who felt so bad he began bawling.

The truck's name was Harry, and Christian, who believes "the notion that nonliving objects possess something like the human soul," wrote us: "He died in his sleep, God rest his soul. I'm excited about the next one."

The House of Balls is located at 212 3rd Avenue North and 2nd Street in the warehouse district of Minneapolis. The studio is open around midnight, by appointment, and Saturday noon to 4 p.m. Call (612) 332-3992 or see it on the web at www.houseofballs.com.

Stupor Bowl Time
Minneapolis

Well here's another thing we're not supposed to talk about or even know about and especially not to discuss with our razor sharp readership of curious persons.

The deal is a semi-secret bicycle race held right under our noses every year on the weekend of the Super Bowl. Mostly under Minneapolitan noses; close enough.

The human engine is liquid-cooled, bringing fluid to the surface for evaporation, and winter machinery in Minnesota needs a nonfreezing solution. Alcohol works in our cellular motors where antifreeze would be a poison. The race has four winners: Men's Stupor, Women's Stupor, Men's Speed, and Women's Speed,

The beer-fueled Stupor Course is shorter than the main course, which was about forty miles long last year. The Stupor Course favors replenishment over punishment. Riders get a chit at each checkpoint, which are a secret to the riders until the race; even the starting points are secret, and when you complete one only then do you get a manifest showing the next leg.

Riders are allowed to take whatever route they think will be fastest that day, taking into account potholes, traffic, hills, ice, crowds, and law enforcement. You get a marker at the speed course checkpoints but at each of the Stupor Stops you drink a pint of beer before you get your marker and your new manifest.

The secrecy is about keeping the big race away from the police, the media, and the crowds, and it works to the point that a few contenders are police and government officials themselves. The average citizen has no idea that a very large competition is taking place on their city streets and in their local bars. The sport is alleycat/messenger racing and this one, in spite of being the coldest and on some of the worst streets, draws nearly five hundred riders from all over the world.

They guard their semi-secret sport as well as they can, and we aren't sure if it actually happens during the Super Bowl game itself or if it's just that week. But just by looking at some of their pictures you get the idea that these folks are not here to celebrate a silly old football game.

The Gum Lady

Valerie Boettcher is the world's undisputed champion gum collector, listed in the 2000 edition of the *Guinness Book of World Records* as having 2,646 different unopened packages; her fame has grown and people have since sent her more. So now it's well over 5,000.

She's become more than a collector these days; she can tell you the various ways gum is made and its history all the way back to the mastica tree in Greece in the year 50, a number so low it looks like a misprint. Her own gum history dates back to when she was fourteen years old and she collected 250 Bazooka wrappers, which she sent in for a Fonzie necklace—the guy in *Happy Days*—and suddenly packets of gum became interesting to her. Today, she's world champ.

She has exotic gums from France, Japan, Denmark, Tahiti, Zimbabwe, Germany, Korea; garlic-flavored gum from Italy. She has gum made in 1918, a 1932 Wrigley's Juicy Fruit, and a rare 1947 Warrens Mint Cocktail. A two-foot by three-foot Chiclets box from Mexico hangs from the light fixture in her dining room. There is gum in the shape of guitars, of brains and lips; gum with names like Chimp Ears and Uncle Sillie's Food Fight. And of course all that gum with sports cards, movie cards, and television cards.

When she first told her husband-to-be about the collection, he said, "You have *what*?" But he's since become a big help; he encouraged her to go public in 1994, telling her if she didn't someday all those trunks full of packets would be lost. And there are a lot of trunks; the basement of their house is nearly full. She is thinking these days of a gum museum, with a room for history and another to show the manufacturing process; and of course a really big room to show off the collection.

She says some 550 companies make gum, 60 of them in Turkey. The United States, England, and Canada are next, and other makers are scattered throughout the world. She has samples from most of them. But what she doesn't have is the very model that started it all: the Jumbo Bazooka, which was made in three or four flavors. She's also missing five flavors of Bubs Daddy. If anyone out there can help, please contact her: Valerie Boettcher, 13310 North 40th Street, Baytown Township, MN 55082.

She chews gum only when pressured by photographers.
PHOTO BY LINDA STUDLEY

World's Tallest Bicycle

Minneapolis

The Black Label Bike Club is more a loose affiliation than a club: no meetings, no schedule, no dues, no membership manual. But of course you wouldn't call yourself the Black Label Bike Loose Affiliation, so it's a club. They build and ride tall bikes, but not the kind that one remembers seeing old pictures of, with the big wheel in front and the little one in

She Rode with John Dillinger

Ruby Rydeen grew up on a farm on County Road 3 in Washington County, about a mile from Big Marine Lake.

The back pasture was forested and extended to the shoreline, and it was her daily chore, at the age of twelve, to go out there with her younger brother Leroy and bring in the cows. They were offered a ride one day by a man in a black pickup; she climbed in first and sat next to John Dillinger. He gave them each a sucker and she remembers that hers was the red one; she doesn't recall what color Leroy got. He let them out at the pasture gate and went on to his cabin on the lake. Ruby remembers Dillinger as a nice man.

It's long been an open secret that Chicago gangsters of the Prohibition era—a time now referred to as if it were a geologic period—had an understanding with the local cops and sheriffs that as long as they stayed straight in these parts they wouldn't be bothered. And it worked for a while, until a couple of intergang hits in 1933 upset the locals and they were forced to act.

back and no chain, variously called velocipedes, high wheels, or penny farthings. These tall bikes are built of an ordinary woman's bicycle frame welded on top of a man's frame, with a chain running from the upper sprocket position down to the rear wheel.

If you are a tall bike biker you will run alongside and push to get it going, and then in a quick and athletic move you will hop up to the horizontal tube of the lower frame—which is now the middle of the

Ruby remembers that the Dillinger cabin had about a dozen chickens in the yard. It wasn't that the boys couldn't afford eggs or that they were trying to fool the neighbors, because everybody knew what they were up to; it's just that chickens make pretty good lookouts, and you can't shut 'em up by tossing steak at them. He bought the chickens from Joseph Dahlquist, Ruby's great-uncle, and he also got his mail at Dahlquist's mailbox. Nobody wanted to know too much, and people tried hard not to see or hear anything. Her older brother Lawrence, wiser to the world than she, was reluctant to go out in the fields when "the boys" were around.

The Dillinger cabin has stood empty above the lake for more than thirty-five years, the chicken house leaning badly behind it. No one seems to know who owns the property, but rumor has it someone recently bought it. Folks are wondering if the historical society will want that chicken house restored to its former glory.

Take County Road 3 to 177th Street, turn west onto Norell, then north onto 182nd. Turn left; the famous but modest buildings sit three hundred feet west of the intersection.

bike—and swing your other foot even higher, through the V up there at eye level, and start pedaling. If you don't have momentum and balance at this critical instant you will fall a fall that will be four times worse than your usual crash from a bicycle. If you should somehow maintain and find yourself in the miracle of street traffic and you later need to stop at a red light, you will make it over to the curb and hang on to the post until the light changes. And then you will have a new problem, starting from a dead stop that far in the air.

That's how it works for most tall bikes, anyway. The world's tallest bike is something else altogether, and in fact there is only one man allowed to even try to ride it, because it's twelve feet up to the seat and he has to lie flat to go under a freeway overpass. It was built by an artist and mechanic, a lean Swede named Per Hanson who is the club president, and it is ridden only by a gymnastic young man named Stranj. (There's a long *a* in that.) He rides it mostly in parades, given that it takes an entourage to get him up there and to bring it safely to a stop and get him back down.

The Hard Times Cafe, a West Bank co-op the city tried unsuccessfully to shut down, serves as the casual meeting ground for the club, but there are inner-city garages and backyards where most of the welding and mechanical work is done; a favorite junkyard yields up frames and chains and parts, some left by friends and supporters. The builders and riders are generally phoneless and footloose, some homeless, some with facial tattoos, body metal, and so forth; at a club get-together in an art gallery they said some members held jousting contests from the high bikes using PVC pipe wrapped with foam. Four out of five of them could remember their grandmother's telephone number.

A college literature professor said about the Hard Times Cafe: "It is an authentic Parisian cafe of the 1920s; it's literary, it's intellectual, it's artistic and it also has real people, the poor and the homeless. People my age talk a lot about diversity; this place is diversity, and it threatens them."

All of which is probably true, but it also provides sustenance to the builders of the World's Tallest Bicycle.

The Hard Times Cafe is located at Riverside Avenue and Cedar Avenue on the West Bank in Minneapolis.

Stranj, tall in the saddle and presumably heading for the *Guinness Book of World Records*.

Cooties

In addition to being the source of three main watersheds—east to the Atlantic, north to Hudson Bay, and south to the Bay of Mexico—Minnesota is also the source of all the world's Cooties; at least all those spelled with a capital C. And Cooties are a water-borne bug anyway: They were created by a fisherman who liked bugs and who carved lures from wood.

He was a Minneapolis letter carrier named William H. "Herb" Schaper, and in 1948 he carved the first Cootie. He was bitten by the bug with the removable parts and invented a game of it. In the fall of 1949 he boxed up a dozen sets and took them to Dayton's department store for consignment. By the end of 1950 Dayton's had sold 5,592 of them. They went national and were a huge success. By 1965 Schaper Manufacturing was selling twenty-five different games from its plant in Golden Valley; a lot of them were also bug games, like Ants in the Pants, Tickle Bee, Inch Worm, Guess'n Bee, and Tumble Bug.

In the first few years Herb carved more than forty thousand sets by hand, four Cooties per game, each with a body, a head, two antennae, two eyes, a tongue, and six legs. He turned the work over to machinery, which in three years built well over a million; by 1978, thirty million had been sold. The current Hasbro version is in plastic and adds a hat, a bowtie, teeth, and lips. The rules are the same: You shake a die and get body parts according to the number; a one gets a torso, a six buys a leg. First complete bug wins.

Lowercase cooties, both the word and the reality, were exotic souvenirs picked up by sailors around the turn of the twentieth century from the Pacific Islands. The Malayans had a similar word meaning dog lice, and the Polynesian word for any old kind of lice is *kutu*. After World War I the term became fairly common for head lice among schoolchildren. The school nurse put an end to the critters but not the term, which was too appealing to be dropped and became a tease word. A girl getting too close to a boy would get boy cooties, and so forth.

And, in a present-day marketing irony, Dayton's is no longer Dayton's but Cooties are still Cooties.

The Grave of Tiny Tim

Minneapolis

On December 17, 1969, when thirty-seven-year-old Herbert Khaury married seventeen-year-old Vicki Budinger, the event was seen live on 21,400,000 American television sets, at that time *The Tonight Show*'s largest audience.

He startled us, did Tiny Tim, even in a time when startling the public was already much the fashion. He had competed in talent contests with no success and then in 1953 seriously prayed for a new vocal style. Bingo. The falsetto. He was quoted: "Not only was it easier on my throat, but I found that I was thrilling myself as well."

He wore white pancake makeup and long hair and could produce remarkable trills and swoops, doing vaudeville favorites in a way that made you wonder if he wasn't actually serious about it. He was first billed as Larry Love, the Singing Canary, and sang for free in Hubert's Museum in Times Square, and in various small clubs in Greenwich Village, Long Island, and New Jersey, sometimes as Julian Foxglove or as Emmett Swink. His first paying gig was at the Cafe Bizarre in the Village in 1962.

His manager changed the name to Tiny Tim, and it worked.

He drew national attention with an appearance on the first *Laugh-In* show in 1968, drawing a downpour of negative mail. He released a single of "Tiptoe Through the Tulips" that year that went to #17 on the pop charts and his first album, *God Bless Tiny Tim*, sold two hundred thousand copies. He became a regular guest on *The Tonight Show.*

His career crested in 1970, the marriage ended in 1977, and his audiences dwindled. There was a resurgence in the 1980s including some successful Las Vegas appearances, and in the 1990s he released a number of albums. His discography lists twenty-one albums on four labels, including appearances with other artists.

He died of an onstage heart attack while playing at the Women's Club of Minneapolis on November 30, 1996. He is survived by his third wife, Sue Gardner, and a daughter from the famous first marriage, Tulip Victoria.

Larry Love, the Singing Canary—aka Tiny Tim.

He is interred in a mausoleum at the Lakewood Cemetery in good company, not far from the Showmen's Rest.

The press at first didn't know what to make of him but they came around to realize he was serious about the music. "A romantic," one wrote, "in the pursuit of a beautiful dream."

He once told an interviewer: "These voices really live within me."

Tunnel of Fudge

Minneapolis

It's perhaps not what you might think. It's a prizewinner that helped launch a successful Minnesota enterprise, a pioneering cake pan company that brought the bundt into the American mainstream.

Early circular cakes were called Bundkuchen in Germany; a Milwaukee cookbook from 1901 offers a recipe for Bundt Kuchen. The pans brought over from Europe were made of delicate ribbed ceramic or heavy cast iron. In 1950 the Minneapolis manufacturer of Nordic Ware, H. David Dahlquist, was approached by members of the local Hassadah Society chapter, who suggested that he might build a pan that could be lighter and more easily constructed. He took a modified a Scandinavian design, trademarked it, and produced it in aluminum.

Sales were slow at first, until a bundt cake took second place in a baking contest sponsored by Pillsbury in 1966. A pan scramble ensued and the cast aluminum pans outsold the Jell-O tin to become the country's most popular pan. Fifty million have been sold by Nordic Ware, bringing great happiness thoughout the nation.

The happiness is variously named Apple Cream Cheese, Chocolate Whiskey, Gingham Bar, Pear, Pumpkin, Glazed Chocolate-Pumpkin, Sour Cream Pumpkin, Firecracker, Key Lime, Lemon, Cranberry Crème Fraîche, Chocolate Rum, Lavender Lemon, plus dozens more. There are bundts for many occasions, including somebody's "big fat Greek wedding." Not necessarily ours or yours, but someone's. Someone in a movie, perhaps.

It is the Tunnel of Fudge that is connected to the original prize winner. A magic something happens when you combine the right amounts of sugar, butter, six eggs, powdered sugar, flour, unsweetened cocoa, and two cups of chopped walnuts. The walnuts are essential, and a glaze of milk and cocoa and powdered sugar make it all the better.

You blend it all just so and bake it at 350 degrees for forty-five to fifty minutes; cool it upright and turn it over. When you slice it you will find the chocolate tunnel in the center, more a solid tube, running all the way around the ring. It just happens. Pillsbury's website has the recipe.

National Bundt Pan Day is November 15. As far as we know there is no Bundt Pan Parade. Perhaps there's a banquet. Around a circular table, one hopes, with a hole in the center.

The House of Mari Mae

Minneapolis

Page 131 of *New Art International* says: "Exuberantly forceful and brightly charismatic, the elaborate folk visions of Mari Mae Newman stretch their roots down through mythic lace of clouds to the raucous and sublime loam of contemporary culture. . . ." And it goes on from there. Maybe a bit overheated, but the accompanying prints of her paintings are really cool.

She had an art stand in their front yard when other kids were selling lemonade; at thirteen she had a solo show and at twenty-five sold a painting to a museum. Her work has been in the papers, on television, and in important collections, and she's established a national name for herself as a self-taught artist, a visionary in the field of what they call outsider or naive art. But she's not exactly uneducated: Her entry in *Who's Who in American Art* lists her as Newman, Mari Alice Mae, Painter, Sculptor, b. Esterville, Iowa, and reveals that she studied at the University of Minnesota and the Minneapolis College of Art and Design and has certificates in cabinetry, upholstery, and jewelry making.

But, as she told a reporter, despite the media attention and getting her works into museums, she's had this problem: ". . . Been doing this since I was five years old, and I have yet to be able to make a living at it. . . ." Over the years she's worked as a dishwasher, parking lot attendant, in factories and meatpacking plants, at a hospital. In 1989 she decided to make her house into her résumé. She painted it as few houses have been painted before; it's become a city landmark in the last decade. Local citizens will direct you to the place.

And it fits all those adjectives the critics use: *colorful, brilliant, vivid, humorous, quirky,* and so forth; the steps and sidewalks are covered with moving rectangles of color, and there is an immense amount of detail in the panels on the front porch. She changes them and sometimes presents images of nonspecific social commentary, which

As they say in the want ads:
"Must see to appreciate."

some take the wrong way, writing angry letters to the newspaper; she shrugs off the controversy. The yard is a landscape of bright-painted tree stumps and the occasional current sculpture, and the roof is entirely of alternating red and white shingles.

It looks like a house in a children's book of fairy tales. If we had a color spread here we could show it off a little, but, lacking that, if you

Showmen's Rest

A block south of the Main Chapel, in a sweet southeast corner of the big Lakewood Cemetery in Minneapolis, is an area set aside for the circus people. It's the Showmen's Rest area, specifically for those in the traveling show business who have perhaps drifted from their early roots and might otherwise simply disappear.

The Midwest Showmen's Association was formed in 1957 to provide a common place for people in the outdoor entertainment trades to connect during the off-season. They are carnival owners, game and ride owners, concessionaires, entertainers, and so forth. In 1963 they chose this spot with fifty gravesites and hold an option on sixty more.

They hold a gathering on Memorial Day. A plaque there bears a poem written by Glanville Smith of the Cold Spring Granite Company. The first verse, of three, reads:

No Ferris wheel with circling lights
Glitters across the quiet nights
Bird music has replaced the sound
Of barker's calls and merry-go-rounds.
Tent canvas folded, stored away
Steeps in no sun for us, this day.

get to Minneapolis you should take a swing by Mari's place. For a small donation she'll even give you a tour of the place; you will be amazed.

Mari Mae Newman's house is at 5117 Penn Avenue South in Minneapolis. Phone (612) 922-6439.

The rest of the poem and other details are on the website, www.midwest-showmens-association.com.

R.I.P.

Cork Truck

Minneapolis

Houston is generally recognized as the Capital City of the Art Car and most people are okay with that; it is, after all, the Metro Petro. And while it may stage the world's largest art car parade, it's not the only parade, and a determined lady in Minneapolis is seeing to it that her city gets its just due; she is not only an artist but also a street museum curator. She has set the standard here with her 1980 Mazda pickup crawling with ten thousand wine-bottle corks, acquired in thirteen years of working in an Italian restaurant. Set in adhesive, generally end-to-end in flowing rows, they give the vehicle a tan corduroy look, inset with a reverse CORK TRUCK across the front bumper and an ART CAR across the tailgate. And a circular design on the hood and other artistic touches that are better seen than described.

Which is the case with most art, of course, but the art critic business is a huge industry that requires no proficiency test or license and, well, we thought, why not have a modest go at it ourselves? Seems the only way to tell if a new style is real art or not is whether or not it seems goofy to the general public. If something comes along that everybody likes right away, then it's not art; but if a few folks really go nuts for it and almost everyone else says why bother, then it's most likely art. And if there's a sense of humor in there somewhere, then it's art for sure.

And these art cars in the parade here that Jan Elftmann organizes, and in the few others around the country, these definitely meet the criteria. Jan herself meets the criteria: She has a fine dress made of wine corks, and she has covered a bowling alley entirely in wine corks—balls, pins, and alley. She has sizable forearms from years of squeezing an adhesive gun. And, of course, every wine cork has a story, so her old beater pickup is carrying an unlikely blend of ten thousand dinners, meetings, parties, and trysts, glued end-to-end and side-by-side and driving around town.

Jan Elftmann and her ten-thousand-story pickup truck.

Other vehicles seen in Minneapolis parades: a Surfin' Car covered with seashells and featuring two beautiful women's heads on the front fenders with seashells for hair; the Bone Car, covered with real bones—but no human ones, a question folks ask her all the time; Miss Vicki, the tulip car designed for Tiny Tim; a truck shingled with pages from James Joyce; the Trophy Car, bearing 150 trophies and awards; a '75 Caddie in the form of a leaping orange horse with a papier-mâché head and legs and a rope tail.

Wild alterations to ordinary vehicles—like the thirteen-foot-tall tail fins on a Houston car named Max the Daredevil Finmobile—seldom seem to add anything to the trade-in value; the upside is that, as art car pioneer Ruthann Godelleri put it, "Unlike galleries and museums, art cars are open twenty-four hours a day, and they're free."

Black and White

He's known among artists and enthusiasts as Scott Seekins, but to the city in general he's the Black and White Guy; all black in winter, all white in summer. He has a severely angular appearance, exaggerated by machete sideburns and a thin slice of mustache, a weave of black curls, and large Buddy Holly glasses. In a white linen dinner jacket, white pants, black leather shoes, and a large Art Deco brooch, he is an eye-catching combination of elements; the artist as art.

He realized in high school that he didn't quite fit in, saying that in the 1960s he was the only person his age in South St. Paul who wasn't a hippie. He went on to art school in Minneapolis and along the way developed an interest in turn-of-the-twentieth-century men's formal styles, eventually settling on seasonal black and white. He found a couple of antique clothing stores on the bus routes between home and school and built a wardrobe fit for a high-tone gentleman of another age. He says, "If you just stand still, you'll be back in style sometime."

He's been hollered at a lot over the years, as in: "Ya look like ya got a cat on yer head, ya [drive-by vulgarity]!" About that, he says, "Conformity is strong in the suburb of Sweden. Each group polarizes into itself and is fearful of the others. . . . They accept you, but they don't. It hurts you in all kinds of ways, relationships, all kinds of things. I'm not a good person to bring home to Mama . . . because of the look. Three times, when I've been going with somebody and then we meet her parents, they take one look at me and they say to their daughter: 'Where have we gone wrong?' Three times! 'Where have we gone wrong?' And in each case, it was over. The girls say it's just too much pressure, they can't handle it. It's way too hard. . . ."

He developed a focus on painting Madonnas in contemporary settings, often with local historical landmarks over their shoulder and often with himself hidden in the background. He's done a thousand

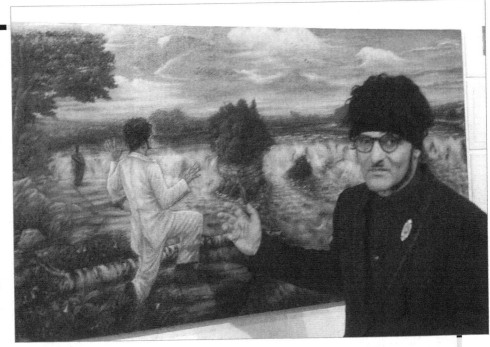

Scott Seekins sees the world in black and white.

paintings of the Madonna in the last twenty years, "more than were done in the Renaissance. I just felt one day that it was a positive image. It's not so much a Catholic thing." He's an expert model railroad detailer, president of the Twin Cities N-Scalers club, and writes articles in the various hobby publications. His interest in early rock, rockabilly, and R&B has landed him guest disc jockey spots on local radio, and he collects reptiles and will bring them to local schools and give talks. He's also a historian, a specialist in World War II, and a fly fisherman. That rarest of Minnesotans, a man without a car, he carries a fly rod on the bus to city lakes.

But it's the outfit, and the big dry-cleaning bills that go with it, that has made him into the city's harbinger of the seasons: Winter ends when Scott changes to his whites, and he alone makes the decision, based strictly on his instincts. Two seasons here: Black and White. And he'll let you know.

If you spot Scott, report your sighting on the website at http://seekingseekins.com.

The Art Car Parade can be seen on the Fourth of July as part of the Greenway Parade of Arts in Minneapolis. It starts at 1 p.m. on Lyndale and follows Lake Street to 5th Street. It is organized by Intermedia Arts; call (612) 871-4444 or visit the website at www.intermediaarts .org or www.corktruck.com.

Mt. Holly
Shakopee

Telephone conversation about the city founded by Mike Haeg, which is one house with a population of four, sitting on a street corner in the town of Shakopee, a southern suburb of Minneapolis:

"We heard about your little town down there in Shakopee—"

"Shakopee is actually a first tier suburb of Mt. Holly."

[Laughing] "Yes, that's the kind of information I need. I like that. . . . So what else can you tell me about Mt. Holly? How did you start your town?"

"We were from here originally . . . and finally decided to buy a house here. We thought if we want our friends to come out, we might as well make it interesting. So I decided to just make my own city.

"And we figured if we were going to be a city we should do the same things they do, so we have a couple of festivals here every year, such as a Pinewood Derby for Adults, and we have an International Film Festival. . . . Two years ago we had an International Short Film Festival and we had eight films from around the world that all starred midgets. And I have a friend who travels and he puts on a Free Soybean Feed once a year; and we put out a little newspaper."

"Yes, and your newspaper, is that the *Mt. Holly Register*?"

"Yep . . . it used to be online. Now it's print and you can send me a stamp and I'll send you an issue for every stamp you send. Or you can come by Mt. Holly, where you can get 'em for free."

"So do you have meetings and jobs?"

"Yes. My son is head of Animal Control and Sanitation—tends to the cat and takes out the garbage. My daughter was the Town Crier but she just moved to City Administrator because now she can read and take notes. And my wife is the First Lady and the Warden. And the City Treasurer. And I am Acting Mayor and Chief of Police . . . and Occasional Town Drunk. I'm on both sides of the badge there."

"Very good."

"And I'm the only taxpayer."

"Well. What a fun town to live in."

"Yes. Come on out sometime; there's free pinball."

Contact city hall at mikehaeg@gmail.com.

(Small as it is, Mt. Holly is not the state's smallest legal metropolis. To experience that excitement one must travel to Funkley, located up there in the northwest part of the state, which is also where you'll find it in this book.)

Twelve-Level Tree House
St. Louis Park

It began back in Springfield, Virginia, when Mark Tucker was a little kid and a tree house behind the family home was taken down by a bulldozer to make room for a school. He never got that tree house thing out of his system. He married a Minnesota woman, they moved here, he built up a business, they had five kids, and all along he meant to build a tree house in the big spreading maple in the yard. When the oldest was sixteen and moved out of the house, Mark realized he should have built that tree house and he'd better get to it soon, before any more left. He put his insurance business on hold and went down to the lumberyard.

And once he started he couldn't stop; he had six levels up there in the first year and his kids thought it was great. He had a grand opening and invited folks up there and in the next few years got the notion to put his office there—called it his branch office, of course—and pretty soon the city was on his case. They wanted handrails and regulation stairs and structural engineers and load limits and reports from foresters and he didn't, and he kept adding levels and additions and

A house irresistible to bureaucrats.

pretty soon the city was threatening to tear the whole thing down, all twelve levels of it. And, like so many of our wild romantic notions and obsessive-impulsive constructions, it became fodder for lawyers.

The court settlement allowed him to have family members plus four up there at any one time, and it has to undergo annual inspections and special inspections after storms and a whole invoice of other governmental mothering—that he has to pay for—but they are letting it stay there. He says it's a good place for the kids and for him to get away and watch TV or read. There were times he wished he'd never built it, but now he's thinking it's pretty cool.

And for all of that, it is an amazing thing to see. As wide as it is tall, it emerges from the ground part mushroom, part pirate ship, and part precarious Gothic castle; it looks like an illustration in a children's story book. It intertwines in the branches, platforms wrapping around the trunk here and decks spreading out onto large branches over there, all very organic. Once up into the main forks of the branches, it climbs forty feet farther into the crown of the big tree, where there is a high observation post and you can see for at least a couple of miles, anyway. They say it creaks in a windstorm like a wooden sailing ship.

The tree house is located at 4800 Minnetonka Boulevard in St. Louis Park. To get there take Minnetonka Boulevard east off Highway 100 for a few blocks. It's on the left side of the road. For information about tours call Mark Tucker at (952) 920-6627 or visit www.slphistory .org/history/tuckerstreehouse.asp.

Pavek Museum of Broadcasting
St. Louis Park

In 1927 you could buy a new Model A Ford for $585. An Amberola radio cost $600. You not only couldn't get the radio in the car, but if you got the radio you couldn't afford the car. In small towns it was not uncommon to find only one radio in the whole community, and if the owner was generous he would put it in the window and let his neighbors listen.

By 1927 Joe Pavek was nineteen years old and it had already been nine years since he built his first radio, which was struck by lightning, burst into flames, and set fire to his mother's curtains, which caused his mother to throw the radio out the window. Joe went on to become a radio repairman, a bookkeeper, a sales manager, and a paint distributor, but he's well known these days because of his fabulous collection of old radios and broadcasting equipment. He started this museum in 1988 and died in 1989; it has been augmented by the Charles Bradley Collection and the Jack Mullin Collection, so that it's now the second largest museum of its type in the world.

★ ★

They have twelve thousand square feet of stuff there you never imagined: a big 1912 rotary spark-gap transmitter like the one used on the *Titanic* to transmit distress signals; an 1896 wireless device invented by Guglielmo Marconi himself; a 1903 Zonophone

I told you kids to turn that thing down.

gramophone; the 1912 Edison Amberola; Airtones, Operadios, Mag-nadynes, Atwater-Kents. There's the Grunow twelve-tube Teledial, the RCA Radiola Super Hetrodyne, the Kennedy Coronet, and the Grebe Synchrophase, whose motto was "Get It Better with a Grebe."

And they have the unbelievable RCA Theremin, the only musical instrument ever made that you didn't touch to play. It's in a small desklike cabinet containing a speaker and sprouting two antennae, one vertical for pitch and one horizontal for volume; as your hand moves along the antenna it wails and moans, rising and falling, loud and soft. The sales brochure says: ". . . Yet, WE . . . ALL . . . YOU . . . can now play, and play beautifully, a wonderfully expressive, marvel-ously simple, absolutely unmechanical musical instrument! Scientists and musicians of note and of standing have gone on record with their opinions that the Theremin may likely revolutionize the whole world of music. . . ." It never happened. The thing wails like a saw.

Joe was about ready to auction off the amazing collection in 1984 when the inventor of the wearable pacemaker, Earl Bakken—the cofounder of Medtronic and a radio junkie himself—stepped up and helped form the museum, which he saw as a great opportunity for education. It opened on the fiftieth anniversary of Orson Welles's *War of the Worlds* broadcast, and although the public is welcome, it func-tions primarily as an educational museum for grade school children. It's booked solid every year; they've done more than three thousand work-shops for more than sixty thousand kids since 1991.

It is one of the five best-kept secrets in Minnesota, or at least it was until this book got published.

The Pavek Museum of Broadcasting is located at 3517 Raleigh Avenue in St. Louis Park. To get there take Highway 100 south, go east on County Route 25, then right on Beltline Road to Raleigh Street. Call (952) 926-8198 or visit www.museumofbroadcasting.org for more information.

Hilltop

It's a spirited little place, eighty acres of land that was once a riding stable, holding not quite eight hundred citizens, most of them living in mobile homes. "Mobile" doesn't necessarily mean homes on wheels, because they aren't. In a 150-mile-an-hour wind they might become more mobile than homes anchored to the planet with basements, but that is pure speculation. No dwellings have left on the wind since the town's inception in 1956.

The town consists of four neat and well-shaded trailer parks, an apartment building, and some built-in-place houses. And a commercial strip along the eastern and southern edges, Central Avenue and Forty-fifth Street, respectively, that includes the well-known Flameburger restaurant. The town is notable in that it is landlocked, surrounded completely by the city of Columbia Heights, an extension of Minneapolis and a city whose thinly disguised purpose is to someday swallow Hilltop whole and get rid of the trailers. In 1959 their city council asked their attorneys to ". . . study ways of erasing Hilltop from the metropolitan map."

Officials there, like officials everywhere, have come to learn the art of the smokescreen statement. They don't openly talk of wiping out the independent Hilltop way of life anymore, but they do speak ominously of "mergers" and "re-adaptive use of land resources." Hilltop residents had offered themselves up for annexation fifty years ago and were rebuffed, so they incorporated and are now happy to remain as their own town. It is a place where, once settled into, families tend to stay.

The town suffered brief fame thirty years ago when three people had a fatal misunderstanding in one of the townhouses, giving Hilltop an annual murder rate of three per 800, or one in every 267. Put into Los Angeles's population of 3.8 million, for example, that ratio would equal 14,000 victims a year. That doesn't happen in L.A., even in a bad year. So Hilltop took over as the nation's most statistically

Eighty acres of independence, surrounded by ordinances.

dangerous city for a short time, proving nothing of course except that you can create anything with statistics, even dark humor. Especially dark humor.

The town's third claim to fame is the Hilltop Chapter of the Barbershop Harmony Society, a group of singers from around the Twin Cities called the Great Northern Union. It is the only chorus to have qualified for twenty consecutive appearances at the international championships; the chorus was ranked in the top ten every time and reached the medals circle seven times.

The group does four-part harmony and has had a lot of fun in the process, and they have released four albums to prove it. At last check, though, none of its seventy members actually resides in Hilltop. One hopes they would at least stop in for an occasional Flameburger.

Hilltop sits north of downtown Minneapolis between Forty-fifth and Forty-eighth Streets, and between Central and Madison Avenues, in Columbia Heights. The Great Northern Union can be found at www .gnunion.com.

Marvy Barber Poles
St. Paul

The people of the William Marvy Company make high-quality barber poles in a handsome building on St. Claire Avenue. The company is doing exactly what it was intended to do in the first place. One wouldn't expect a successful enterprise to become a curiosity, but this one has been featured on every national television network, been on Charles Kuralt's television show a couple of times, and is mentioned in his book and a number of other books. And there have been photos and interviews in newspapers across the country.

William Marvy was a man with a better idea, and he built a business from not much and took it to the top of the industry and then outlasted every shred of competition. The company hasn't wavered from the original approach and they still build barber poles that will last into the next century. They are now the only barber pole maker in the western hemisphere.

Marvy got into the business in 1922. He was thirteen years old when he took a job at a barber supply house and was in his twenties when he opened his own shop. He thought the barber poles he sold were overly heavy and not as durable as they could be. He went to work building a lighter corrosion-resistant one of aluminum and stainless steel, with the highest quality electric motors available; on New Year's Day of 1950 his two young sons threw the switch on the first "Six Ways Better" pole.

His son Robert still runs the company and has three sons of his own who carry on the family tradition; William Marvy could be the unintended Hank Williams of the barber pole business. We have no way of knowing if he would take that as a compliment.

Barber pole serial #75,001 hangs on a hook back in the assembly room with note taped to it, "DO NOT SELL"; pole #75,000 is in the Smithsonian Institute in Washington, DC, and is one of two in their collection. There is a Marvy pole in the White House barber shop. As of this writing they have made more than eighty-two thousand of

Still made in Minnesota and still the best.

them, in various sizes. And they have a parts inventory that enables them to repair and renovate nearly any pole ever made in the United States.

In 1960 they expanded into the disinfectant and sterilizing aspects of the beauty and barber business. Pole production has slowed somewhat in these later years, possibly because the poles last so long, but it's hard to imagine a town without one.

Marvy barber poles can be seen in just about every city that has a barber. To see Marvy's collection call (651) 698-0726 or stop by the shop at 1540 St. Clair Avenue in St. Paul. Check them out at www .wmmarvyco.com.

Onyx John
St. Paul

He's the world's largest onyx sculpture, carved in Mexican stone by a Swedish sculptor named Carl Milles who was inspired by a ceremony he had witnessed in Ponca City, Oklahoma. The sculpture shows five Native Americans seated about a fire holding sacred pipes, while rising from the smoke is a very tall figure Milles called the *God of Peace*, whom Milles pictured to be speaking to all peoples.

The word *God* apparently became a little too strong for some St. Paul activists, and in a 1994 multicultural ceremony the work was renamed *Vision of Peace*. To St. Paulites in general he's always been called Onyx John. He would be a compelling and magnificent figure under any name, weighing sixty tons and standing thirty-six feet tall in the Memorial Hall of the St. Paul City Hall and Ramsey County Courthouse. He rotates sixty-six degrees to either side on his base, making a full turn in two and a half hours. He is reflected in the gold mirror ceiling above him, doubling the grandeur and the mystery.

The ceiling is gold because of the Great Depression. The building was commissioned in 1928 with a $4 million public bond set for its construction. The stock market crashed the following year, causing labor and materials to become suddenly cheap and available. What

He's the world's tallest onyx man,
and he's okay with that.

would have been a most interesting Art Deco building—American Perpendicular on the outside and Zigzag Moderne inside—ended up as a stunning expression of these styles dressed in first-class elegance.

The exterior of the building is clad in Indiana limestone and Wisconsin Rosetta black granite. Cut stone reliefs—representing Law, Order, Education, Commerce, Transportation, Industry, Agriculture, Peace, and Justice (no mention of Self-Esteem)—flank the main entrances on Fourth and Kellogg Streets. Narrow vertical lines of windows and spandrels slice the tower into twenty-story stone shafts.

Sixteen tall bronze shafts set against blue-black Belgian marble in the long three-story Memorial Hall, dedicated to the veterans from Ramsey County who were lost in battle, are a polished backdrop to the sculpture. It's the kind of room that makes people speak in hushed tones.

The council chambers on the third floor are finished in exotic woods and are graced with four large wall murals depicting the beginnings of the city. The hardware, the doors, the wall and ceiling materials; the entire building is stunning, once you get used to the idea that such a fashionable structure could stand so modestly in downtown St. Paul.

The building was designed by Holabird & Root of Chicago and finished in 1932. The sculpture, a separate project, was unveiled in 1936. Most rational folks agree that this building and the great stone Federal Courthouse (called the Landmark Center) two blocks away, plus the Louis Sullivan bank down in Owatonna, are the three primo buildings in Minnesota. They may be classified as curiosities in the sense that no curious person should pass up the chance to see them.

Visit St. Paul City Hall and Ramsey County Courthouse at 15 West Kellogg Street in St. Paul or check out the website at www.stpaul.gov/index.aspx?NID=2085.

Skivvies Unlimited
St. Paul

We expect a good museum to have an intriguing underground dungeon and at the Minnesota Historical Society it's as good as it gets. Beneath the sidewalks of St. Paul lies the world's largest known stash of underwear, a cornucopia of whalebone corsets, girdles, brassieres, hoops, wire bras, pantaloons, panty girdles, long johns, colorful union suits, boxers, petticoats, and a Stars and Stripes bra and girdle from 1946.

The 3,500-piece collection was a gift from the Munsingwear Corporation, who were the nation's first to mass produce and publicly advertise comfortable underwear. They ran shocking magazine ads showing entire families gathered around the fireplace in their form-fitting cream-colored union suits.

Unmentionables became mentioned and Munsingwear became a full-bore participant in the Roaring Twenties. They bought a Hollywood lingerie company and printed ads featuring young ladies in early pushup bras, the copy breathing sly phrases like, "Time to give nature a nudge and look more beautiful from the inside out."

In another a circus strongman holds aloft eight guys, every one in a union suit, with a kid on top holding a Munsingwear banner. The text says: "Munsing Union Suits please because of . . . the satisfactory way in which they fit and cover the form without gaping or binding at the crotch."

Daring copy indeed, all in sync with fledgling jazz at the turn of the century, back when divorces were one per thousand couples and the national debt was $12.45 per person. And unsung new weaving machines could plate silk on wool and create elastic itchless fabrics for undergarments possessed of "a soft but smooth under surface that will not irritate the flesh of the wearer," in the memorable phrase of Mr. George Munsing.

He was an engineering genius and acquired patents right and left, even getting one for an egg beater. His company was at one time the largest employer of women in the nation.

He also built five buildings in Minneapolis, the original one now on the National Historic Register, while his fabric legacy rests in climate controlled chambers across the river in the Sister City.

You wonder if in his busy life Mr. Munsing ever thought about his contacts and if they found it intimidating to be wearing his shorts.

You can see the collection at the Minnesota History Center at 345 West Kellogg Boulevard in St. Paul. The museum's hours are Tuesday 10 a.m. to 8 p.m., Wednesday through Saturday 10 a.m. to 5 p.m., and Sunday noon to 5 p.m. Call (651) 259-3000 or visit www .minnesotahistorycenter.org for more information.

Iguana
St. Paul

A remarkable steel sculpture lies on the lower entrance plaza to the Science Museum of Minnesota: a 3,900-pound, forty-foot lizard, life-like, poised as if ready to make a sudden move on any approaching meaty object, such as yourself; you find yourself comforted by the fact that you might be quicker than some of the people around you.

He was welded together of thirteen thousand railroad spikes, the head of each spike a single scale on his extraordinary hide, by an artist named Nick Swearer, from Northfield. (Anyone who has ever worked on a section gang would appreciate an artist working with rail spikes having the name *Swearer*.) Nick began the sculpture when he was fifteen, using his own iguana as a model, and it took four years to finish, working every day after school; art patrons Betty and John Musser paid him $10,000 for it and donated it to the museum. The beast has been a great favorite in this city for more than twenty years.

When the museum made ready to move to their new building in 1999 they threw a big party for Iggy, as he's called, and then a few days later hoisted him onto a flatbed trailer and paraded him through crowds in downtown Minneapolis and St. Paul to his new spot near the river.

A lizard beyond your expectations.

A huge iguana welded of rail spikes. Amazing such a rough concept could turn out to be such a tour de force, so graceful and so appealing. Kids climb all over him. His snout is smooth from people patting it as they pass. Nick told the newspaper he never oiled it; "He is oiled by human oil, and he would be a red rust if he were not touched so much. . . . It shows how much people love him."

The Science Museum of Minnesota is located at 120 West Kellogg Boulevard, across from RiverCentre in downtown St. Paul. Museum hours are Tuesday through Wednesday 9:30 a.m. to 5 p.m., Thursday through Saturday 9:30 a.m. to 9 p.m., and Sunday 9 a.m. to 5 p.m. Monday closed. Call (651) 221-9444 or visit www.smm.org for more information.

Tiger Jack

He was born in New York, on Long Island, in 1907; his mother died when he was seven and he was sent to live with relatives near Danville, Virginia. He came to Minnesota during the Great Depression, as he used to say, "in a boxcar, with a tag on my ankle," which he later revealed was partly true and partly poetic license.

He spent one night in a St. Paul mission and woke up the next day determined to become a boxer, so he went to a 7th Street gym and said he was a hotshot from Ohio who'd had so many fights he couldn't count 'em all. The going rate was two and three dollars a fight; his first one was in borrowed trunks and shoes. He said, "I throwed glove and throwed glove and throwed glove. In two weeks I'd whipped everyone in my weight." He came by his *nom de guerre* when the sheriff's brother told him after a good fight that he had been a tiger out there, and it stuck. For two years he shined shoes and made door-to-door sales in daylight and boxed at night.

He married his wife, Nurceal, in 1946, and in 1949 they opened a small variety store on Rondo and Farrington Street: Rondo was the main street of a thriving black commercial district in those days, home to the Blind Pig Cafe, the Busy Bee Grocery, Booker T's Restaurant, the Blue Moon, Baby Muriel's, the Love Tailor Shop, the Dew Drop, Walker Williams Pool Hall and Grocery. And Field's Drug Store, Coleman's Little Harlem Restaurant, the Square Deal Liquor Store. They were all swept away when Interstate 94 was shoved through in the mid-1960s, and Rondo became a frontage road named Concordia.

Tiger Jack Rosenbloom was the only businessman to survive in the neighborhood; he moved the shack to the high corner where Dale Street crosses the freeway and shined shoes and sold charcoal, kerosene, candy, and greeting cards. At Christmas, he said, "I got a black Jesus and a white Jesus; some folks want one and some want the other."

A steadfast man becomes an institution.

He became the most famous and most popular man in St. Paul, and he stayed that way for thirty years. He was quotable. He favored hard work and spoke against government handouts: "If Tiger Jack was mayor," he said, "it would be harder for one of these people to receive a dime than for a dead man to stand up and walk." Governor Rudy Perpich declared December 29, 1978, "Tiger Jack Day." He got an anniversary card from Hubert Humphrey. His son Lucky is the chairman of the Minnesota Black Republican Coalition.

He said, "I'm no yes man, no get-by man. No one uses Tiger Jack. Everything I say is truth and logic." A local reporter asked him on his ninetieth birthday how his health was; he said, "Like an alligator." He also told him: "Tiger's commandments. Put 'em down: Be

(Continued on next page)

(Continued from previous page)

true. Your word is your word. Respect your fellow man. Respect your license."

He had an ability to touch people through word and deed and he kept his life simple, never went into debt, preached hard work and honesty, and sent eight children to school on the profits from an eight-by-ten-foot charcoal and shoeshine shack. In April of his ninety-fourth year the city named a street after him and his wife: "Mr. and Mrs. Tiger Jack Street." He died that August on the birthday of his daughter Mona, who had preceded him. He knew he would go that day; he said his good-byes and told people Mona would call him home, and so she did.

The family gave his shack on Dale and the freeway to the city; they say it's going to become a historic site.

Tiger's Shack has been moved to the Minnesota History Center at 345 West Kellogg Boulevard in St. Paul. The museum's hours are Tuesday 10 a.m. to 8 p.m., Wednesday through Saturday 10 a.m. to 5 p.m., and Sunday noon to 5 p.m. Call (651) 259-3000 or visit www.minnesota historycenter.org for more information.

The Museum of Questionable Medical Devices
St. Paul

Bob McCoy is president of the Minnesota Skeptics, who post a standing offer of $10,000 to anyone who can furnish solid evidence supporting the existence of ghosts, but he is better known as the curator of the nation's largest museum of quackery gear. It began in 1983 when he and a friend salvaged twelve phrenology machines from the 1920s and started a phrenology parlor in a shopping mall.

* *

The machines look like outsized hooded hair dryers; for a modest few dollars they'd read your cranial lumps and tell you things about yourself—your intelligence, spirituality, chastity, suavity, wit, ideality, and twenty-nine other qualities—and if you weren't pleased with how you tested out Bob said he could rearrange your lumps: "I have a mallet handy."

He began acquiring other wacky machines from garage sales and other collectors, and from places like the defunct St. Louis Medical Quackery Museum. The collection has grown to 325 unique and interesting ways for a person to make a complete fool of himself, or herself. There's soap that sudses off your extra pounds, and weight reduction glasses that you wear standing in front of lights flashing prismatic colors in your face. He has the 1918 G-H-R Electric Thermitis Dilator, which is a rectally inserted electric "prostate warmer" that plugs into a wall outlet and stimulates the male "abdominal brain"; the foot-operated breast-enlarging Nemectron Machine, a pump that attaches to the kitchen sink and allows a lady to enlarge her bust while she washes the dishes. (Fellas: a real thoughtful gift for that special gal.)

The Crosley Xervac is a vacuum-powered hair restorer; the Spectro-Chrome machine, invented in 1920 by one Dinshah P. Ghaliali, could cure patients of almost any malady through the proper use of pure and intense colored light, broken down from sunlight. William Reich's 1940 invention, called the Orgone Energy Accumulator, is a "storehouse of orgasmic energy," an ordinary box of fiberboard and steel wool with a galvanized metal lining; sit in there for the prescribed thirty minutes and . . . wow. You've just sat in a box for a while.

The turn of the twentieth century brought on a burst of actual scientific progress, which fueled a huge market for charlatans, including those pushing things like radium water. Few people knew that Madame Curie, one of the pioneers in research on radioactivity, had her fingers fall off before she died; a captain of the steel industry, Eben MacBurney Byers, boasted that he had drunk 1,400 bottles of radium water in two years. He died in 1930 after his jaw fell off.

The phrenology machine—precursor to the
Minnesota Multiphasic Personality Test.

But flummery didn't disappear in the 1930s—in the 1960s the Ruth Drown radio therapy machine enticed thousands to have their saliva analyzed while it emitted healing rays. In 1995 the FDA seized a "radio" machine from a health store that claimed it could cure AIDS; it was nothing more than a plastic box with knobs. Holistic magazines are still full of this stuff: For thirty-nine dollars plus S&H you can get an electric pain relief zapper, the same item that's called a barbecue grill spark igniter and available for less than ten bucks at a chain store.

Bob McCoy is now semi-retired, and his fabulous and famous collection has been moved to the Collections Room at the Science Museum of Minnesota, where it is a big hit.

The museum is located at 120 West Kellogg Boulevard, across from RiverCentre in downtown St. Paul. Museum hours are Tuesday through Wednesday 9:30 a.m. to 5 p.m., Thursday through Saturday 9:30 a.m. to 9 p.m., and Sunday 9:30 a.m. to 5 p.m. Monday closed. Call (651) 221-9444 or visit www.smm.org for more information.

Mickey's Diner

St. Paul

One of the few businesses in the metro area that has remained unchanged through the last forty years, Mickey's is one of those things—like the violin, for instance—that they got right early on and so why fool with it.

It's had close calls, the closest just a few years back when they expanded the St. Paul Companies insurance headquarters, but after the dust settled there it still sat, on a skinny strip of land at the corner of St. Peter and 7th, its back up against a gigantic new masonry wall; it has Art Deco attitude there in its resolute cream-and-red railroad car getup. It looks like that wall will come down before Mickey's leaves.

And it could happen that way because Mickey's was hauled in from New Jersey in 1938 and is on the National Register of Historic Places, one of only two diners in the nation so honored. It's been in four movies and quite a few notables have sat there; we could start dropping

Mickey's motto: "You are what you eat—be all you can be."

names but we won't. But it's as much theater as it is restaurant—and, as one of the few places left to stay open twenty-four hours, as much necessity as luxury. If you need a breakfast suggestion, a lot of us go for the Twos: two eggs, two sausage, two cakes. For dinner, the Mulligan stew or the half-pound hamburger steak, with onions. Soup of the day is ham and bean, every day. The coffee mugs are like the building itself: sturdy and exactly right for the purpose. So is the coffee.

The waitresses are generally feisty and don't put up with a lot of nonsense; they'll tell you to get a job if they figure you're unemployed out of sheer laziness. If you're tipsy and out of line they'll tell you to behave. One is from Wisconsin, a Packers fan, and she says she doesn't give a rip about the Vikings and that they've never amounted to anything anyways, and when a regular customer said she should be careful not to say that too loud in there, she threw her good-sized shoulders back and said: "I don't care if they don't like it. Bring 'em on. C'mon! Get a shiner at Mickey's Diner! Haha!"

Mickey's Diner is located at 36 West 7th Street and Cedar Avenue in downtown St. Paul. It's always open. For more information call (651) 222-5633 or visit www.mickeysdiningcar.com.

Food on a Stick
St. Paul

The Minnesota State Fair is the largest state fair in the country and it features most of the things that any of the other fairs feature, including hogs the size of full-grown steers, steers up there at a ton, heavy as bison, and pumpkins the size of easy chairs. The puke-inducing rides, the slingshot launching folks up into the goose flyways, the ring-the-bell mallets, darts and balloons, floating ducks, and all the rest. National rock and country acts in the grandstand, stages all up and down the midway, people carrying huge stuffed animals.

What really separates this fair from a lot of the others, however, is that, for ten days at the end of summer, it is likely the world's largest market for boiling oil and sharp sticks. There is an incredible array of food offered on a stick here, over seventy-five varieties at the 2011 State Fair, including Deep Fried Candy Bars, Cheese on a Stick, Chocolate Covered Cheese, Chocolate Covered Bananas, five kinds of Pickles on Sticks, the Field and Stream (walleye and prime rib), Pizza on a Stick, Scotch Eggs, Teriyaki Ostrich, Alligator—either breaded or as Naked Alligator on a Stick—Ooey Gooey Chocolate Chip Cookie Dough on a Stick, and Big Fat Bacon on a Stick. And to cleanse the palate for some stick-mounted Fudge Puppies and Taffy Pops, try Watermelon on a Stick. An item-on-a-stick offered at the 2006 fair

The undisputed grand patriarch of stick food.

was Pepto-Bismol on a Stick, now available at the Medical Tent. Seriously. It's a sealed packet taped to a popsicle stick.

Recently we have seen traditional family dinners on a stick, like Swedish Meatballs with Mashed Potatoes on a Stick and Spaghetti and Meatballs on a Stick. It gives some the uneasy feeling there might be something amiss in the trackwork here and that civilization as we know it may be coming off the rails a bit.

It's probably a good thing for all of us that the fair only comes once a year; and that, at least so far, we have no chains of boiled-in-oil food-on-a-stick restaurants.

The Minnesota State Fair runs for the last ten days of summer, including Labor Day. The fairgrounds are located on Snelling Avenue and Como Avenue north of Interstate 94 in St. Paul.

Dan Patch
Savage

Asked to name the country's greatest superstar athlete ever, sports fans might say Babe Ruth or Joe Louis, or perhaps Johnny Unitas. They might also say Michael Jordan, Joe Montana, or Tiger Woods. But none of these greats ever had a railroad named after them, or a make of automobile, or a brand of cigar, or a dance, or a washing machine. None retired unbeaten. And none died at the age of twenty, either.

Dan Patch did all of these and more. He was born in Oxford, Indiana, on April 29, 1896, with legs so crooked he couldn't stand up to nurse. Neighbors suggested he be put out of his misery but his owner, Dan Messner, turned him over to a local trainer named Johnny Wattles, who had patience and, apparently, foresight. They didn't put Dan Patch into competition until he was a full-grown four-year-old, and in his case full grown was big. He stood sixteen hands at the withers, sixty-four inches, and weighed 1,165 pounds. In his first few seasons of harness racing he broke every record a harness horse could break, including net worth.

In 1900 he was sold to M. E. Sturgis of Buffalo, New York, for $20,000, the most ever paid for a pacer up until then, and two years later was bought by Marion Willis Savage of Hamilton, Minnesota, for the breathtaking sum of $60,000. Enough money to buy ninety-two new 1902 Oldsmobile Runabouts, none of which would have been nearly as fast or as dependable as Dan Patch pulling a two-wheel sulky.

He took the country by storm, becoming a household name and the rage of the age, always the winner, riding in his own railroad car with his portrait painted on the side. His luxurious barn was named the Taj Mahal. Marion Savage donated a percentage of his winnings to the church in the horse's own envelopes, making Dan Patch the only horse ever to become a Methodist, and the only Methodist ever to live in the Taj Mahal.

His crowning achievement came on a blazing hot 8th of September, 1906, in front of ninety-three thousand people in the stands at the Minnesota Fairgrounds. By that time no owner would put a horse up against him and he was running against the clock. The crowd was keyed up to see history made, and they went berserk with happiness when the great horse crossed the finish line in a stunning one minute and fifty-five seconds. People wept with joy and threw their hats into the air; the record was tied thirty-two years later but has never been broken.

The town of Hamilton changed its name to Savage in 1904, and in 1908 construction began on the Dan Patch Line, running from Savage to the south end of the Minneapolis streetcar tracks; it would ultimately become a belt line connecting six major railroads radiating south and west of the city.

Dan Patch died on July 11, 1916, from an enlarged heart; Marion Savage died the next day, from a broken one. Dan Patch Days are celebrated every summer in Savage, and even down in Oxford, Indiana, they still celebrate Dan Patch Day on November 2. They have a big street party and dance the Dan Patch Two-Step.

For more information about Dan Patch Days call (952) 440-6255 or visit www.danpatchdays.org. For more information about Dan Patch visit the Dan Patch Historical Society at www.danpatch.com.

You Can't Always Get What You Want

In 1964 the Rolling Stones made their first tour of the United States; one of the stops on the way was at Danceland, a ballroom out on Lake Excelsior, west of the Twin Cities. The gig didn't really go that well and the band was actually booed, which may have said more about the crowd than the band, depending on your viewpoint.

There is a man in the nearby small town of Excelsior named Jimmy, sometimes referred to as Mister Jimmy, who has been there as long as almost anyone can remember. He lives with his brother and walks around town, often chewing on an unlit cigar, checking things out, talking to people. He lights the Christmas lights on the main street; he's sort of the honorary town ambassador. He may or may not have an occupation, but that's not relevant to the story. What is relevant is that on the morning after the Stones gig at Danceland, Jimmy was in the Beacon Drug Store, apparently minding the counter for a few minutes, when Mick Jagger walked in. He ordered a cherry Coke and said he was looking for some item and Jimmy took it upon himself to help, not knowing who he was dealing with at the time, and who would have, back then?

They searched the shelves for whatever it was Mick was seeking without success but were finally able to come up with something else that would probably work just as well, and in fact, maybe even better. As Mick was paying for it, Jimmy made the offhand comment that "I guess you can't always get what you want, but if you try, sometimes you can get what you need."

In the song he wrote from that remark, "You Can't Always Get What You Want," Jagger has changed the Beacon to the Chelsea and altered the exchange somewhat, but he left Jimmy's name the same. Almost forty years later, and neither one has undergone a career change.

You can probably find Jimmy somewhere on the streets of Excelsior and Mick somewhere with the Rolling Stones. And if you can't find either one maybe you'll find what you need.

The House of Santas
Stillwater

It's a big English Tudor house of a mint-green color on the corner of Wilkins and Owens; in the yard stands a fifteen-foot Santa, alongside you-know-who the you-know-what-nosed reindeer. And even fully aware that you are about to enter a place with twenty-one rooms holding six thousand Santas, it still isn't something you're ready for.

You enter a scene that feels uneasily like you are in a movie—not just on the set but in the movie already, and you aren't quite sure it's Disney; it might be Quentin Tarantino. Feels like anything could happen here. And they do come to life; a pair of life-sized fellows flanking the couch bend at the waist, raise an arm, and turn to the right a couple of times. A dance line on the mantel starts singing and doing the hula as they are turned on, a cacophony of Clauses. Others come to life with a clap of the hands, singing and yo-ho-hoing. There are international, political, and occupational Santas, cowboys and sailors and photographers. A glass case of biker Santas, on Harleys, naturally, and a pink bathroom full of pink Santas. A black Santa playing "Jingle Bell Rock" on a saxophone; a talking Vincent Price Santa. There is a Santa from Germany that is a hundred years old. You cannot find a corner anywhere to rest the eye without it falling on a Santa Claus; they are there in every size from half an inch tall on up, and they are there in incredible profusion.

The lady in charge of all this is Lois Kohns, a disarming person who likes to smile; she is married to exactly the right guy for this, Dick, who not only helps with the collecting and displays but also has a repair shop in the garage where he rebuilds the rough old antiques that come in. The menacing aspect of the scene melts away as she talks, not only of all the Santas but all the rest of it: the globe that says MERRY CHRISTMAS in whatever country's language you touch; the White House presidential ornaments; how it takes them two months to get ready for the Christmas tourists. Thousands of them, these days.

There is a room in the house where there are no Santas; it's the daughter's bedroom, upstairs, and it's an ordinary bedroom except

Dick and Lois with six thousand fat guys in red overcoats.

maybe for her thousand Barbie dolls, all in the original boxes. Dick says, "This stuff keeps us going, keeps us excited about life. The worst thing I can think of is sitting in front of a television, doing nothing, waiting to die."

You leave marveling at the reach of the human imagination, to recast a fat white guy with white hair and whiskers into so many different incarnations. You wonder what future archaeologists would think if these were the only remnants of us found half a million years hence: "They had computers, but they worshipped fat guys in thick overcoats, looks like. One might have expected something more sophisticated."

The House of Santas is located at 1020 North Owens Street in Stillwater. Tours are available from Thanksgiving to January 15. For tour information call (651) 439-6110 or (651) 439-0066. There is an admission fee.

Butter Sculptures

If you drink milk and use dairy products and your father is a Minnesota dairy farmer or you have close ties to the dairy industry, and you are a reasonably attractive unmarried female high school graduate under the age of twenty-four, you are eligible to become a candidate for the title of Princess Kay of the Milky Way; statistically, you are more likely to be eligible to train as a navy fighter pilot and fly an F-18 Hornet than to become Princess Kay.

There are eleven dairy regions in the state and each sends a candidate to the state fair; one becomes princess and the rest are her court, but each is given a golden day in the sun, metaphorically, when her likeness is sculpted in butter. An artist named Linda Christensen starts with an eighty-five-pound block of it, eighteen by eighteen by twenty-four inches, and with knives and wooden paddles of varying sizes and small wire loops removes all the butter that doesn't look like the young lady.

The sitting takes place at thirty-eight degrees Fahrenheit, with the two of them on a revolving turntable inside a glass-walled cooler at the state fair. They are dressed in parkas and scarves and insulated boots, sometimes with three or four shirts, while huge crowds of people stand outside in the blazing heat and watch. The process takes six to eight hours. One model said, "We take an hour break for lunch, and we take a break every hour and a half or whenever the sculptor's nose starts running." It is one of the five main attractions at the fair, proving that Minnesotans do indeed know how to have a good time, regardless of what you may have heard.

The young women get to keep their likenesses, which contain roughly 192,000 calories; some give them to local pancake dinners and corn roasts and others save them for centerpieces at their weddings. One has kept her bust in a plastic bag in her freezer since 1980 and another cut just the face off and kept that in the freezer;

She's big, she's beautiful, and she's all butter.
COURTESY OF MIDWEST DAIRY ASSOCIATION

every time she lifted the lid there she was, looking up at herself.

Ms. Christensen has had this part-time job since 1972, when she was a student at the Minneapolis College of Art and Design. Since then she had done more than three hundred beauty queen butters, as well as a life-sized Elvis, Dolly Parton, and Michael Jackson for the Mid-South Fair in Memphis.

Butter sculpting used to be more common. Teddy Roosevelt made the famous "walk softly and carry a big stick" speech here at the Minnesota State Fair in 1901. When he returned in 1910, a local dairy had done a life-sized statue of him in butter wearing a pith helmet, his foot on the neck of a lion. (Did they think he meant a big stick of butter?)

You can watch Linda (2012 marks her fortieth anniversary) sculpt the princesses in the Empire Building at the Minnesota State Fair, which runs for the last ten days of summer, including Labor Day. The fairgrounds are located on Snelling Avenue and Como Avenue north of Interstate 94 in St. Paul. Call the Midwest Dairy Association at (800) 642-3895 or visit www.midwestdairy.com for more information.

Franconia Sculpture Park
Taylors Falls

It's both sculpture garden and workshop, open year-round and free to the public. It sits on sixteen acres of what was grazing land, on the west bluffs of the St. Croix River, a long-grass field bracketed by woods, with strange and dramatic objects spotted around. The materials and textures are generally the same as you would see on a neighboring abandoned farm: wood, rusting steel, stone, concrete. Occasional plaster on chicken wire, and some fiberglass. Colorful surfaces here and there and some surprises, like the elephant of steel reinforcing rods dancing on a welded steel ball, or the forty-foot-tall roller coaster.

They are produced by artists mostly from Minnesota and New York but also from South Carolina, Louisiana, and Oregon, plus the United Kingdom, Colombia, Peru, and the Czech Republic; more than sixty-five pieces, with titles such as *Hitta Straight Stick, Witta Crooked Stick, Kawishshiwi Memory, I'll Know When They Come, Lizard Lounge, Abstreet.* And *Johnny Appleseed, Got the Power: Minnesota, Into the Blue, Constructed Memory.* A large wooden wave rises over the grass, twenty feet high and seventy-six feet long, built by a man from Minneapolis.

Artists and interns come here to work and to learn, supported mostly by grants and donations. The founder and manager is sculptor John Hock. He says, "We don't have a set ideology. We just want to support anyone who wants to work in any medium. The crazier the better." But with most of the materials donated by local junkyards, machine shops, lumberyards, and quarries, or salvaged from construction sites, there emerges a certain rough continuity. And working with all this weight is as much common labor as it is artistic vision. Outdoor art in Minnesota is art that has been suffered for, and art that will itself suffer, sitting out there in the ice and cold and the lightning strikes. This place would make a good setting for a movie, especially one with big lightning strikes.

(Continued on page 300)

People who build straw houses shouldn't play with fire.

"Where's my car? I can't find my car!"

Mummy without a Visa

He's very compelling; lying there, mottled dark brown, looking like he's made of solid-ified dirt—which of course we all are—with large eyes closed and a head that seems too big for the skinny body. He's in a glass case in a gray-painted room; an explana-tion titled MUMMIFICATION hangs on the wall alongside an X ray of the guy. He's lying on his back in the bottom half of a sarcophagus; kids are leaning on the case. He is infinitely still; he moved 3,500 years ago and hasn't moved since.

This guy could never imagine he would someday be lying in a glass case with seasons of schoolchildren parading past, pointing and making comments. If you could go back in time and tell him that he would someday rest in a big museum and his picture would be on the Internet, he'd never believe you.

For a city to have a mummy was kind of a mark of the big leagues back around 1925, kind of like a symphony orchestra, or gangsters. The tomb of King Tutankhamun had been opened in 1922 and the Egyptian craze was in full swing; and the St. Paul Institute, which is now the Science Museum of Minnesota, didn't have a mummy. A sixty-six-year-old lawyer named Simon Percy Crosby volunteered to go see if he could find one, and he did. Nobody knows where or how he bought it or how much he had to pay for it, which makes one sus-pect that Mr. Crosby was probably a pretty good lawyer. He shipped it back to himself and donated it to the institute.

It was in its mummy wrap but the hard-shell case didn't come with it, so they had a craftsman build the sarcophagus; it was painted as sort of a modern take on the Egyptian motif—modern in those days being Art Deco. They had no idea who this mummy was or what he did for a living or even where he was found.

So for a while they had it on display but not right out there where you'd see it, and they had a small plaque, mounted low, explaining that the fellow hadn't come with a pedigree. The museum staff eventually got to work and found the brain had been removed, which dated it to the later years of mummification, and they concluded the guy's head was shaved and he did a lot of barefoot walking but not much manual labor. There were other clues as well, and they were able to establish he'd been a priest, maybe thirty-five years old.

So they moved it out into the more public areas and it was a big hit, and stayed that way when they moved from the auditorium into a mansion and then into their own building. Now it's in the institute's downtown quarters overlooking the Mississippi, and some aren't that crazy about having a dead guy around for people to gawk at, so it's in a special exhibit about the history of the museum. Sort of a "we used to do it this way but we don't anymore" kind of setting, like an exhibit of plowing with oxen, only it's about we used put dead people out there to look at but we don't do it now. But we do have to admit it's sort of fascinating.

The mummy can be found in the Collections Room of the Science Museum of Minnesota, which is located at 120 West Kellogg Boulevard across from RiverCentre in downtown St. Paul. Museum hours are Tuesday through Wednesday 9:30 a.m. to 5 p.m., Thursday through Saturday 9:30 a.m. to 9 p.m., and Sunday 9:30 a.m. to 5 p.m. Monday closed. Call (651) 221-9444 or visit www.smm.org for more information.

(Continued from page 296)

Franconia Sculpture Park is on the corner of US Highway 8 and Highway 95 at 29836 St. Croix Trail North, about three miles west of Taylors Fall. It is free and open to the public every day year-round. Call (651) 257-6668 or visit www.franconia.org for more information.

Wiener Dog Hurdles
Wayzata

For many of us the essence of high-tone humor lies in the perverse staging of contests wherein even the winner will end up looking foolish, like three-legged racing or blueberry pie eating—contests for which the entrants are unlikely to possess any inner grace or aptitude. We wouldn't say a search for foolishness was the driving force behind the establishment of the annual wiener dog hurdles in Wayzata. But it's likely.

They started the racing event in 1984 with seventeen dachshunds. There are now upward of one hundred dogs entered, too many beasts to run all at once, so they stage heats, five racers per heat. The Miniature Dachshunds run with the regular full-sized Dachshunds and they all wear little capes, like silks on thoroughbreds, with their numbers on them. The course runs down the 300 block of Lake Street with a starting gate but no lane markings, about thirty yards long, with three short hurdles crossing the field at measured intervals. A short hurdle is one a Dachshund can't crawl under and can barely jump over, a 6-inch hurdle. There is also the Leap into the Chair, a timed event wherein the owner sits in a chair some distance from the gate and the dog is released, runs, and leaps into the waiting lap. And for the purists who crave sheer speed, there is the straight-ahead full-bore Sprint Race with no leaping involved.

There are two persons per dog, one at each end. Parents generally handle the dogs at the gate and children call to them from the finish line, often waving treats. The gates open, the announcer says, "AND THEY'RE OFF!" and all pandemonium breaks loose; kids shrieking, parents yelling, dogs barking and running all over. They get to that first hurdle and some leap right over and others stop dead, and yet others go running around the end, which is to say off the track. They don't get docked for this, but the dog who end-arounds the hurdles will seldom be later seen in the winners' circle—except in one recent race when all five dogs ran around all three hurdles.

At the Leap into the Chair event a lot of dogs who have been trained to stay off the furniture come busting out of the gate and then skid to a stop at the chair, unable, literally, to make the leap. And, as if all that isn't enough, they usually add a costume contest.

You wouldn't buy a wiener dog to run down antelope. They all discovered eons ago that they liked the sound of human laughter better than they liked the taste of antelope meat, and they set their genetic code to that course. And once a year, here beside an ancient glacial lake, their deepest primeval dreams come true as their owners and people they don't even know laugh until they are nearly sick.

The dogs race as part of James J. Hill Days in Wayzata. Call the chamber of commerce at (952) 473-9595 for race times or visit www .wayzatachamber.com/dach.htm.

index

index

index

index

index

about the authors

Denise Remick was raised in St. Paul's storied East Side. She hopped a westbound freight train to Seattle on a summer break from college and has followed an abiding interest in people and places ever since, once leading a horse expedition from Minnesota to Colorado (they didn't quite make it). She has worked as a cartographer and is currently employed as a production artist in a Minneapolis ad agency. She is the daughter of the lady who rode with John Dillinger.

Russ Ringsak was raised in Grafton, North Dakota, back in the good old days when snowdrifts reached second-story windows. He was a registered architect in Minnesota when he bought an over-the-road semi tractor in 1977, a career move that ultimately led him to driving trucks and writing for the *Prairie Home Companion* radio show. He calls himself "one of the country's most semi-famous truck drivers." His great-grandfather owned the *Rosebud,* the steamboat upon which Mark Twain was once employed.